ISBN 978-1-330-81957-9
PIBN 10109571

# My King

AND

# His Service

BY

FRANCES RIDLEY HAVERGAL

---

MY KING
ROYAL COMMANDMENTS
ROYAL BOUNTY
ROYAL INVITATION
LOYAL RESPONSES

---

*46270X*

PHILADELPHIA:
HENRY ALTEMUS
1892

# BIOGRAPHICAL SKETCH

OF

# FRANCES RIDLEY HAVERGAL.

A GENTLE SPIRIT, a temperament alive to all innocent joys, to all the harmonies of life and literature, a deep and earnest faith, a loving self-surrender to the Saviour who was the object of that faith—these are the qualities which make Frances Ridley Havergal a character of exceptional interest, not only to professing Christians, but to all who recognize and revere the spirit of the Gospel teachings. For having the gift of expression—a simple and pellucid style through which the soul poured itself out in either prose or verse—the qualities which endeared her to the friends who knew her in person won her a world-wide circle of friends among those who only knew her through her published writings.

Miss Havergal was born December 14th, 1836, and died June 3d, 1879. She was the daughter of Rev. William Henry Havergal, famous as a writer of sacred music. The story of her life, as revealed

(iii)

to us in the "Memorials" edited by her sister in 1880 seems uneventful enough in incident. Its landmarks are two heavy bereavements, and the changes in outward circumstances ensuing therefrom. One might think that the first of these epoch-marking bereavements was the death of her mother, which occurred in 1848. Yet Frances herself confesses that this event "did not make at first the impression upon me which might have been expected." We must not take her too literally, however. It is undoubtedly from this period that we may roughly date the kindling of that intense religious enthusiasm which burns in all her life and poetry, and which remained unquenched to the last. At the same time, the first poignant and crushing grief that she experienced was the sudden death of her father at Easter, 1870. His widow (for he had married a second time) continued to live at Leamington with the daughters; and the main support of the family devolved upon Frances, who had already won wide fame as a hymn-writer. In 1878 the death of Mrs. Havergal broke up the little circle, and Frances, with her sister Maria, afterwards her biographer, removed from Leamington into Wales, but she outlived her beloved second mother only a little over a year.

This life—tranquil as it seems on the surface—was disturbed in its inner depths by many conflicting currents of religious feeling. "I am quite sure," she tells us in her Autobiography, "that *nothing* in the way of earthly and external trials could have been to me what the inner darkness and strife and utter weariness of spirit, through the greater part of these years, have been. Many have thought mine a comparatively thornless path; but often when the path was smoothest, there were hidden thorns within, and wounds bleeding and rankling." Evidently she had, in a less morbid degree, that extreme sensitiveness of conscience which drove Cowper mad. Through a life of the utmost purity and even sanctity, a life devoted to good works, to philanthropical endeavors of all sorts, she was disturbed by the sense of continual back-slidings. "I remember," she tells us again, "I remember longing to be able to say 'O God, my heart is fixed' in bitter mourning over its weakness and wavering."

It is pleasant to know that these dark shadows were eventually lifted. In her maturer years the early disquiet was succeeded by a calm trust and confidence, thus faithfully mirrored in the prelude to "Under His Shadow."

> So now, I pray Thee, keep my hand in Thine
> And guide it as Thou wilt. I do not ask
> To understand the "wherefore" of each line:
> Mine is the sweeter, easier, happier task
> Just to look up to Thee for every word,
> Rest in thy love and trust and know that I am heard.

Miss Havergal's verses were collected and reissued in two volumes in 1884. But hitherto her prose writings have been strangely neglected by publishers.

In these prose writings, even more than in her poems, Miss Havergal has shown us her best and truest self. Simple and direct as they are in method, they go straight from the heart to the heart. The author's tenderness, reverence and humility, her ardent love for her Lord and for her neighbor are all reflected in her prose. Independently of their religious value, these writings have a distinct liter ary interest as revealing the inner workings of a unique and winning personality. It is no wonder that in this country alone they have sold to the extent of some half a million copies.

It may be added that the little volume of Poems entitled "Loyal Responses" has been included among the prose works because it was expressly prepared as part of the "royal" series of which "My King" was the initial volume. As the earlier books called attention to the utterances from the Throne, so the later one embodies the responses of its loyal subjects, and forms an integral portion of the scheme.

# MY KING

OR

# DAILY THOUGHTS

FOR

# The King's Children

# FIRST DAY.

---

## The Source of the Kingship.

'Because the Lord hath loved His people, He hath made thee king over them.'—2 CHRON. ii. 11, ix. 8.

CHRIST said to His Father, 'Thou lovedst me before the foundation of the world.'[1] At that mysterious date, not of time, but of everlasting love, God 'chose us in Him.'[2] Before the world began, God, that cannot lie,[3] gave the promise of eternal life to Him for us, and made with Him for us 'a covenant ordered in all things, and sure.'[4] The leading provisions of that covenant were, a Lamb for our atonement, and a King for our government—a dying and a living Saviour. This God the Father did for us, and His own divine interest is strongly indicated in the typical words, 'God will provide *Himself* a Lamb,'[5] and 'I have provided *me* a King.'[6] So the Source of the Kingship of Christ is God Himself, in the eternal counsels of His love. It is one of the grand 'thoughts of God.'[7]

---

1 John xvii. 24.  2 Eph. i. 4.  8 Titus i. 2,
4 2 Sam. xxiii. 5.  5 Gen. xxii. 8.  6 1 Sam. xvi. 1.
7 Ps. cxxxix. 17.

5

Having provided, He appointed and anointed His King: 'Yet have I set (margin, anointed) my King upon my holy hill of Zion.'[1] What a marvellous meeting-place is thus found in the Kingship of Jesus for God's heart and ours! He says in His majestic sovereignty, 'I have set *my* King;' and we say in lowly and loving loyalty, 'Thou art *my* King.'[2]

God has appointed His King 'to be ruler over Israel *and* over Judah.' Thus He gives His children a great bond of union. For 'one King shall be King to them all,'[3] and He shall 'gather together in one the children of God which were scattered abroad.'[4] 'Satan scatters, but Jesus gathers.' Shall we then let the enemy have his way, and induce us to keep apart and aloof from those over whom our beloved King reigns also? Let us try this day to recollect this, and make it practical in all our contact with His other subjects.

*Why* has God made Jesus King? Who would have guessed the right answer? '*Because* the Lord loved His people.' So the very thought of the Kingship of Christ sprang from the everlasting love of God to His people.[5] Bring that wonderful statement down to personal reality,—'His people,' that is, *you and me.* God made Jesus King over you, because He loved you, and that with nothing less than the love wherewith He loved Him [6] Which is the more wonderful—the love that devised such a gift, or the gift that was devised by such love! Oh, to realize the glorious value of it!

---

[1] Ps. ii. 6.  [2] Ps. xliv. 4.  [3] Ezek. xxxvii. 22.
[4] John xi. 52.  [5] Jer. xxxi. 3.  [6] John xvii. 26.

May we, who by His grace know something of God's gift of His Son as our Saviour, learn day by day more of the magnificent preciousness of His gift of His Anointed One as our King!

———•———

## SECOND DAY.

———

## The Promise of the King.

'I will be thy King.'—Hos. xiii. 10.

HE knows our need of a king. He knows the hopeless anarchy, not only of a world, but of a heart, 'without a king.'[1] Is there a more desolate cry than 'We have no king'?[2]—none to reverence and love, none to obey, none to guide and protect us and rule over us, none to keep us in that truest freedom of whole-hearted loyalty. Have we not felt that we really want a strong hand over our hearts?·that having our own way is not so good as another's way, if only that other is one to whom our hearty and entire confidence and allegiance can be and are given? Has there not been an echo in our souls of the old cry, 'Give me a king'?—a cry that nothing can still but this Divine promise, '*I* will be thy king!'[3]

But the promise has been given; and now, if the

---

[1] Hos. iii. 4.　　[2] Hos. x. 3.　　[3] Hos. xiii. 10.

old desolate wail of a kingless heart comes up in an hour of faithless forgetfulness, His word comes like a royal clarion, 'Now, _why_ dost thou cry out aloud? Is there no king in thee?'[1] And then the King's gracious assurance falls with hushing power, 'I will be _thy_ King.'

How glad we are that He Himself is our King! For we are so sure that He is able even to subdue all things unto Himself[2] in this inner kingdom, which we cannot govern at all. We are so glad to take Him at His word, and give up the government into His hands, asking Him to be our King in very deed, and to set up His throne of peace in the long disturbed and divided citadel,[3] praying that He would bring every thought into captivity to His gentle obedience.[4]

We have had enough of revolutions and revolts, of tyrants and traitors, of lawlessness and of self-framed codes. Other lords (and oh, how many!) have had dominion over us [5] He has permitted us to be their servants, that now, by blessed and restful contrast, we may know His service.[6] Now we _only_ want 'another King, one Jesus.'[7] He has made us willing in the day of His power,[8] and that was the first act of His reign, and the token that 'of the _increase_ of His government and peace there shall be no end'[9] in our hearts.

Lord, be Thou my King this day! Reign more absolutely in me than ever before. Let the increase

---

[1] Mic. iv. 9.  [2] Phil. iii. 21.  [3] Rom. vii. 19.
[4] 2 Cor. x. 5.  [5] Isa. xxvi. 13.  [6] 2 Chron. xii. 8.
[7] Acts xvii. 7.  [8] Ps. cx. 3.  [9] Isa. ix. 7.

of Thy government be continual and mighty in me,
so that Thy name may be glorified in me now and
forever.[1]

> Reign over me, Lord Jesus!
> Oh, make my heart Thy throne!
> It shall be thine forever,
> It shall be Thine alone!

———•———

## THIRD DAY.

———

## Allegiance to the King.

'Thou art my King.'—Ps. xliv. 4.

FIRST, *can* I say it?
Is Jesus in very deed and truth 'my King'?
Where is the proof of it? Am I living in His kingdom of 'righteousness and peace and joy in the
Holy Ghost' now?[2] Am I speaking the language
of that kingdom? Am I following 'the customs
of the people'[3] which are not His people? or do I
'diligently learn the ways of His people'?[4] Am I
practically living under the rule of His laws? Have
I done heart homage to Him? Am I bravely and
honestly upholding His cause, because it is His, not
merely because those around me do so? Is my
allegiance making any practical difference to my
life to-day?
Next, *ought* I to say it?

1 2 Thess. i. 12.    2 Rom. xiv. 1.    3    4 er. xii. 16.

What! any question about that? The King, who came Himself to purchase me from my tyrant and His foe;[1] the King, who laid aside His crown and His royal robes, and left His kingly palace, and came down Himself to save a rebel;[2] the King, who, though He was rich, yet for my sake became poor, that I 'through His poverty might be rich,'[3]— *ought* I to acknowledge Him? is it a question of '*ought* I?' God has 'called me unto His Kingdom and glory;'[4] He 'hath translated me into the kingdom of the Son of His love;'[5] and shall the loyal words falter or fail from my lips, 'Thou art my King'?

Lastly, *do* I say it?

God has said to me, 'He *is* thy Lord, and worship thou Him.'[6] Do my lips say, ' My Lord and My God'?[7] Does my life say, 'Christ Jesus, *my* Lord,'[8]—definitely and personally, '*my* Lord'? Can I share in His last sweet commendation to His disciples, the more precious because of its divine dignity, 'Ye call me Master and Lord, *and ye say well*, for so I am'?[9] Have I said, 'Thou *art my* King'[10] to Jesus Himself, from the depth of my own heart, in unreserved and unfeigned submission to His sceptre? Am I ashamed or afraid to confess my allegiance in plain English among His friends or before His foes?[11] Is the seal upon my brow so unmistakable that always and everywhere I am known to be His subject? Is 'Thou art my King'[12]

---

[1] Acts xx. 28.
[2] Phil. ii. 7.
[3] 2 Cor. viii. 9.
[4] 1 Thess. ii. 12.
[5] Col. i. 13.
[6] Ps. xlv. 11.
[7] John xx. 28.
[8] Phil. iii. 8.
[9] John xiii. 13.
[10] Ps. lxxxi. 15, margin.
[11] Matt. x. 32.
[12] Acts iv. 13.

blazoned, as it ought to be, in shining letters on the whole scroll of my life, so that it may be 'known and read of all men '?[1]

Answer Thou for me, O my King! 'Search me and try me,'[2] and show me the true state of my case, and then for Thine own sake pardon all my past disloyalty, and make me by Thy mighty grace from this moment totally loyal! For 'Thou *art* my King.'[3]

———•———

## FOURTH DAY.

———

## Decision for the King.

'Ye sought for David in times past to be king over you. Now, then, do it.'—2 SAM. iii. 17, 18.

'IN time past, when Saul was king over us, thou wast he that leddest out and broughtest in Israel.'[4] Chosen, anointed, given by God, continually leading and caring for us, yet not accepted, not crowned, not enthroned by us;[5] our real allegiance, our actual service, given to another![6] Self has been our Saul, our central tyranny; and many have been its officers domineering in every department.[7]

'Ye sought for David in times past to be king over you.' Well we might, for the bondage of any other lord was daily harder.[8] Well we might,

---

[1] 2 Cor. iii. 2.    [2] Ps. xxxviii. 15, P. B. V.; ib. cxxxix. 23.
[3] Ps. xxv. 11.    [4] Sam. v. 2.    [5] Ps. lxxxix. 19, 20; Isa. lv. 4.
[6] Rom. vi. 16.    [7] Rom. vii. 23.    [8] Isa. xiv. 3.

with even a dim glimpse of the grace and glory of the King who waited for our homage. We sought, first, only for something—we hardly knew wha —restlessly and vaguely; then for some One, who was not merely 'the Desire of all nations,' but our own desire.[1] And yet we did not come to the point: we were not ready for His absolute monarchy, for we were loving and doing the will of our old tyrant.[2]

But 'the time past of our life may suffice us to have wrought the will' of self—Satan—the world.[3] We do not want 'to live the rest of our time' to any but One Will.[4] We come face to face with a great NOW! 'Now, then, do it!'[5] 'Now, then,' let us, with full purpose of heart, dethrone the usurper and give the diadem to Him 'whose right it is,' a blood-bought and death-sealed right.[6]

He does not force allegiance,—He waits for it. The crown of our own individual love and loyalty must be offered by our own hands.[7] We must 'do it.' When? Oh, now! *Now* let us come to Jesus as our King. *Now* let us, first in solemn heart surrender, and then in open and unmistakable life-confession, yield ourselves to Him as our Sovereign, our Ruler.

What a glorious life of victory and peace opens before us when this is done! What a silencing of our fears lest the time to come should nevertheless be as the time past! 'Now, then, do it: FOR the Lord hath spoken of David, saying, By the hand of

---

1 Hag. ii. 7.　　2 1 Kings xviii. 21.　　3 1 Pet. iv. 3.
4 1 Pet. iv. 2.　　5 2 Sam. iii. 18.　　6 Ezek. xxi. 26, 27.
7 2 Sam. v. 3.

my servant David I will save my people Israel out of the hand of the Philistines, and out of the hand of all their enemies.'[1]

Now, do not let us 'take away from the words'[2] of this promise, and merely hope that our King *may* save us from *some* of our enemies.   The Lord hath said, '*will* save from *all*.'   Let us trust our true David this day to fulfil the word of the Lord, and verily we shall not fail to find that according to our faith it shall be unto us.[3]

## FIFTH DAY.

## Tbe First to Meet the king.

'For thy servant doth know that I have sinned; therefore, behold, I am come the first this day of all the house of Joseph to meet my lord the king.'—2 SAM. xix. 20.

YES, I have sinned.   I *know* that I have sinned.   Whether I feel it more or less does not touch the fact : I *know* it.   And what then ?  'THEREFORE, behold, I am come the first this day of all  .  .  . to meet my Lord the King.'

Just because I *know* that I have sinned, I come to Jesus.   He came to call sinners,[4] He came to save sinners,[5] so He came to call and to save me.  'This is all my desire.'[6]

---

[1] 2 Sam. iii. 18.      [2] Rev. xxii. 19.      [3] Matt. ix. 29.
[4] Matt. ix. 13.       [5] 1 Tim. i. 15.      [6] 2 Sam. xxiii. 5.

Just because I know that *I* have sinned, I may and must come 'the first of all.' Thousands are coming, but the heart knoweth his own bitterness.[1] So, not waiting for others, not coming in order, but 'first of all,' by the pressure of my sore need of pardon, I come. There is no waiting for one's turn in coming to Jesus.

'The first of all,' because it is against '*my* lord the King' that I have sinned. I am His servant, so I have the greater sin.[2] 'The first of all, because I have so much to be forgiven, and have already been forgiven so much, that I must, I do, love much;[3] and love, even of a sorrowing sinner, seeks nearness, and cannot rest in distance.[4]

'Therefore,' also, 'I am come *this day*.' I dare not and could not wait till to-morrow. No need to wait, even till to-night! Now! He is passing by,[5] and I must 'haste to meet' Him.[6] 'While he is near,'[7] I will tell Him all.

I am come to *meet* Him, not merely to *go* to Him;[8] for He is always coming to meet us. He was on His way before I had said, 'I will arise and go.'[9] I come, because He comes to me.

Yet I could not come with this terrible knowledge that I have sinned, but that I know something more. I know that He hath said, 'Come unto me.'[10] I know that He hath said, 'Him that cometh I will in no wise cast out.'[11] This is enough; therefore I am come to my Lord the King.

Not to His servants, but to Himself. Even those

---

1 Prov. xiv. 10.  2 Ps. cxvi. 16.  3 Luke vii. 47.
4 Col. ii. 13.  5 Matt. xx. 30.  6 2 Sam. xix. 16.
7 Isa. lv. 6.  8 Zech. ix. 9.  9 Luke xv. 18.
10 Matt. xi. 28.  11 John vi. 37.

who stand near Him may accuse and condemn, but the King Himself will receive me graciously;[1] for with Him there is forgiveness, and mercy, and plenteous redemption.[2]

And though the oath of an earthly sovereign may be broken, my King (in glorious contrast to the imperfect human type) 'keepeth His promise for ever.'[3] His covenant will He not break, nor alter the thing that is gone out of His lips.[4] Therefore the eternal life which He hath promised me is secured to me forever, for He hath said,[5] 'I give unto them eternal life, and they shall never perish, neither shall any man pluck them out of my hand.'[6]

# SIXTH DAY.

## The Condescension of the King.

'Behold, thy King cometh unto thee.'—Zech. ix. 9.

THAT our King should let us come to Him is condescension indeed. But have we praised Him for His still more wonderful condescension: 'Thy King *cometh unto thee*'?[7] 'Unto *thee*,' rebel, traitor, faithless subject, coward and cold-hearted follower; for where is the life that has not fallen

---

[1] Hos. xiv. 2.  [2] Ps. cxxx. 4, 7.  [3] Ps. cxlvi. 5. (P. B. V.)
[4] Ps. lxxxix. 34.  [5] 1 John ii. 25.  [6] John x. 28.
[7] Isa. xlviii. 8.

under these charges, when seen in the double light of the King's perfect law and the King's great love? Yes, he cometh unto *thee*, and it is enough to break our hearts when we get one contrasted glimpse of this undeserved grace and unparalleled condescension.

His great promise has had its first fulfilment 'unto thee.' It is a finished fact of sevenfold grace. Thy King has come, and His own voice has given the objects of His coming,—'to do Thy will, O God;'[1] 'to fulfil' the law;[2] 'to call sinners to repentance;'[3] 'to seek and to save that which was lost;'[4] 'that they might have life, and that they might have it more abundantly;'[5] 'a light into the world, that whosoever believeth on me should not abide in darkness.'[6] What He came to do He has done, for 'He faileth not.'[7] On this we may and ought to rest quietly and undoubtingly, for 'the Lord hath *done* it.'[8]

But you want a further fulfilment,—you want a present coming of your King. You have His most sweet word, 'I will come to you;'[9] and you respond, 'Oh, *when* wilt Thou come unto me?'[10] Are you ready to receive the King's own answer now? Do you so desire His coming, that you do not want it postponed at all? Can you defer all other comers, and say in reality, '*Let* my Beloved come'?[11]

He has but one answer to that appeal. Hush!

---

[1] Heb. x. 9.    [2] Matt. v. 17.    [3] Matt. ix. 13.
[4] Luke xix. 10.    [5] John x. 10.    [6] John xii. 46.
[7] Zeph. iii. 5.    [8] Isa. xliv. 23.    [9] John xiv. 18.
[10] Ps. ci. 2.    [11] Cant. iv. 16.

listen ! believe ! for the King speaks to you : 'I am come into my garden, my sister, my spouse.' [1] He *is* come. Do not miss the unspeakable blessing and joy of meeting Him and resting in His presence, by hurrying away to anything else, by listening to any outward call.[2] Stay *now*, lay the little book aside, kneel down at your King's feet, doubt not His word, which is 'more sure' than even the 'excellent glory'[3] that apostles beheld, and thank Him for coming to you. Commune with Him now of all that is in your heart,[4] and 'rejoice greatly,' for, 'behold, thy King cometh unto thee.'

> ' Jesus comes to hearts rejoicing,
>     Bringing news of sin forgiven;
> Jesus comes in sounds of gladness,
>     Leading souls redeemed to heaven.

> ' Jesus comes again in mercy,
>     When our hearts are bowed with care;
> Jesus comes again, in answer
>     To an earnest, heartfelt prayer.'
>                     GODFREY THRING.

---

1 Cant. v. 1.
3 2 Pet. i. 19.
2 Cant. ii. 3.
4 1 Kings x. 2.

## SEVENTH DAY.

---

## Ⓣhe Ⓘndwelling of the Ⓚing.

'Is not her King in her?'—Jer. viii. 19.

WAITING for a royal coming,—What expectation, what preparation, what tension! A glimpse for many, a full view for some, a word for a favoured few, and the pageant is over like a dream. The Sovereign may come, but does not stay.

Our King comes not thus: He comes not to pass, but to '*dwell* in the midst of thee;'[1] not only in His Church collectively, but in each believer individually.[2] We pray, 'Abide with us,'[3] and He answers in the sublime plural of Godhead, 'We will come unto him, and make our abode with him.'[4] Even this grand abiding with us does not extend to the full marvels of His condescension and His nearness, for the next time He speaks of it He changes the 'with' to 'in,' and thenceforth only speaks of 'I *in* you,' 'I in him,' 'I in them.'[5]

Now do not let us say, 'How can this be?'[6] but, like Mary, 'How shall this be?'[7]　The means,

---

[1] Zech. ii. 10.　　[2] 2 Cor. vi. 16.　　[3] Luke xxiv. 29.
[4] John xiv. 23.　　[5] John xv. 4, 5; ib. xvii. 23.
[6] John iii. 9.　　[7] Luke i. 34.

though not the mode, of the mystery is revealed
for our grasp of adoring wonder : ' That Christ may
dwell in your heart by faith.'[1] It is almost too
wonderful to dare to speak of. Christ Himself, my
King, coming to me, into me ! abiding, dwelling in
my very heart ! Really staying there all day, all
night, wherever I am, whatever I am doing ; here in
my poor unworthy heart at this very moment !
And this only because the grace that flowed from
His own love has broken the bars of doubt, and
because He has given the faith that wanted Him
and welcomed Him. Let us pause a little to take
it in !

The more we have known of the plague of our
own heart,[2] the more inconceivably wonderful this
indwelling of Christ will appear,—much more
wonderful than that He chose a manger as His
royal resting-place,[3] for that had never been defiled
by sin, and had never harboured His enemy. It is
no use trying to comprehend this incomprehensible
grace of our King,—we have only to believe His
promise, saying, 'Amen ; the Lord God of my Lord
the King says so too.'[4]

There should be three practical results of this
belief :—1. *Holiness.* We must see to it that we
resolutely ' put away '[5] all that ought not to be in
His royal abode.[6] ' Having, therefore, these promises, dearly beloved, let us cleanse ourselves from
*all* filthiness of the flesh and spirit, perfecting
holiness in the fear of God.'[7] 2. *Confidence.*

---

[1] Eph. iii. 17.     [2] 1 Kings viii. 38.     [3] Luke ii. 7.
[4] 1 Kings i. 36.     [5] Eph. iv. 31.     [6] 1 Cor. iii. 16, 17.
[7] 2 Cor. vii. 1.

What does the citadel fear when an invincible general is within it?  'The Lord thy God in the midst of thee is mighty; He will save.'[1]  He is 'the wall of fire round about,' and 'the glory in the midst of her;'[2] and 'he that toucheth you toucheth the apple of His eye.'[3] 3. *Joy.* Yes!  'Be glad and rejoice with all the heart,'[4] 'sing and rejoice, O daughter of Zion; for, lo, I come, and I will dwell in the midst of thee, saith the Lord.'[5]

---

## EIGHTH DAY.

---

## full Satisfaction in the King.

' Yea, let him take all, for as much as my lord the king is come again in peace to his own house.'—2 SAM. xix. 30.

IT is when the King has really come in peace to His own home in the 'contrite and humble spirit '[6] (not before),—when He has entered in to make His abode there[7] (not before),—that the soul is satisfied with Him[8] alone, and is ready to let any Ziba take all else, because all else really seems nothing at all in comparison to the conscious possession of the Treasure of treasures.[9]

Sometimes this is reached at once, in the first flush of wondering joy at finding the King really 'come in peace '[10] to the empty soul which wanted to be

---

1 Zeph. iii. 17.          2 Zech. ii. 5.          3 Zech. ii. 8.
4 Zeph. iii. 14.          5 Zech. ii 10.          6 Isa. lvii. 15.
7 John xiv. 23.          8 Ps. xxii. 26.          9 Matt. xiii. 46.
10 Isa. xxxiii. 6.

'His own house.'[1] Sometimes very gradually,—as year after year we realize His indwelling more and more, and find again and again that He is quite enough to satisfy us in all circumstances; that the empty corners of the 'house' are filled one after another; that the old longings have somehow gone away, and the old ambitions vanished; that the old tastes and interests in the things of the world are superseded by stronger tastes and interests in the things of Christ; that He is day by day more really *filling* our lives,[2]—we 'count' (because we really find) one thing after another 'but loss for the excellency of the knowledge of Christ Jesus my Lord,'[3] till He leads us on to the rapturous joy of the 'Yea, doubtless,' and '*all* things!'

Now, have we got as far as saying '*some* things,' without being quite sure about '*all* things'? Do you see that it all hinges upon Jesus coming into the heart as 'His *own* house,'—*altogether* 'His own'?[4] For if there are some rooms of which we do not give up the key,—some little sitting-room which we would like to keep as a little mental retreat, with a view from the window, which we do not quite want to give up,—some lodger whom we would rather not send away just yet,—some little dark closet which we have not resolution to open and set to rights,—of course the King has not full possession; it is not all and really 'His own;' and

---

1 Heb. iii. 6.       2 Eph. i. 23.
3 Phil. iii. 8.       4 Acts xxvi. 29.

the very misgiving about it proves that He has
*therefore* not yet 'come again in peace.'   It is no
use expecting 'perfect peace,'[1] while He has a secret
controversy[2] with us about any withholding of
what is 'His own'[3] by purchase.   Only throw open
*all* the doors,[4] 'and the King of Glory shall come
in,'[5] and then there will be no craving for other
guests.   He will 'fill this house with glory,'[6] and
there will be no place left for gloom.

Is it not so?   Bear witness, tell it out, you with
whom the King dwells in peace?   Life is filled with
bright interests, time is filled with happy work or
peaceful waiting, the mind is filled with His beautiful words and thoughts, the heart is filled with His
presence, and you 'abide satisfied'[7] with Him!
Yes, 'tell it out!'

> The human heart asks love; but now I know
>     That my heart hath from Thee
> All real, and full, and marvellous affection,
> So near, so human! yet Divine perfection
> Thrills gloriously the mighty glow!
>     Thy love is enough for me!
>
> There were strange soul-depths, restless, vast and broad,
>     Unfathomed as the sea;
> An infinite craving for some infinite stilling;
> But now Thy perfect love is perfect filling!
> Lord Jesus Christ, my Lord, my God,
>     Thou, Thou art enough for me.

---

[1] Isa. xxvi. 3.          [2] Mic. vi. 2.          [3] Acts v. 2.
[4] Rev. iii. 20.          [5] Ps. xxiv. 9.          [6] Hag. ii. 7.
[7] Prov. xix. 23.

# NINTH DAY.

## Tbe Sorrow of tbe king.

'The king himself also passed over the brook Kidron.'[1]—
2 SAM. xv. 23.

'JESUS went forth with His disciples over the
brook Cedron.'[2]  How precisely the Old Testament shadow corresponds with the New Testament
fulfilment! The King, in sorrow and humiliation, is
here brought before us, passing from his royal home,
from all his glory and gladness,—passing over into
exile and unknown distresses.[3]

There is no need for imagination in dwelling on
His sorrows. The pathos of the plain words
is more than enough; no pen has power to
add to it. Let us listen to them just as they stand,
—not hurrying over them because they are only
texts, and we know them all beforehand; they are
the Holy Ghost's sevenfold testimony to the sorrow
of the King.

'A man of sorrows and acquainted with grief,'[4]
'I am poor and sorrowful.'[5] 'The sorrows of death

---

[1] Kidron means ' obscurity '; Cedron is ' black ' or ' sad.'
[2] John xviii. 1.  [3] 2 Sam. xviii. 20.
[4] Isa. liii. 3.  [5] Ps. lxix. 29.

compassed me.' 'The sorrows of hell compassed me.'[1] 'Behold and see if there be any sorrow like unto my sorrow.'[2] 'He began to be sorrowful and very heavy.'[3] 'My soul is exceeding sorrowful, even unto death.'[4] Oh, stay a little that you may take it in! hear Jesus saying to you, 'Hear, I pray you, and behold my sorrow?'[5]

'Surely He hath borne our griefs, and carried our sorrows.'[6] The sorrows of the past, the very sorrow that may be pressing heavily at this moment; all yours, all mine; all the sorrows of all His children all through the groaning generations; all that were 'too heavy'[7] for them,—Jesus bore them all. 'Is it nothing to you?'[8] It is when the Lord says, 'Now will I gather them' (the rebels and wanderers), that He adds, 'And they shall sorrow a little for the burden of the King of princes.'[9] Have we this proof that He has indeed gathered us? For '*all* the people,' except the rebels, 'passed over with the king.'[10] Do we know anything of this passage over Cedron, the brook of sadness, with Him? Possibly it seems presumptuous to think of sharing 'the fellowship of His sufferings,'[11] that mysterious privilege! But mark, it was not only the mighty Ittai and 'all his men,' the nobles and the veterans, that passed over, but 'all the little ones that were with him '[12] too. And so 'the little ones, the weak ones,'[13] the least member of His body, may thus

---

1 Ps. xviii. 4, 5.     2 Lam. i. 12.     3 Matt. xxvi. 37.
4 Matt. xxvi. 38.     5 Lam. i. 18.     6 Isa. liii. 4.
7 Ps. xxxviii. 4.     8 Lam. i. 12.     9 Hos. viii. 10.
10 2 Sam. xv. 23.     11 Phil. iii. 10.     12 2 Sam. xv. 22.
13 1 Cor. xii. 26, 27.

'continue with '[1] Jesus; and nothing brings one closer to another than a shared sorrow.

But look forward! Because He has drunk 'of the brook in the way, therefore shall He lift up the head.'[2] Already the 'exceeding sorrowful'[3] is exchanged for 'Thou hast made Him (the King) exceeding glad;'[4] and when the ransomed and gathered of the Lord shall return with everlasting joy,[5] 'their King also shall pass before them.'[6]

---

## TENTH DAY.

---

## Going Forth with the King.

'The king said, Wherefore wentest thou not with me?'— 2 SAM. xix. 25.

'WITH me!'[7] To be with our King will be our highest bliss for eternity; and surely it is the position of highest honour and gladness now. But if we would always *be* with Him, we must sometimes be ready to *go* with Him.[8]

'The Son of God goes forth to war' now-a-days. Do we go with Him? His cross is 'without the gate.' Do we go 'forth unto Him without the camp, bearing His reproach'?[9] Do we really go with Him every day and all day long, following 'the Lamb whithersoever He goeth'?[10] What

---

[1] Luke xxii. 28.      [2] Ps. cx. 7.      [3] Matt. xxvi. 38.
[4]      [5]      [6]

about this week—this day? Have we loyally gone with our King wherever His banner, His footsteps, go before?[1]

If the voice of our King is heard in our hearts, 'Wherefore wentest *thou* not with me?'—thou who hast eaten 'continually at the King's table,'[2]—thou who hast had a place among 'the King's sons,'[3]—thou unto whom the King has shown 'the kindness of God,'[4] we have no 'because' to offer. He would have healed the spiritual lameness that hindered,[5] and we might have run after Him. We are without excuse.

It is only now that we can go with Jesus into conflict, suffering, loneliness, weariness. It is only now that we can come to the help of the Lord against the mighty[6] in this great battlefield. Shall we shrink from opportunities which are not given to the angels? Surely, even with Him in glory, the disciples must 'remember the words of the Lord Jesus, how he said'[7] to them, 'Ye are they which have continued *with me* in my temptations,'[8] with a thrill of rapturous thanksgiving that such a privilege was theirs.

There will be no more suffering with Him in heaven, only reigning with Him;[9] no more fighting under His banner, only sitting with Him on His throne.[10] But to-day we may prove our loving and grateful allegiance to our King in the presence of His enemies, by rising up and going forth with

---

[1] 1 Pet. ii. 21.　　[2] 2 Sam. ix. 13.　　[3] 2 Sam. ix. 11.
[4] 2 Sam. ix. 3.　　[5] 2 Sam. xix. 26.　　[6] Judges v. 23.
[7] Acts xx. 35.　　[8] Luke xxii. 28.　　[9] 2 Tim. ii. 12.
[10] Rev. iii. 21.

Him,—forth *from* a life of easy idleness or selfish
business,—forth *into* whatever form of blessed fellowship in His work, His wars, or, it may be, of His
sufferings, the King Himself may choose for us.[1]
We have heard His call, ' Come *unto* me.'    To-day
He says, ' Come *with* me.'[2]

> True-hearted, whole-hearted! Faithful and loyal,
>   King of our lives, by Thy grace we will be!
> Under Thy standard exalted and royal,
>   Strong in Thy strength we will battle for Thee.

---

## ELEVENTH DAY.

---

# Tbe Smiting of tbe king.

'I will smite the king only.'—2 SAM. xvii. 2.

IT may be that this futile threat of a wicked man
against the king was like the saying of Caia-
phas,—'not of himself,'[3] but written for our learning 'more about Jesus.'[4]    A deadly stroke was to
be aimed at ' the king only,' for he was ' worth ten
thousand ' of the people;[5] if he were smitten, they
should escape.    Do the words of David in another
place tell of his great Antitype's desire that it
should be so?    ' Let Thine hand, I pray Thee, O
Lord my God, be on me, . . . but NOT on Thy
people.'[6]    ' For the transgression of my people was

---

[1] 2 Cor. vi. 1; Phil. iii. 10.    [2] Cant. iv. 8.    [3] John xi. 51.
[4] Rom. xv. 4.    [5] Cf. 1 Kings xxii. 31; 2 Sam. xviii. 3.
[6] 1 Chron. xxi. 17.

the stroke upon Him '[1] (*margin*); therefore not
upon us, never upon us.   The lightning that strikes
the conductor instead of the building to which it is
joined, has spent its fiery force and strikes no more.

Not the hand of an impotent foe, but the sharp
sword of the omnipotent Lord of hosts, was lifted
to smite His Shepherd,—our Shepherd-king,[2] The
Great,[3] The Chief,[4] The Good[5] (and The Beautiful,
as the original implies).   Think of the words,
'stricken, smitten of God,'[6] with their unknown
depths of agony, and then of Jesus, Him whom we
love,[7] fathoming those black depths of agony *alone !*
'*Jesus, smitten of God!*'[8] can we even *say* the words,
and not feel moved as no other grief could move
us?   Do not let us shrink from dwelling upon it;
let us rather ask the Holy Spirit, even now, to show
us a little of what this awful smiting really was,—
to show us our dear Lord Jesus Christ, in this tremendous proving of His own and His Father's love,
—to whisper in our hearts as we gaze upon the
Crucified One, 'Behold *your* King !'[9]

'The King *only*.'   For, 'by Himself He purged
our sins.'[10] Certainly we had nothing to do with it
then !   Certainly no other man or means had anything to do with it ! and certainly nothing and no
one now can touch that great fact, so far out of
reach of human quibbling and meddling, that
Jesus, 'His own self, bare our sins in His own body
on the tree.'[11]   Is not the fact that He ' with whom

---

[1] Isa. liii. 8.   [2] Zech xiii. 7.   [3] Heb. xiii. 20.
[4] 1 Pet. v. 4.   [5] John x. 11.   [6] Isa. liii. 4.
[7] 1 Pet. i. 8.   [8] Isa. lxiii. 3.   [9] John ix. 14.
[10] Heb. i. 3.   [11] 1 Pet. ii. 24.

we have to do,'[1] *was smitten of God instead of us,*
enough ? What else can we want to guarantee our
salvation ?

'The King *only.*' For the sorrow of our King is
shared with His people; but in the smiting we
have no part. We can only stand 'afar off,'[2] bowed
and hushed in shuddering love, as the echoes of the
awful stripes that fell on Him float down through
the listening centuries, while each throb of the
healed heart replies, 'For me! for me!'[3]

'I have trodden the wine-press *alone,* and of the
people there was none with me.'[4]

## TWELFTH DAY.

# The Kinship of the King.

'The king is near of kin to us.'—2 SAM. xix. 42.

NOT only in the Prophet raised up 'from the
midst of thee, of thy brethren,'[5] and in the
High Priest, 'thy brother,'[6] 'taken from among
men,'[7] do we see the kinship of Christ; but in the
divinely chosen King the same wonderful link is
given—'One from among thy brethren shalt thou
set king over thee: thou mayest not set a stranger
over thee, which is not thy brother.'[8]

---

[1] Heb. iv. 13.  [2] Matt. xxvii. 55.  [3] Isa. liii. 5.
[4] Isa. lxiii. 3.  [5] Deut. xviii. 15.  [6] Ex. xxviii. 1.
[7] Heb. v. 1.  [8] Deut. xvii. 15.

How very close this brings us to our glorious Lord! And yet, when we have exhausted all that is contained in the very full and dear idea of ' brother,' we are led beyond, to realize One who ' sticketh *closer* than a brother,'[1] because no earthly relationship can entirely shadow forth what Jesus is. And whatever relationship we most value or most miss, will be the very one which, whether by possession or loss, will show us most of Him, and yet fall short of His ' reality.' For we always have to go beyond the type to reach the antitype

The King is so ' near of kin,' that we may come to Him as the tribes of Israel did, and say, ' Behold, we are Thy bone and Thy flesh ; '[2] finding many a sweet endorsement of the type in His word. So near of kin, that He is ' in all things ' ' made like unto His brethren ; '[3] and whatever is included in the flesh and blood of which we are partakers, sin only excepted, ' He also Himself likewise took part of the same.'[4]

So ' near of kin to us,' and yet God ! Therefore every good thing that we find in near human relationships, we shall find in Jesus in the immeasurable proportion of the divine to the human. Is not this worth thinking out, each for ourselves?—worth seeking to enter into?

But will He acknowledge the kinship ? He hath said, ' Whosoever shall do the will of my Father which is in heaven, the same is my brother and sister and mother.'[5] ' How beautiful to be Christ's little sister! ' said a young disciple. For of course

---

[1] Prov. xviii. 24.　　　　[2] 2 Sam. v. 1.　　　　[3] Heb. ii. 17.
[4] Heb. ii. 14.　　　　[5] Matt. xii. 50.

He really means it. Will not this make our prayer more fervent, ' Teach me to do Thy will ' ?[1]

If the King is indeed near of kin to us, the royal likeness will be recognizable. Can it be said of us, 'As thou art, so were they; each one resembled the children of a king!'?[2] Nor let us shrink from aiming at the still higher standard, 'The King's daughter is all glorious *within*'[3]

We must not dwell only on a one-sided kinship. If ' He is not ashamed to call' us ' brethren,'[4] shall we ever be ashamed to call Him Master? If He is ready to give us all that is implied or involved in near kinship, should we fail to reciprocate with all the love and sympathy and faithfulness which the tie demands on our side?

Also, if we do realize this great privilege, let us prove our loyal love to our Brother-King by 'looking for and hasting unto the coming of the day'[5] of His return. Let us not incur the touching reproach, 'Ye are my brethren, ye are my bones and my flesh: wherefore then are ye the last to bring back the King?'[6]

> Joined to Christ in mystic union,
>     We Thy members, Thou our Head,
> Sealed by deep and true communion,
>     Risen with Thee, who once were dead.
> · Saviour, we would humbly claim
> All the power of this Thy name.
>
> Instant sympathy to brighten
>     All their weakness and their woe,
> Guiding grace their way to lighten,
>     Shall Thy loving members know,

---

[1] Ps. cxliii. 10.  [2] Judges viii. 18.  [3] Ps. xlv. 13.
[4] Heb. ii. 11.  [5] 2 Pet. iii. 18.  [6] 2 Sam. xix. 12.

All their sorrows Thou dost bear,
All Thy gladness they shall share.

Everlasting life Thou givest,
    Everlasting love to see;
They shall live because Thou livest,
    And their life is hid with Thee.
Safe Thy members shall be found,
When their glorious Head is crowned!

## THIRTEENTH DAY.

## The Desire of the King.

'So shall the King greatly desire thy beauty.'—Ps. xlv. 11.

CAN this be for us? What beauty have we that
the King can desire? For the more we have
seen of His beauty,[1] the more we have seen of our
own utter ugliness. What, then, can He see?
'My comeliness which I had put upon thee.'[2]
'The beauty of the Lord our God upon us.'[3] For
'He will beautify the meek with salvation.'[4] And
so the desire of the King is set upon us.

Perhaps we have had the dreary idea, 'Nobody
wants me!' We never need grope in that gloom
again, when the King Himself desires us! This
desire is love active, love in glow, love going forth,
love delighting and longing. It is the strongest

[1] Isa. vi. 5.    [2] Ezek. xvi. 14.    [3] Ps. xc. 17.    [4] Ps. cxlix. 4.

representation of the love of Jesus,—something far beyond the love of pity or compassion ; it is taking pleasure in His people ;[1] delighting in them ;[2] willing (*i. e.* putting forth the grand force of His will) that they should be with Him where He is, with Him now, with Him always.[3]  It is the love that does not and will not endure separation,—the love that cannot do without its object.  ' *So* shall the King desire thy beauty.'

He gave us a glimpse of this gracious fervour when He said, ' With desire I have desired to eat this passover with you before I suffer.'[4]  With Gethsemane and Calvary in fullest view, His heart's desire was to spend those few last hours in closest intercourse with His disciples.  ' *So* ' did He desire them.

Now, if we take the King at His word, and really believe that He thus desires us, can we possibly remain cold-hearted and indifferent to Him ?  Can we bear the idea of disappointing His love,—*such* love,—and meeting it with any such pale, cool response as would wound any human heart, ' I do not know whether I love you or not ! '

Oh, do let us leave off morbidly looking to see exactly how much we love (which is just like trying to warm ourselves with a thermometer, and perhaps only ends in doubting whether we love at all), and look straight away at His love and his desire![5] Think of Jesus actually wanting you, really desiring your love, not satisfied with all the love of all the angels and saints unless you love him too,—

---

[1] Ps. cxlix. 4.    [2] Isa. lxii. 4.    [3] John xvii. 24; ib. xii. 26.
[4] Luke xxii. 15.    [5] Heb. xii. 2.

needing that little drop to fill His cup of joy! Is
there no answering throb, no responsive glow?

> ' Lord, let the glow of Thy great love
> Through my whole being shine ! '

Perhaps it is upon the emphatic '*so*,' as pointing
to the context, that the intensity of the emphatic
'*greatly*' hinges. It is when the bride forgets her
own people and her father's house,[1]—that is, when
her life and love are altogether given to her Royal
Bridegroom,—that He ' shall *greatly* desire ' her
beauty. When His glorious beauty has so filled our
eyes, and His incomprehensible love has so filled
our hearts,[2] that He is first, and most, and dearest
of all,—when we can say not merely, ' The desire
of our souls is to Thy name,'[3] but ' There is *none*
upon earth that I desire beside Thee,'[4]—when thus
we are, to the very depth of our being, really and
entirely our Beloved's, then we may add, in solemn,
wondering gladness, 'And His desire is toward
me.'[5]

> O love surpassing thought,
> So bright, so grand, so clear, so true, so glorious ;
> Love infinite, love tender, love unsought,
> Love changeless, love rejoicing, love victorious !
> And this great love for us in boundless store ;
> Christ's everlasting love ! What wouldst thou more?

---

[1] Ps. xlv. 10.     [2] Eph. iii. 19.     [3] Isa. xxvi. 8.
[4] Ps. lxxiii. 25.     [5] Cant. vii. 10.

# FOURTEENTH DAY.

---

## The Sceptre of the King.

'The king held out the golden sceptre.'—ESTH. viii. 4.

JESUS is He 'that holdeth the sceptre,'[1]—the symbol first of kingly right and authority, and next of righteousness and justice. 'A sceptre of righteousness is the sceptre of Thy kingdom,'[2]—'a right sceptre.'[3] And yet the golden sceptre was held out as the sign of sovereign mercy to one who, by 'one law of his to put him to death,' must otherwise have perished, 'that he may live.'[4] Thus, by the combination of direct statement and type, we are shown in this figure the beautiful, perfect meeting of the 'mercy and truth' of our King, the 'righteousness and peace' of His kingdom [5]

Again and again the Holy Ghost repeats this grand blending of seemingly antagonistic attributes, confirming to us in many ways this strong consolation.[6]

How precious the tiny word *and* becomes, as we read, 'He is just, *and* having salvation.'[7] 'A

---

[1] Amos i. 5.  [2] Heb. i. 8.  [3] Ps. xlv. 6.
[4] Esth. iv. 11.  [5] Ps. lxxxv. 10; ib. lxxii. 2, 3.
[6] Heb. vi. 18.  [7] Zech. ix. 9.

merciful *and* faithful High Priest.'[1] 'A just God,
*and* a Saviour.'[2] We do not half value God's *little*
words.

To 'the King's enemies' the sceptre is a 'rod of
iron'[3] (for the word is the same in Hebrew).
They cannot rejoice in the justice which they defy.
To the King's willing subjects it is indeed golden,
a beautiful thing, and a most precious thing. We
admire and glory in His absolute justice and righteousness; it satisfies the depths of our moral being,
—it is so strong, so perfect.

His justice is, if we may reverently say so, the
strong point of His atoning work. The costly
means of our redemption were paid for 'at the full
price.'[4] He fulfilled the law. There was nothing
wanting in all the work which His Father gave Him
to do. He finished it.[5] And His Father was
satisfied. Thus He was just towards His Father,
that He might be faithful and just to forgive us our
sins.[6] It is no weak compassion, merely wrought
on by misery, but strong, grand, infinite, and equal
justice and mercy, balanced as they never are in
human minds. For only the ways of the Lord are
thus 'equal.'[7]

And oh, how 'sweet is Thy mercy'! and just
because of the justice, how 'sure'![8] Esther said,
'If I perish, I perish.'[9] So need not we, 'for His
mercy endureth for ever.'[10] And so, every time we
come into the audience chamber of our King, we

---

[1] Heb ii. 17.      [2] Isa. xlv. 21.
[3] Ps. xlv. 5; ib. ii. 9.      [4] 1 Chron. xxi. 24; Matt. v. 17.
[5] John xvii. 4; Isa. xlii. 21.      [6] 1 John i. 9.
[7] Ezek. xviii. 25.      [8] Ps. cix. 20, P. B. V; Isa. lv. 3.
[9] Esth. iv. 16.      [10] Ps. cxxxvi. 1.

know that the golden spectre will be held out to us, first 'that we may live,'[1] and then for favour after favour. 'Let us therefore come boldly unto the throne of grace, that we may obtain mercy, and find grace to help in time of need.'[2]  Not stand afar off and think about it, and keep our King waiting; but, like Esther, 'let us draw near,'[3] and 'touch the top of the sceptre.'[4]

## FIFTEENTH DAY.

## Cleaving to the King.

'The men of Judah clave unto their king.'—2 SAM. xx. 2.

FOR it is not a matter of course that coming is followed by cleaving.   Even when the King Himself, in His veiled royalty, walked and talked with His few faithful followers, 'many of his dis ciples went back, and walked no more with Him.'[5] There was no word of indignation or reproach, only the appeal of infinite pathos from His gracious lips, 'Will ye also go away?'[6]

Let this sound in our ears to-day, not only in moments of temptation to swerve from truest-hearted loyalty and service, but all through the business of the day; stirring our too easy-going

---

[1] Esth. v. 2; iv. 11; viii. 3, 4.    [2] Heb. iv. 16.    [3] Heb. x. 22.
[4] Esth. v. 2.    [5] John vi. 66.    [6] John vi. 67.

resting into active cleaving; quickening our
following afar off[1] into following hard after Him ;[2]
rousing us to add to the blessed assurance, ' Thine
are we, David !' the bolder and nobler position,
'and *on Thy side !* '[3]

For this cleaving is not a mere terrified clinging
for safety,—it is the bright, brave resolution,
strengthened, not weakened, by the sight of waver-
ers or renegades, to be on His side, come what may,
because He *is* our King, because we love Him, because His cause and His kingdom are so very dear
to us. -

We cannot thus cleave, without loosening from
other interests. But what matter ! Let us be noble
for Jesus, like the men of might who 'separated
themselves unto David,' and who 'held strongly
with him in his kingdom.'[4] Shall we be mean
enough to aim at less, when it is *our Lord Jesus* who
would have us entirely ' with Him '?[5]

It is, after all, the easiest and safest course. The
especial friends and 'the mighty men which be-
longed to David,'[6] not only did not follow the
usurping Adonijah, but they were never tempted to
do so. 'But me, even me thy servant, . . . hath
he not called.'[7] There is many a temptation, very
powerful and dangerous to a camp-follower, which
the enemy knows it is simply useless to present to
one of the body-guard. Our Father leads us '*not*
into temptation,'[8] when He leads us closer to Jesus.

The Bible never speaks of ' good resolutions,'

---

[1] Matt. xxvi. 58.  [2] Ps. lxiii. 8.  [3] 1 Chron. xii. 18.
[4] 1 Chron. xii. 8 ; 1 Chron. xi. 10, marg.  [5] Cant. iv. 8.
[6] 1 Kings i. 8.  [7] 1 Kings i. 26.  [8] Matt. vi. 13; 1 Sam. xxii. 23.

but again and again of ' purpose.'[1] And this is
what we want, that 'with purpose of heart' we
should ' cleave unto the Lord.'[2] Have we this
distinct purpose to-day? Do we really *mean*, God
helping us, to cleave to our King to-day? Do not
let us dare to go forth to the certain conflicts and
temptations of the day with this negative but real
disloyalty of want of *purpose* in the matter. And
' if our heart condemn us,'[3] let us at once turn to
Him who says, 'I have *caused to cleave* unto me
the whole house of Israel.'[4] His grace shall enable
us to cleave unto our King.

---•---

## SIXTEENTH DAY.

---

# Tbe Joy of tbe king.

' David the king also rejoiced with great joy.'—I CHRON.
xxix. 9.

DO not let us think of the joy of our King over
His people as only future. While we cannot
look forward too much to the day when He shall
present us 'faultless before the presence of His
glory with exceeding joy,'[5] let us not overlook the
present gladness which we, even we, who have so
often grieved Him, may give to our King.
Elsewhere we hear of the joy of angels over

---

[1] 2 Tim. iii. 10.   [2] Acts xi. 23.   [3] 1 John iii. 20.
[4] Jer. xiii. 11.   [5] Jude 24.

repenting sinners;[1] here we have a glimpse of the joy of the King of angels over His consecrated ones. Look at the whole passage,—it is full of typical light,—and let us take it ' for our learning.'[2]

' Who then is willing to consecrate his service this day unto the Lord?'[3] Silence is negative here: there must be a definite heart-response if we *are* willing. Are you? If so, when? The King's question says nothing of some day, but of ' this day.' And the question *is* put to you: if never before, it is sounding in your ears now. Shall your service be His, ' this day,'[4] and henceforth? or *not?*

The result of willing consecration of ourselves and our service is always joy. ' The people rejoiced, for that they offered willingly;'[5] but was it not far more, far sweeter, that their king ' also rejoiced with great joy'? How they must have felt when He said, ' Now have I seen with joy Thy people which are present here, to offer willingly unto Thee!'[6]

For when a heart and life are willingly offered and fully surrendered to Him, He sees of ' the travail of His soul'[7] in it; it is a new accomplishment of the work which He came to do: and what then? He ' is satisfied.' If motive were wanting to yield ourselves unto Him,[8] would it not be more than supplied by the thought that it will be satisfaction and joy to Him ' who loved us and washed us from our sins in His own blood'?[9] It seems just the one blessed opportunity given to us of being

---

[1] Luke xv. 10.     [2] Rom. xv. 4.     [3] 1 Chron. xxix. 5.
[4] Josh. xxiv. 15.     [5] 1 Chron. xxix. 9.     [6] 1 Chron. xxix. 17.
[7] Isa. liii. 11.     [8] Rom. vi. 13.     [9] Rev. i. 5.

His true cup-bearers,[1] of bringing the wine of joy
to our King; and in so doing He will make our
own cups to run over.[2]

As our own hearts are filled with the intense joy
of consecration to our Lord, a yet intenser glow
will come as we remember that His joy is greater
than ours, for He is anointed 'with the oil of gladness above' His 'fellows.'[3]

Shall not 'this day' be 'the day of the gladness
of His heart'?[4]   Will you not consecrate your
service to-day unto Him?[5]   For then 'He will
save, He will rejoice over *thee* with joy; He will
rest in His love; He will joy over *thee* with
singing.'[6]

> Take myself, and I will be,
> Ever, *only*, ALL, for Thee!

---

## SEVENTEENTH DAY.

## Rest on tbe Morb of tbe iking.

'The word of my lord the king shall now be for rest' (*margin*).—2 SAM. xiv. 17.

HERE is the whole secret of rest from the very
beginning to the very end.   The *word* of
our King is all we have and all we need for deep,
utter heart-rest, which no surface waves of this

---

[1] 1 Kings x. 5.   [2] Ps. xxiii. 5.   [3] Ps. xlv. 7.
[4] Cant. iii. 11.   [5] 1 Chron. xxix. 5.   [6] Zeph. iii. 17.

troublesome world can disturb.[1] What gave 'rest from thy sorrow and from thy fear'[2] at the very first, when we wanted salvation and peace? It was not some vague, pleasing impression, some indefinable hush that came to us (or if it was, the unreality of the rest was soon proved), but some word of our King which we saw to be worthy of all acceptation;[3] we believed it,[4] and by it Jesus gave us rest.[5]

There is no other means of rest for all the way but the very same. The moment we simply believe any word of the King, we find that it is truly 'for rest,'[6] about the point to which it refers. And if we would but *go on taking* the King's word about every single thing, we should *always* find it, then and there, 'for rest.' Every flutter of unrest may, if we look honestly into it, be traced to not entirely and absolutely taking the King's word. His words are *enough* for rest at all times, and in all circumstances; therefore we are sinning the great sin of unbelief whenever we allow ourselves in any phase of unrest. It is not infirmity, but sin, to neglect to make use of the promises which He meant for our strong consolation and continual help.[7] And we ought not to acquiesce in the shadows which are only around us, because we do not hear, or hearing do not heed, God's call into the sunshine.

Take the slightest and commonest instances. If we have an entire and present belief in 'My grace is sufficient for thee,'[8] or, 'Lo, I am with

---

1 Job. xxxiv. 29.     2 Isa. xiv. 3.     3 1 Tim. i. 15.
4 2 Thess. ii. 13.     5 Heb. iv. 2, 3.     6 Mark. ix. 23.
7 Heb. vi. 18.     8 2 Cor. xii. 9.

you alway,'[1] should we feel nervous at anything He calls us to do for Him? Would not that word be indeed 'for rest'[2] in the moment of need,—'rest from the hard bondage' of service to which we feel unequal?[3] Have we not sometimes found it so, and if so, why not always? I see nothing about 'sometimes' in any of His promises. If we have an entire and present belief that 'all things work together for good,'[4] or that He leads us 'forth by the right way,'[5] should we feel worried when some one thing seems to work wrong, and some one yard of the way is not what we think straightest?

We lean upon the word of the King for everlasting life,[6] why not for daily life also? For it shall '*now* be for rest;' only try it to-day, 'now,' and see if it shall not be so! When he says 'perfect peace,'[7] He cannot mean imperfect peace. 'The people rested themselves upon the words of Hezekiah king of Judah.'[8] Just so simply let us rest upon the words of our King, Jesus!

---

[1] Matt. xxviii. 20.  [2] Phil. iv. 19.  [3] Isa. xiv. 3.
[4] Rom. viii. 28.  [5] Ps. cvii. 7.  [6] 1 John ii. 25.
[7] Isa. xxvi. 3.  [8] 2 Chron. xxxii. 8.

## EIGHTEENTH DAY.

---

## The Business of the King.

'The king's business required haste.'—1 SAM. xxi. 8.

AND yet there is no other business about which average Christians take it so easy. They 'must'[1] go their usual round, they 'must' write their letters, they 'must' pay off their visits and other social claims, they 'must' do all that is expected of them; and then, after this and that and the other thing is cleared off, they will do what they can of the King's business.[2] They do not say 'must' about that, unless it is some part of His business which is undertaken at second-hand, and with more sense of responsibility to one's clergyman than to one's King. Is this being 'faithful and loyal and single hearted?'[3] If it has been so, oh, let it be so no more! How can 'Jesus *Only*'[4] be our motto, when we have not even said 'Jesus *first*'?[5]

The King's business *requires* haste. It is always pressing, and may never be put off. Much of it has to do with souls which may be in eternity to-morrow;[6] and with opportunities which are gone

---

[1] Luke xiv. 20.
[2] Luke ix. 59, 61.
[3] Eph. vi. 5, 6.
[4] Matt. xvii. 8.
[5] Matt. vi. 33.
[6] Luke xii. 20.

for ever if not used then and there; there is no
'convenient season'[1] for it but 'to-day.'[2]  Often it is
not really done at all, because it is not done in the
spirit of holy haste.  We meet an unconverted
friend again and again, and beat about the bush,
and think to gain quiet influence and make way
gradually, and call it judicious not to be in a hurry,
when the real reason is that we are wanting in holy
eagerness and courage to do the King's true business
with that soul, and in nine such cases out of ten
nothing ever comes out of it; but 'As thy servant
was busy here and there, he was gone.'[3]  Have we
not found it so?

Delay in the Lord's errands is next to disobedience,
and generally springs out of it, or issues in it.
'God commanded me to make haste.'[4]  Let us see
to it that we can say, 'I made haste, and delayed
not to keep Thy commandments.'[5]

We never know what regret and punishment
delay in the King's business may bring upon ourselves.  Amasa 'tarried longer than the set time
which he (the king) had appointed him,'[6] and the
result was death to himself.  Contrast the result in
Abigail's case, where, except she had hasted, her
household would have perished.[7]

We find four rules for doing the King's business,
in His word.  We are to do it,—first, 'Heartily;'[8]
second, 'Diligently;'[9] third, 'Faithfully;'[10] fourth,
'*Speedily*.'[11]  Let us ask Him to give us the grace

---

1 Acts xxiv. 25.    2 Heb. iii. 13.    3 1 Kings xx. 40.
4 2 Chron. xxxv. 21.    5 Ps. cxix. 60.    6 2 Sam. xx. 5.
7 1 Sam. xxv. 34.    8 Col. iii. 23.    9 Ezra vii. 23.
10 2 Chron. xxxiv. 12.    11 Ezra vii. 21.

of energy to apply them this day to whatever He
indicates as our part of His business, remembering
that *He* said 'I *must* be about my Father's business.'[1]

Especially in that part of it which is between
Himself and ourselves alone, let us never delay.
Oh, the incalculable blessings that we have already
lost by putting off our own dealings with our King!
Abigail first 'made haste'[2] to meet David for mere
safety; soon afterwards, she again ' hasted and arose
and went after the messengers of David, and became
his wife.'[3]

Thus hasting, we shall rise from privilege to
privilege, and ' go from strength to strength.'[4]

What shall be our word for Jesus ?　Master, give it day by day;
Ever as the need arises, teach Thy children what to say.
Give us holy love and patience ; grant us deep humility,
That of self we may be emptied, and our hearts be full of
　　Thee;
Give us zeal and faith and fervour, make us winning, make us
　　wise,
Single-hearted, strong and fearless ;—Thou hast called us, we
　　will rise!
Let the might of Thy good Spirit go with every loving word;
And by hearts prepared and opened, be our message always
　　heard !

---

[1] Luke ii. 49.　　　　　　　[2] 1 Sam. xxv. 18.
[3] 1 Sam. xxv. 42.　　　　　[4] Ps. lxxxiv. 7.

# NINETEENTH DAY.

---

# The Readiness of the king's Servants.

' Thy servants are ready to do whatsoever my lord the king shall appoint.'—2 SAM. xv. 15.

THIS is the secret of steady and unruffled gladness in ' the business of the Lord, and the service of the King,'[1] whether we are ' over the treasures of the house of God,'[2] or, ' for the outward business over Israel.'[3]

It makes all the difference ! If we are really, and always, and equally ready to do *whatsoever*[4] the King appoints, all the trials and vexations arising from any change in His appointments, great or small, simply do not exist. If He appoints me to work there, shall I lament that I am not to work here?[5] If he appoints me to wait in-doors to-day, am I to be annoyed because I am not to work out-of-doors? If I meant to *write* His messages this morning, shall I grumble because He sends interrupting visitors, rich or poor, to whom I am to *speak* them, or ' show kindness '[6] for His sake, or

---

[1] 1 Chron. xxvi. 30.   [2] 1 Chron. xxvi. 20.   [3] 1 Chron. xxvi. 29.
[4] John ii. 5.   [5] Josh. i. 16.   [6] 2 Sam. ix. 3.

at least obey His command, 'Be courteous'?[1] If all my 'members'[2] are really at His disposal, why should I be put out if to-day's appointment is some simple work for my hands or errands for my feet, instead of some seemingly more important doing of head or tongue?

Does it seem a merely ideal life? Try it! begin at once; before you venture away from this quiet moment, ask your King to take you 'wholly' into His service, and place all the hours of this day quite simply at His disposal, and ask Him to make and keep you *ready* to do just exactly what He appoints. Never mind about to-morrow;[3] one day at a time is enough. Try it to-day, and see if it is not a day of strange, almost *curious* peace, so sweet that you will be only too thankful, when to-morrow comes, to ask Him to take it also,—till it will become a blessed habit to hold yourself simply and 'wholly at Thy commandment' 'for *any* manner of service.'[4]

Then will come, too, an indescribable and unexpected sense of freedom, and a total relief from the self-imposed bondage of 'having to get through' what we think lies before us. For, 'of the chil dren of Israel did Solomon make no bondmen.'[5]

Then, too, by thus being ready, moment by moment, for whatsoever He shall appoint, we realize very much more that we are not left alone, but that we are dwelling 'with the King for His work.'[6] Thus the very fact of an otherwise vexa-

---

[1] 1 Pet. iii. 8.    [2] Rom. vi. 13.    [3] Jas. iv. 14.
[4] 1 Chron. xxviii. 21.    [5] 1 Kings ix. 22.    [6] 1 Chron. iv. 23.

tious interruption is transmuted into a precious proof of the nearness of the King.[1]  His interference implies His interest and His presence.

The 'whatsoever' is not necessarily active work. It may be waiting ( whether half an hour or half a lifetime ), learning, suffering, sitting still.  But, dear fellow-servants of 'my Lord the King,' shall we be less ready for these, if any of them are His appointments for to-day?  'Whatsoever the king did pleased all the people.'[2]

'Ready' implies something of preparation,—not being taken by surprise.  So let us ask Him to prepare us for all that He is preparing for us.  And may 'the hand of God give' us 'one heart to do the commandment of the King!'[3]

> 'Lord, I have given my life to Thee,
> And every day and hour is Thine;
> What Thou appointest let them be;
> Thy will is better, Lord, than mine.'
>
> A. L. WARING.

---

[1] Ps. cxxxix. 5.      [2] 2 Sam. iii. 36.      [3] 2 Chron. xxx. 12.

# TWENTIETH DAY.

## The Friendship of the King.

'He that loveth pureness of heart, for the grace of his lips
the king shall be his friend.'—PROV. xxii. 11

'WHO can say, I have made my heart clean, I
am pure'?[1]  Who must not despair of the
friendship of the King if this were the condition?[2]
But His wonderful condescension in promising His
friendship bends yet lower in its tenderly devised
condition.  Not to the absolutely pure in heart,[3] but
to the perhaps very sorrowfully longing lover of that
pureness, come the gracious words, ' The King shall
be his Friend.'

Yet there must be some proof of this love; and
it is found in 'the grace of His lips.'  'For out of
the abundance of the heart the mouth speaketh.'[4]
Here, again, we stop and question our claim; for
our speech has not always been 'with grace;'[5] and
the memory of many a graceless and idle word
rises to bar it.[6]  How then shall the King be our
Friend?  Another word comes to our help : ' Grace

---

[1] Prov. xx. 9.　　　[2] Hab. i. 13.　　　[3] Matt. v. 8.
[4] Matt. xii. 34.　　　[5] Col. iv. 6.　　　[6] Matt. xii. 36.

is poured into *thy* lips,'[1]—grace that overflowed in
gracious words,[2] such as never man spake,[3] perfectly
holy and beautiful ; and we look up to our King
and plead that He has Himself fulfilled the condition in which we have failed,—that this is part of
the righteousness which He wrought for us, and
which is really unto us and upon us, because we
believe in Him ;[4] and so, for the grace of His own
lips, the King shall be our Friend.

Who has not longed for an ideal and yet a real
friend,—one who should exactly understand us,[5] to
whom we could tell everything,[6] and in whom we
could altogether confide,—one who should be very
wise and very true,[7]—one of whose love and unfailing interest we could be certain ?[8]   There are other
points for which we could not hope,—that this
friend should be very far above us, and yet the very
nearest and dearest, always with us,[9] always thinking of us, always doing kind and wonderful things
for us ;[10] undertaking and managing everything ;[11]
forgetting nothing, failing in nothing ;[12] quite certain never to change and never to die,[13]—so that
this one grand friendship should fill our lives, and
that we really never need trouble about anything
for ourselves any more at all.[14]

Such is our Royal Friend, and more; for no
human possibilities of friendship can illustrate what
He is to those to whom He says, 'Ye are my
friends.'[15]   We, even we, may look up to our

---

1 Ps. xlv. 2.   2 Luke iv. 22.   3 John vii. 46.
4 Rom. iii. 22.   5 Ps. cxxxix. 2.   6 Mark vi. 30.
7 Rev. xix. 11.   8 John xiii. 1.   9 Matt. xxviii. 20.
10 Ps. xl. 17.   11 Isa. xxxviii. 14.   12 Zeph. iii. 5.
13 Mal. iii. 6.   14 1 Pet. v. 7.   15 John xv. 14.

glorious King, our Lord and our God, and say,
'This is my Beloved, and this is my Friend!'[1]
And then we, even we, may claim the privilege of
being 'the King's companion'[2] and the 'King's
friend.'[3]

---

# TWENTY-FIRST DAY.

---

## The Light of the King's Countenance.

'In the light of the king's countenance is life.'—PROV.
xvi. 15

BUT first fell the solemn words, 'Thou hast set
our secret sins in the light of Thy countenance'[4] That was the first we knew of its brightness; and to some its revelation has been so terrible,
that they can even understand how the Lord 'shall
destroy' the wicked 'with the brightness of His
coming.'[5] Yet, though we feel that 'His eyes
were as a flame of fire,'[6] we found also that our
'King that sitteth in the throne of judgment, scattereth away all evil with His eyes;'[7] and that it
was when we stood in that light, that we found the
power of the precious blood of Jesus, the Anointed
One, to cleanse us from all sin.[8]

---

[1] Cant. v. 16.     [2] 1 Chron. xxvii. 33.     [3] 1 Kings iv. 5.
[4] Ps. xc. 8.     [5] 2 Thess. ii. 8.     [6] Rev. i. 14.
[7] Prov. xx. 8.     [8] 1 John i. 7.

This gives new value to the promise, 'They *shall* walk, O Lord, in the light of Thy countenance;'[1] for it is when we walk in the light that we may claim and do realize the fulness of its power and preciousness,—not for fitful and occasional cleansing, but for a glorious, perpetual, present cleansing from all sin. Do not let us translate it into another tense for ourselves, and read,[2] '*did* cleanse last time we knelt and asked for it,' but keep to the tense which the Holy Ghost has written, and meet the foe-flung darts of doubt[3] with faith's great answer, 'The blood of Jesus Christ His Son cleanseth (*i. e. goes on cleansing*) us from all sin.'

Thus the light of His countenance shall save us. Look at Ps. xliv. 3, where we see it as the means of past salvation,[4] and then at Ps. xlii. 5, where the Psalmist anticipates praise for its future help;[5] while the two are beautifully linked by the marginal reading of the latter, which makes it present salvation: 'Thy presence *is* salvation.'

Then follows peace. The waves are stilled, and the storm-clouds flee away noiselessly and swiftly and surely, when He lifts up the light of His countenance upon us, and gives us peace.[6] For this uplifting is the shining forth of His favour,[7]—the smile instead of the frown; and as we walk in the light of it, the peace will grow into joy, and we shall be even here and now 'exceeding glad with Thy countenance,'[8] while every step will bring us nearer to the resurrection joy of Christ Himself,

---

1 Ps. lxxxix. 15.    2 Rev. xxii. 18, 19.    3 Eph. vi. 16.
4 Ps. xliv. 3.    5 Ps. xlii. 5.    6 Num. vi. 26.
7 2 Sam. xxiii. 4.    8 Ps. xxi. 6.

saying with Him, 'Thou shalt make me full of joy with Thy countenance.'[1]

So we shall find day by day, that in the light of the King's countenance is cleansing, salvation, peace, joy;—and do not these make up life, the new life, the glad life of the children of the King?

'Lord, lift Thou up the light of Thy countenance upon us'[2] this day, and in it let us have life, yea, 'Life more abundantly.'[3]

'He that followeth me shall not walk in darkness, but shall have the light of life.'[4]

---

# TWENTY-SECOND DAY.

---

## The Tenderness of the King.

'And the king commanded, saying, Deal gently for my sake with the young man, even with Absalom.'—2 SAM. xviii. 5.

EVEN with Absalom! Even with the heartless, deliberate traitor and rebel.[5] We must recollect clearly what he was, to appreciate the exquisite tenderness of David in such a command to his rough war captains in such untender times. For the sake of his people and his kingdom, he must send them forth against him, but the deep love gushes out in the bidding, 'Deal gently for my sake.'

It was no new impulse. When Amnon was mur-

---

[1] Acts ii. 28.  [2] Ps. iv. 6.  [3] John x. 10.
[4] John viii. 12.  [5] 2 Sam. xv. 2-11.

dered, the king 'wept very sore,' and 'mourned for his son every day,'[1] and yet, when the fratricide had fled, 'the soul of King David longed to go forth unto him,'[2] and 'the king's heart was toward Absalom.'[3] And when God's own vengeance fell upon the wicked son, David's lamentation over him is perhaps unparalleled in its intensity of pathos among the records of human tenderness.[4]

Turn to the Antitype, and see the divine tenderness of our King. Again and again it gleams out, whether He himself wept, or whether He said, 'Weep not,'[5]—whether in the tender look, the tender word, or the tender touch of gentlest mercy. The Gospels are full of His tenderness. There is not room here even for the bare mention of the instances of it; but will you not give a little time to searching quietly for them, so that, reading them under the teaching of the Holy Spirit,[6] you may get a concentrated view of the wonderful tenderness of Jesus, and yield your heart to be moved by it, and your spirit to be so penetrated by it, that you may share it and reflect it? Remember that in such a search we learn not only what He did and said, nor only what He was, but what He *is;* and in all His recorded tenderness we are looking into the *present* heart of Jesus, and seeing what we shall find for ourselves as we have need. For He is 'this same Jesus'[7] to-day.

Then let us glance at the volume of our own experience. Who that has had any dealings with

---

1 2 Sam. xiii. 36, 37.   2 2 Sam. xiii. 39.   3 2 Sam. xiv. 1.
4 2 Sam. xviii. 33.   5 Luke xix. 41; ib. vii. 13; ib. xxii. 61.
6 John xiv. 26.   7 Acts i. 11.

Christ at all, but must bear witness that He has indeed dealt gently with us. Has not even suffering
been sweet when it showed us more of this?[1] What
if He had ever 'dealt with us after our sins'![2] But
He never did, and never will.[3] He hath dealt
gently and will deal gently with us, for His own
sake, and according to His own heart, from the first
drawings of His loving-kindness, on throughout the
measureless developments of his everlasting love.[4]
Not till we are in heaven shall we know the full
meaning of 'Thy *gentleness* hath made me great.'[5]

May we not recognize a command in this, as well
as a responsibility to follow the example of the
'gentleness of Christ'?[6] Perhaps next time we are
tempted to be a little harsh or hasty with an erring
or offending one, the whisper will come, 'Deal
gently, for My sake!'

> Return!
> O erring, yet beloved!
> I wait to bind thy bleeding feet, for keen
> And rankling are the thorns where thou hast been;
> I wait to give thee pardon, love, and rest.
> (Is not my joy to see thee safe and blest?)
> Return! I wait to hear once more thy voice,
> To welcome thee anew, and bid thy heart rejoice!
>
> Return!
> O chosen of my love!
> Fear not to meet thy beckoning Saviour's view;
> Long ere I called thee by thy name, I knew
> That very treacherously thou wouldst deal;
> Now I have seen thy ways,—yet I will heal.
> Return! Wilt thou yet linger far from Me?
> My wrath is turned away, I have redeeméd thee!

---

[1] Lam. iii. 32.  [2] Ps. ciii. 10.  [3] Job xi. 6.
[4] Jer. xxxi. 3.  [5] Ps. xviii. 35.  [6] 2 Cor. x. 1.

# TWENTY-THIRD DAY.

## The Token of the King's Grace.

'To-day thy servant knoweth that I have found grace in thy
sight, my lord, O king, in that the king hath fulfilled the
request of his servant.'—2 SAM. xiv. 22.

AN answered prayer makes us glad for its own
sake. But there is grace behind the gift
which is better and more gladdening than the gift
itself. For which is most valued, the 'engaged
ring,' or the favour of which it is the token?
Setting aside judicial answers to unspiritual prayers,[1]
which an honest conscience will have no difficulty
in distinguishing, the servants of the King may take
it that His answers to their requests are proofs and
tokens of His grace and favour,[2]—of His real, and
present, and personal love to themselves individually.

When they are receiving few or none, they should
search for the cause, lest it should be some hidden
or unrecognized sin.[3] For 'if I regard iniquity in
my heart, the Lord will not hear me;'[4] so *never*
let us go on comfortably and easily when He is silent
to us. And instead of envying others who get

---

[1] Ps. cvi. 15; Hos. xiii. 11, etc.   [2] 1 John iii. 22.
[3] Job x. 2.            [4] 1 Sam. xxviii. 6; Ps. xix. 12; ib. lxvi. 18.

'such wonderful answers,' 'let us search and try our ways.'[1]

Personal acceptance comes first. We must be 'accepted in the Beloved'[2] before we can look to be answered through the Beloved. Is there a doubt about this, and a sigh over the words? There need not be; for now, at this moment, the old promise stands with its unchangeable welcome to the weary: 'Him that cometh to me I will in no wise cast out.'[3] Then, if you come, now, at this moment, on the strength of His word, you *cannot* be rejected; and if not rejected, there is nothing but one blessed alternative—'accepted!'

*Then* come the answers! As surely as the prayers go up from the accepted one, so surely will the blessings come down. When Esther had touched the golden sceptre, '*then* said the king unto her, What wilt thou, queen Esther? and what is thy request? it shall be even given thee to the half of the kingdom.'[4] But there is no 'half' in our King's promise. He says, 'All things' and 'whatsoever.'[5] And He *does* 'do exceeding abundantly above all that we ask or think,' and more than fulfils our little scanty requests.[6]

And *then*, by every fresh fulfilment we should receive ever new assurance of our acceptance,—*then* (shall it not be 'to-day'?), as we give thanks for each gracious answer, we may look up confidingly and joyfully, and say, 'Thy servant *knoweth* that I have found grace in thy sight.' For He says,

---

1 Lam. iii. 40.
3 John vi. 37; Heb. vii. 25.
5 Matt. xxi. 22; John xiv. 13.

2 Eph. i. 6.
4 Esth. v. 3.
6 Eph. iii. 20; 1 Kings x. 13.

'See, I have hearkened to thy voice, and have accepted thy person.'[1]

> Accepted, Perfect, and Complete,[2]
> For God's inheritance made meet![3]
> How true, how glorious, and how sweet![4]

---

## TWENTY-FOURTH DAY.

---

# The Omniscience of the King.

'There is no matter hid from the king.'—2 SAM. xviii. 13.

THE very attributes which are full of terror to 'the King's enemies,'[5] are full of comfort to the King's friends. Thus His omniscience is like the pillar, which was 'a cloud and darkness' to the Egyptians, but 'gave light by night' to the Israelites.[6]

The king's own General complained of a man who did not act precisely as he himself would have acted. In his reply he uses these words, 'There is no matter hid from the king.' The appeal was final, and Joab had no more to say. When others say, like Joab, '"*Why* didst thou not" do so and so?' and we know or find that full reasons cannot be given or cannot be understood, what rest it is to fall back upon the certainty that our King knows

---

[1] 1 Sam. xxv. 35.  [2] Eph. i. 6.  [3] Col. i. 28.
[4] Col. ii. 10.  [5] Ps. xlv. 5.  [6] Ex. xiv. 20.

all about it !   When we are wearied out with trying
to make people understand, how restful it is that no
explanations are wanted when we come to speak to
Him !¹   'All things are naked and opened unto
the eyes of Him with whom we have to do ;'² and
the more we have to do with Him, the more glad
and thankful we shall be that there is 'not anything'
hid from the King.³

In perplexities,—when we cannot understand
what is going on around us—cannot tell whither
events are tending—cannot tell what to do, because
we cannot see into or through the matter before us,
—let us be calmed and steadied and made patient
by the thought that what is hidden from us is not
hidden from Him.   If He chooses to guide us
blindfold, let Him do it !⁴   It will not make the
least difference to the reality and rightness of the
guidance. ⁵

In mysteries,—when we see no clue—when we
cannot at all understand God's partial revelation—
when we cannot lift the veil that hangs before His
secret counsel—when we cannot pierce the holy
darkness that enshrouds His ways, or tread the
great deep of His judgments where His footsteps
are not known,⁶—is it not enough that even these
matters are not hid from our King?   'My father
will do nothing, either great or small, but he will
show it me.'⁷   ' For the Father loveth the Son, and
showeth Him all things that Himself doeth.' ⁸

Our King could so easily reveal everything to us,

---

1 Job xxiii. 10.　　2 Heb. iv. 13.　　8 1 Kings x. 3.
4 Isa. xlii. 16.　　5 Ps. cvii. 7.
6 Ps. xcvii. 2; ib. xxxvi. 6; ib. lxxvii. 19.　　7 1 Sam. xx. 2.
8 John v. 20.

and make everything so clear! It would be nothing to Him to tell us all our questions. When he
does not, cannot we trust Him, and just be satisfied
that He knows, and would tell us if it were best?
He has 'many things to say' unto us, but He waits
till we can bear them.[1]

May we be glad that even our sins are 'not hid'
from Him? Yes, surely, for He who knows all
can and will cleanse all. He has searched us and
known us,[2] as we should shrink from knowing
ourselves, and *yet* He has pardoned, and *yet* He
loves![3]

---

## TWENTY-FIFTH DAY.

---

## The Power of the king's Word.

'Where the word of a king is, there is power.'—ECCL. viii. 4.

THEN the question is, *Where* is it? 'Let the
word of Christ dwell *in you* richly,'[4] and
'there,' even 'in you,' will be power.

The Crowned One, who is now 'upholding all
things by the word of His power,'[5] hath said, 'I
have given them Thy word.'[6] And those who have
received this great gift, 'not as the word of men,
but, as it is in truth, the word of God,' know that

---

[1] John xvi. 12.         [2] Ps. cxxxix. 1.         [3] Isa. xlviii. 8.
[4] Col. iii. 16.         [5] Heb. ii. 9; ib. i. 3.         [6] John xvii. 14.

'there is power' with it, because it 'effectually worketh also' in them.[1]

They know its life-giving power, for they can say, 'Thy word hath quickened me;'[2] and its life-sustaining power, for they live 'by every word that proceedeth out of the mouth of God.'[3] They can say, 'Thy word have I hid in my heart, that I might not sin against Thee;'[4] for in proportion as the word of the King is present in the heart, *'there is power'*[5] against sin. Then let us use this means of absolute power more, and more life and more holiness will be ours.

'His word was with power'[6] in Capernaum of old, and it will be with the same power in any place now-a-days. His word cannot fail; it 'shall not return void;' it *'shall* prosper.'[7] Therefore, when our 'words fall to the ground,'[8] it only proves that they were not His words. So what we want is not merely that His power may accompany our word, but that we may not speak our own at all, but simply and only the very 'word of the King.' Then there will be power in and with it. Bows drawn at a venture[9] hit in a way that astonishes ourselves, when God puts His own arrows on the string.[10]

There is great comfort and help in taking this literally. Why ask a little when we may ask much? The very next time we want to speak or write 'a word for Jesus' (and of course that ought to be to-day),[11] let us ask Him to give us not merely a general

1 1 Thess. ii. 13.    2 Ps. cxix. 50.    3 Matt. iv. 4.
4 Ps. cxix. 11.    5 John vi. 63.    6 Luke iv. 32.
7 Isa. lv. 11.    8 1 Sam. iii. 19.    9 1 Kings xxii. 34.
10 Ps. xlv. 5.    11 Heb. iii. 13.

idea what to say, but to give us literally every single word, and 'they shall be withal fitted in thy lips.'[1]

For He will not say, 'Thou hast asked a hard thing,'[2] though it is far more than asking for the mantle of any prophet. He says, 'Behold, I have put My words in thy mouth.'[3] This was not for Jeremiah alone, for soon after we read, 'He that hath My word, let him speak My word faithfully'[4] (for we must not overlook our responsibility in the matter); and then follows the grand declaration of its power, even when spoken by feeble human lips: 'Is not My word like as a fire? saith the Lord; and like a hammer that breaketh the rock in pieces?'[5] 'Behold, I will make My words in thy mouth fire'[6]

If we are not even 'sufficient of ourselves to *think* anything as of ourselves,'[7] how much less to *speak* anything! 'Have I now any power at all to say anything? The word that God putteth in my mouth, that shall I speak.'[8] We would rather have it so, 'that the excellency of the power may be of God, and not of us'[9] Our ascended King has said, 'All power is given unto Me. Go ye *therefore*.'[10] That is enough for me; and 'I trust in Thy word.'[11]

Resting on the faithfulness of Christ our Lord,
Resting on the fulness of His own sure word,
Resting on His power, on His love untold,
Resting on His covenant secured of old.

---

[1] Prov. xxii. 18.    [2] 2 Kings ii. 10.    [3] Jer. i. 9.
[4] Jer. xxiii. 28.    [5] Jer. xxiii. 29.    [6] Jer. v. 14.
[7] 2 Cor. iii. 5.    [8] Num. xxii. 38.    [9] 2 Cor. iv. 7.
[10] Matt. xxviii. 18, 19.    [11] Ps. cxix. 42.

# TWENTY-SIXTH DAY.

---

## The Name of the King.

'A King shall reign. And this is His name whereby He shall be called, THE LORD OUR RIGHTEOUSNESS.' —JER. xxiii. 5, 6.

WE cannot do without this most wonderful name. It can never be an old story to us. It is always a ' new name '[1] in freshness and beauty and power. It is our daily need and our daily joy. For strength it is indeed 'a strong tower; the righteous runneth into it, and is safe.'[2] For sweetness it is ' as ointment poured forth.'[3] In it we see at once the highest height and the deepest depth; Jehovah, God of God, Light of Light, and our need of a righteousness which is not our own at all, because we have none. We stand as upon an Alpine slope, face to face with the highest, grandest, purest summit above, and the darkest, deepest valley below, seeing more of the height because of the depth, and more of the depth because of the height.

Jesus our King ' hath by inheritance obtained a

---

[1] Rev. iii. 12.     [2] Prov. xviii. 10.     [3] Cant. i. 3.

more excellent name "[1] than angels, for His Father has given Him his own name,—' He shall be called Jehovah.'[2] But this alone would be too great, too far off for us; it might find echoes among the harpings of sinless angels, but not among the sighings of sinful souls. And so the name was completed for us, by the very word that expresses our truest, deepest, widest, most perpetual need, and the Holy Ghost revealed the Son of God to as ' Jehovah our Righteousness.'

Do not let us be content with theoretically understanding and correctly holding the doctrine of justification by faith. Turn from the words to the reality, from the theory to the Person, and as a little, glad, wondering child, look at the simple, wonderful truth. That ' the Righteousness of God ' (how magnificent!) is ' unto all and upon all them that believe; "[3] therefore, at this very moment, unto and upon you and me, instead of our own filthy rags,[4] so that we stand clothed and beautiful[5] in the very sight of God, *now;* and Jesus can say, ' Thou art all fair, my love,'[6] *now!* That it is not any finite righteousness, which might not quite cover the whole,—might not be quite enough to satisfy God's all-searching eye; not *a* righteousness, but *The* Righteousness of God;[7] and this no abstract attribute, but a Person, real, living, loving,—covering us with His own glorious apparel,[8] representing us before His Father, Christ Jesus Himself ' made

---

[1] Heb. i. 4.   [2] Jer. xxiii. 6, marg.   [3] Rom. iii. 22.
[4] Isa. lxiv. 6.   [5] Zech. iii. 4, 5.   [6] Cant. iv. 7.
[7] Phil. iii. 9.   [8] Isa. lxiii. 1.

unto us Righteousness ! '[1]  This to-day and this for ever, for ' His name shall endure for ever.'[2]

It is in His kingly capacity that this glorious name is given to Him.    For only by ' *submitting* ourselves to the Righteousness of God,'[3] can we have ' the blessedness of the man unto whom God imputeth righteousness without works.'[4]    There can be no compromise,—it must be His only or ours only.   He must be our King, or He will not be our Righteousness.

---

## TWENTY-SEVENTH DAY.

---

## Working with the King.

' There they dwelt with the king for his work.'—1 CHRON. iv. 23.

' THERE ! '—Not in any likely place at all, not in the palace, not in ' the city of the great king,'[5] but in about the last place one would have expected, 'among plants and hedges.'[6]   It does not even seem clear why they were 'there' at all, for they were potters, not gardeners,—thus giving us the combination of simple labour of the hands, carried on in out-of-the-way places ; and yet they were dwellers with the king, and workers with the king.

---

[1] 1 Cor. i. 30.      [2] Ps. lxxii. 17.      [3] Rom. x. 3.
[4] Rom. iv. 6.      [5] Ps. xlviii. 2.      [6] 1 Chron. iv. 23.

The lesson seems twofold,—First, that anywhere and everywhere we too may dwell ' with the King for His work.' We may be in a very unlikely or unfavourable place for this,—it may be in a literal country life, with little enough to be seen of the ' goings '[1] of the King around us; it may be among hedges of all sorts, hindrances in all directions; it may be, furthermore, with our hands full of all manner of pottery for our daily task. No matter! The King who placed us ' there' will come and dwell there with us; the hedges are all right, or He would soon do away with them,[2] and it does not follow that what seems to hinder our way[3] may not be for its very protection; and as for the pottery, why, that is just exactly what He has seen fit to put into our hands, and therefore it is, for the present, ' His work.'[4]

Secondly, that the dwelling and the working must go together. If we are indeed dwelling with the King, we shall be working for Him, too, ' as we have opportunity.'[5] The working will be as the dwelling,—a settled, regular thing, whatever form it may take at His appointment. Nor will His work ever be done when we are not dwelling with Him. It will be our own work then, not His, and it will not ' abide.'[6] We shall come under the condemnation of the vine which was pronounced ' empty,' because ' he bringeth forth fruit unto himself.'[7]

We are to dwell with the King ' for His work;' but He will see to it that it shall be for a great deal

---

[1] Ps. lxviii. 24.     [2] Job iii. 23.    [3] Matt. xxi. 33.
[4] Mark xiii. 34.    [5] Gal. vi. 10.    [6] 1 Cor. iii. 14.
[7] Hos. x. 1.

besides,—for a great continual reward according to
His own heart and out of His royal bounty,—for
peace, for power, for love, for gladness, for likeness to Himself.

'Labourers together with God!'[1] 'workers
together with him!'[2] 'the Lord working with' us![3]
admitted into divine fellowship of work!—will not
this thought ennoble everything He gives us to do
to-day, even if it is 'among plants and hedges'!
Even the pottery will be grand!

'Be strong, all ye people of the land, saith the
Lord, and work, FOR I am with you, saith the Lord
of hosts.'[4]

---

## TWENTY-EIGHTH DAY.

---

## The Recompense of the King.

'Why should the king recompense it me with such a
reward?'—2 SAM. xix. 36.

BARZILLAI 'had provided the king of suste
nance while he lay at Mahanaim,'[5] exiled from
his royal city. When the day of triumphant return
came, David said to him, 'Come thou over with me,
and I will feed thee with me in Jerusalem.'[6] This
was the 'reward.'

But what a privilege and delight it must have

---

[1] Cor. iii. 9.　　　[2] 2 Cor. vi. 1.　　　[3] Mark xvi. 20.
[4] Hag. ii. 4.　　　[5] 2 Sam. xix, 32.　-　[6] 2 Sam. xix. 33.

been to the loyal old man! And to come nearer, what a continual joy it must have been to the women who 'ministered'[1] to the exiled King of heaven 'of their substance.' How *very* much one would have liked a share in that ministry!

Is there *any* loving wish which our King does not meet? Was it not most thoughtful of Him to appoint His continual representatives, so that we might always and every one of us have the opportunity of ministering *to Him!* These opportunities are wider than we sometimes think; some limit His ' gracious Inasmuch '[2] to services for His sake to the poor only. Yet the 'strangers'[3] whom He bids us love, may be rich in all but the friendliness and kindness which we may show them; and the 'sick' may be those among our own dear ones who need our ministry. Why should we fancy it is only those who are *not* near and dear to us, to whom we may minister ' as unto Him '?[4]

- But oh, what little services are our cups of cold water![5] and how utterly ashamed we feel of ever having thought any of them wearying or irksome, when we look at ' the recompense of the reward,'[6]— '*such* a reward!' Is there one of us whose heart has not thrilled at the mere imagining of what it will be to hear 'the King say, Come, ye blessed!'[7] Then what will it be to enter into the fulness of the reward, to ' come over with '[8] Him, and dwell with Him always in 'the holy Jerusalem,' and ' go no more out.'[9]

---

[1] Luke viii. 3.    [2] Matt. xxv. 40.    [3] Deut. x. 19.
[4] Eph. vi. 7.    [5] Mark ix. 41.    [6] Heb. xi. 26.
[7] Matt. xxv. 34.    [8] 2 Sam. xix. 33.    [9] Rev. xxi. 10; ib. iii. 12.

' *Why* should the king recompense it me with such a reward ? '　' *Why* should thy servant dwell in the royal city with thee ? '[1]　For there is such a tremendous disproportion between the work and the reward, though such a glorious proportion between His love and His reward.

And yet there is a beautiful fitness in it.　The banquet of everlasting joy for those who gave Him meat ;[2] the river of His pleasures for those who gave Him drink ;[3] the mansions in the Father's home for those who took the stranger in ;[4] the white robes for those who clothed the naked ;[5] the tree of life and ' no more pain ' for those who visited the sick ;[6] the ' glorious liberty '[7] for those who came unto the prisoner ; the crown of all, the repeatedly promised ' with Me '[8] for those who were content to be with His sorrowful or suffering ones for His sake.　*Why* all this?　I suppose we shall keep on asking that for ever !

---

## TWENTY-NINTH DAY.

## The Salvation of the King.

' The Lord is our King;　He will save us.'—Isa. xxxiii. 22.

THE thought of salvation is constantly connected with that of kingship.　Type, illustration,

---

[1] 1 Sam. xxvii. 5.　[2] Matt. xxv. 35, etc.　[3] Ps. xxxvi. 8.
[4] John xiv. 2.　[5] Rev. vii. 13.　[6] Rev. xxii. 2 ; ib. xxi. 4.
[7] Rom. viii. 21.　[8] John xvii. 24.

and prophecy combine them. 'Thou shalt anoint him . . . that he may save my people'[1] 'By the hand of my servant David I will save my people.'[2] 'The king saved us.' 'A King shall reign ; in His days Judah shall be saved.'[3] 'Thy King cometh, . . . having salvation.'[4]

Because Jesus is our Saviour, He has the right to be our King; but again, because He is King, He is qualified to be our Saviour; and we never know Him fully as Saviour till we have fully received Him as King. His kingship gives the strength to His priesthood. It is as the Royal Priest of the order of Melchisedec that He is 'able to save.'[5] Thus He is 'a Saviour, and a Great One,' 'mighty to save.'[6]

Our King has not only 'wrought,' and 'brought,' and 'made known His salvation,'[7] but He Himself *is* our salvation.[8] The very names seem used interchangeably. Isaiah says, 'Say ye to the daughter of Zion, Behold, thy *Salvation* cometh ;'[9] Zechariah bids her rejoice, for 'Behold, thy *King* cometh.'[10] Again, Isaiah says, 'Mine eyes have seen the *King*;'[11] and Simeon echoes, 'Mine eyes have seen thy *Salvation*,'[12] as he looks upon the infant Jesus, the Light to lighten the Gentiles; reminding us again of David's words, 'The Lord is my light and my salvation.'[13]

It is because we need salvation, because we are

---

[1] 1 Sam. ix. 16.
[2] 2 Sam. iii. 18; ib. xix. 9.
[3] Jer. xxiii. 5, 6.
[4] Zech. ix. 9.
[5] Heb. vii. 1, 17; ib. vii. 25.
[6] Isa. xix. 20; ib. lxiii. 1.
[7] Isa. lxiii. 5.  [8] Ps. xcviii. 2.  [9] Isa. lxii. 11.
[10] Zech. ix. 9.  [11] Isa. vi. 5.  [12] Luke ii. 30.
[13] Ps. xxvii. 1.

surrounded by enemies and dangers, and have no
power to help ourselves, and have no other help or
hope, that He says, 'I will be thy King; where is
any other that may save thee?'[1]  There is no other.
'He saw that there was no man,'[2] and He says,
'There is no Saviour beside me.'[3]

What is our response?  David begins a Psalm by
saying, 'Truly my soul waiteth upon God: from
Him cometh my salvation;'[4]  but he quickly raises
the key, and sings, 'He *only* is my salvation.'[5]
Perhaps we have long been quite clear that He *only*
is our salvation from 'everlasting destruction;'[6]
but are we equally clear that He *only* is (not will be,
but *is*) our present salvation from everything from
which we want to be saved?—from every danger,
from every snare,[7] from every temptation,[8] from
'the hand of *all* our enemies,'[9] from our sins?[10]  In
death we would cling to the words, 'Christ Jesus
came into the world to save sinners.'[11]  Why not in
life equally cling to, and equally make real use of,
the promise, 'He shall save His people from their
sins,'[12]—not merely from sin in general, but definitely
'from *their* sins,' personal and plural sins?  'Is my
hand shortened at all that it cannot redeem? or
have I no power to deliver?'[13]

His salvation is indeed finished, His work is perfect;[14] and yet our King is still 'working salvation
in the midst of the earth,'[15] applying the reality of
His salvation (if we will only believe His power) to

[1] Hos. xiii. 10.　　　[2] Isa. lix. 16.　　　[3] Hos. xiii. 4.
[4] Ps. lxii. 1.　　　　[5] Ps. lxii. 2.　　　　[6] 2 Thess. i. 9.
[7] Ps. xci. 3.　　　　[8] 2 Pet. ii. 9.　　　　[9] 2 Sam. iii. 18.
[10] Tit. ii. 14.　　　　[11] 1 Tim. i. 15.　　　[12] Matt. i. 21.
[13] Isa. l. 2.　　　　　[14] Deut. xxxii. 4.　　[15] Ps. lxxiv. 12.

the daily details of our pilgrimage and our warfare. We need it not only at last, but now—every hour, every minute. And the King 'shall deliver the needy when he crieth,'[1] 'and shall save the souls of the needy.'[2]

May He say to your soul this day, 'I am *thy* salvation.'[3]

> Look away to Jesus,
>   Look away from all!
> Then we need not stumble,
>   Then we shall not fall.
> From each snare that lureth,
>   Foe or phantom grim,
> Safety this ensureth,
>   Look away to Him!

## THIRTIETH DAY.

# Good Tidings to the king's household.

'We do not well: this day is a day of good tidings, and we hold our peace; if we tarry till the morning light, some mischief will come upon us; now, therefore, come, that we may go and tell the king's household.'—2 KINGS vii. 9.

JUST the last persons who would seem to need 'good tidings,'[4] and the last, too, who would seem likely to have them to convey! But oh, how

---

[1] Ps. lxxii. 12.  [2] Ps. lxxii. 13.
[3] Ps. xxxv. 3.  [4] 2 Kings vii. 3.

true the figure is! how many among the King's own household need the good tidings which these lepers brought! For they are starving so near to plenty,[1] and poor within reach of treasure,[2] and thinking themselves besieged when the Lord has dispersed the foe for them. Is it not often the spiritual leper, the conscious outcast, the famine-stricken, possessionless soul, who takes the boldest step into the fullest salvation, and finds deliverance and abundance and riches beyond what the more favoured and older inmate of the King's household knows anything about?

It may be one of the enemy's devices,[3] that we sometimes hold back good tidings, just because we shrink from telling them to the King's household. How many who do not hesitate to speak of Jesus to little children or poor people, or even to persons who openly say, 'We will not have this man to reign over us,'[4] never say one word to their fellow-subjects about the blessed discoveries that the Holy Spirit has made to them of the fulness of His salvation,[5] and the reality of His power, and the treasures of His word, and the satisfaction of His love, and the far-reaching fulfilments of His promises, and the real, actual deliverance, and freedom, and victory, which He gives,[6] and the strength and the healing that flow through faith in His name![7]

Satan even perverts humility into a hinderance in this, and persuades us that of course our friend knows as much or more of this than we do, and

---

[1] Ps. lxxxi. 10-16.     [2] 1 Cor. iii. 21, 22.     [3] 2 Cor. ii 11.
[4] Luke xix. 14.     [5] John xvi. 14, 15.     [6] Rom. viii. 37.
[7] Acts iii. 16.

that telling of what we have found in Jesus, may seem like or lead to talking about ourselves. Yet perhaps all the while that friend is hungering and feeling besieged, while we are withholding good tidings of plenty and deliverance.[1] Verily, 'we do not well.'[2] Have there not been days when the brightest of us would have been most thankful for the simplest word about Jesus, from the humblest Christian?—days when even 'the mention of His name' might have been food and freedom!

It does not in the least follow that members of Christian families need no such 'good tidings' because of their favoured position. They may need it all the more, because no one thinks it necessary to try and help *them*. 'As we have therefore opportunity, let us do good unto *all* men, specially unto them who are of the household of faith.'[3]

And when? The constantly recurring word meets us here again, '*Now!*'

---

[1] Prov. xi. 24-26.     [2] James iv. 17.     [3] Gal. vi. 10.

## THIRTY-FIRST DAY.

---

## The Prosperity of the King.

'A King shall reign and prosper.'—JER. xxiii. 5.

IF we are really interested, heart and soul, in a person, how delighted we are to have positive assurance of his prosperity, and how extremely interested and pleased we feel at hearing anything about it! Is not this a test of our love to our King? Are we both interested and happy in the short, grand, positive words which are given us about His certain prosperity? If so, the pulse of our gladness is beating through to the very heart of God, for 'Jehovah hath pleasure in the prosperity of His servant.'[1]

His prosperity is both absolute and increasing. Even now, 'Thy wisdom and prosperity exceedeth the fame that I heard.'[2] If we could get one glimpse of our King in his present glory and joy, how we who love Him would rejoice for Him and with Him![3] And if we could get one great view of the wide but hidden prosperity of His kingdom *at this moment*, where would be our discouragement and faint-

---

[1] Ps. xxxv. 27.     [2] 1 Kings x. 7.     [3] 1 Pet. iii. 22.

heartedness! Suppose we could see how His work is going on in every soul that he has redeemed out of every kindred and tongue all over the world,[1] with the same distinctness with which we see it in the last trophy of His grace for which we have been praising Him, would it not be a revelation of entirely overwhelming joy? Many Christians now-a-days are foregoing an immense amount of cheer, because they do not take the trouble to inquire, or read, or go where they can hear about the present prosperity of His kingdom. Those who do not care much, can hardly be loving much or helping much.

But we *do* care about it; and so how jubilantly the promises of His *increasing* prosperity ring out to *us!* 'He *must* increase.'[2] 'He *must* reign, till He hath put all enemies under his feet.'[3] 'Of the increase of His government and peace there shall be *no* end.'[4]

All our natural delight in progress finds satisfaction here,—no stagnation, no reaching a dead level; we are on an ever-winning side, bound up with an ever-progressing cause. A typical light on this point flashes from the story of David. He 'went on and grew great,'[5] or, as the margin has it, 'going and growing;' which we cannot forbear connecting with the promise to ourselves, 'Ye shall *go* forth and *grow* up.'[6] And then we are told that He 'waxed greater and greater' (marg.), 'went on going and *increasing*.'[7]

But we must not be merely on-lookers. Let us

---

[1] Rev. v. 9.    [2] John iii. 30.    [3] 1 Cor. xv. 25.    [4] Isa. ix. 7.
[5] 2 Sam. v. 10.      [6] Mal. iv. 2.      [7] 1 Chron. xi. 9.

see to it, first, that there be increasing prosperity in His kingdom in our hearts. Pray that He may not only reign but prosper in that domain. And next, let us see to it that we are doing all we can to further His prosperity all around us. Translate our daily prayer, 'Thy kingdom come,'[1] into daily, burning, glowing action for its prosperity.

---

[1] Matt. vi. 10.  [2] Ps. xxiii. 5.  [3] 2 Sam. xix. 33.  [4] Gal. iv. 5.
[5] Cant. ii. 4.  [6] Cant. v. 1.  [7] Cant. i. 12.

# ROYAL COMMANDMENTS

OR

## MORNING THOUGHTS

FOR

### The King's Servants

# FIRST DAY.

---

## 𝕷oving 𝕬llegiance.

'Master!'—JOHN xx. 16.

I THINK this is the very epitome of love. Love
understands love; it needs no talk. Sunlight
needs no paraphernalia of pipes, and wicks, and
burners; it just shines out, direct and immediate.
And the dewdrop flashes it back in the same way.
The sparkle may be tiny, but it is true and immediate; it needs no vehicle.

'I have called thee by thy name.'[1] That was
quite enough. The powerful sunshine of His love
was focussed into that white beam of sevenfold
light, and the whole soul was concentrated into the
responsive love-flash, 'Master!'

When that word has truly gone up from the soul
to Christ, then we have felt what we can never put
into any other words. It is the single diamond of
soul-expression,[2] and we have cast it at His feet for
ever.

He accepts it; for how wonderfully sweetly falls
His direct answer, 'Ye call Me Master and Lord:

---

[1] Isa. xliii. 1.　　　[2] Ps. xvi. 2.

and ye say well; for so I am."[1]  Think of this seal
of approval being set upon the name we so love to
give Him.  'Ye say *well.*'

He reserves it to Himself, for He says, 'One is
your Master, even Christ.'[2]  It is sacred to Him in
all its depths of meaning.  He has put His hand
upon our offering, claiming it as only His own;[3]
and now it can never be another's.

It includes the whole attitude of soul towards
our beloved Lord.

1. *Love.*—There is a great hush; we have not
any words at all.  We cannot even tell Him we
love Him, because we are dazzled with a glimpse of
His love,[4] and overwhelmed with our unworthiness
of it.  Our eyes fill, and our bosom heaves.  The
tide has risen too high for verbal prayer or praise;
we have to be 'silent in love'[5]—the very silence
being an echo of the eternal depth of calmness of
the exceeding great love in which He rests.  There
is only one word which does not jar with the still
music of such a moment,—'Master!'

2. *Adoration.*—For the breathing of the name is
all we can do to express the unexplainable recognition of His glory.[6]  Already He is 'admired in all
them that believe'[7] with the admiration of aston-
ishment.  'We praise Thee, we bless Thee, we
worship Thee, we glorify Thee, we give thanks to
Thee for Thy great glory.'  And yet we only
uttered the one word, 'Master!'

3. *Allegiance.*—The true utterance of it is the

---

[1] John xiii. 13.      [2] Matt. xxiii. 8, 10.   [3] 1 Sam. xxv. 35.
[4] 2 Sam. 1. 26; Eph. iii. 19.            [5] Zeph. iii. 17, margin.
[6] John i. 14.        [7] 2 Thess. i. 10 (Gr.)

very oath of allegiance. We cannot, must not, dare not, will not, henceforth serve 'two masters,'[1] nor the still more subtle 'many masters '[2] The word has been breathed into His heart, and He will treasure it there, and keep it for us. It *has been said*, and the sound-waves can never be recalled; they will vibrate through the universe for ever. God grant that no traitorous whisper may ever cross them!

4. *Confidence.*—We have found One whom we can trust implicitly, and rest upon entirely. We have put our lives into His hand. We have burned the bridge behind us, because we are quite sure He is the Captain of our salvation.[3] We have entered His service *for ever.*[4] We have given our allegiance unreservedly, because we confide in Him unreservedly.[5] There is no question about it. 'I know whom I have believed,'[6] and therefore I say, 'Master!'

5. *Obedience.*—All a mockery without this! Not only our lips, but our lives must say, 'Master!' And by His own grace they shall say it; the name shall be emblazoned on every page of our lives. For Jesus Himself will 'make it plain' upon our tablets, so 'that he may run that readeth it '[7] This is the test, the fruit, the manifestation of love.[8] But oh, how sweet that we may fearlessly say the word which pledges us to it, knowing that the Master Himself will enable us to fill it up with the practical obedience which, above all things, we

---

[1] Matt. vi. 24.  [2] Jas. iii. 1; Isa. xxvi. 13.  [3] Heb. ii. 10.
[4] Ex. xxi. 6.  [5] 1 Chron. xii. 18.  [6] 2 Tim. i. 12.
[7] Hab. ii. 2.  [8] John xiv. 15; 2 Cor. v. 14, 15.

want so intensely to yield to Him! It is like throwing our alpenstock up to a higher ledge of rock, and then giving ourselves up to the strong arm of the guide to draw us up after it.

Never shall we have to say, like the Amalekite's servant, ' My master left me! '[1] He is our *good* Master,[2] our ' *own* Master'[3] and He will reveal to His weak servants all that He means in His own faithful endorsement of the name[4] which His Spirit has taught us to call Him.[5]

'O Master, at Thy feet
I bow in rapture sweet!
Before me, as in darkling glass,
Some glorious outlines pass
Of love, and truth, and holiness, and power,
I own them Thine, O Christ, and bless Thee for this hour.'

## SECOND DAY.

## Seeking for His Commandments.

' Keep and seek for all the commandments of the Lord your God.'—I CHRON. xxviii. 8.

IS not this precept too often halved? We acknowledge our obligation to keep, but what about *seeking for* all the commandments of the Lord our God? Are we doing this?

---

[1] 1 Sam. xxx. 13.     [2] Mark x. 17.     [3] Rom. xiv. 4.
[4] John xiii. 13.     [5] 1 Cor. xii. 3.

'Thy commandment is exceeding broad,'[1] and
our horizon must be continually widening if He is
making us to go in the path of His commandments.[2]
Even when, by His grace, we have been led to take
the seven beautiful steps in that path mentioned in
that grand gush of Bible love, the 119th Psalm,
believing them,[3] learning them, longing for them,
loving them,[4] delighting in them, keeping them,[5]
and not forgetting them,[6] there remains yet this
further step, *seeking for all of them.*

Perhaps we have even a little shrinking from this.
We are afraid of seeing something which might
be peculiarly hard to keep; it seems as if it might
be enough to try to keep what commandments we
have seen without seeking for still more, and as if
seeing more to keep would only involve us in
heavier obligations and in more failures to keep
them. And we almost wish we had never seen this
added command, forgetting that shedding of blood
was needed for sin 'through ignorance.'[7] But we
have seen it, even if we never noticed it before; it
is shown us to-day, and we have no alternative but
obedience or disobedience to it.

Does not a loving child like to find out what
its dear father wishes it to do? does it not feel sorry
that it did not know all he wished in time to avoid
doing just the contrary? How little we must love
His will if we would rather not know it, lest it
should clash with our own![8] Even to take the
lowest ground, all His commandments are ' for our

---

[1] Ps. cxix. 96.    [2] Ps. cxix. 35.    [3] Ps. cxix. 66.
[4] Ps. cxix. 73, 131, 127.    [5] Ps. cxix. 47, 115.    [6] Ps. cxix. 176.
[7] Lev. iv. 27-35.    [8] Ps. xl. 8.

good,'[1] and 'in keeping of them there is great reward;'[2] so that we are clearly missing unknown
good or unknown reward by remaining in ignorance
of any of them.   Nay, more, ' it is your life'[3] to
observe to do *all* the words of His law.

We need not fear being left to struggle with newly
discovered impossibilities; for, with the light that
reveals a command, the grace to fulfil it will surely
be given.   It is very humbling when the Spirit's
light flashes upon some command of our God which
we have never ' observed,' much less ' done ;'[4] and
yet it is a very gracious answer to the prayer, ' Teach
me to do Thy will.'[5]

In reading His word, let us steadily set ourselves
to seek for all His yet unnoticed commandments,
noting day by day what we find ; and thus knowing
more of His will, will be a step towards doing more
of it.   Let us not be content with vaguely praying,
' Lord, what wilt thou have me to do?'[6] but set to
work to see what He has already *said*[7] we are to do,
and then, ' Whatsoever he saith unto you, do it.'[8]

---

[1] Deut. x. 13.      [2] Ps. xix. 11.      [3] Deut. xxxii. 47.
[4] Deut. xi. 32 ; xv. 5, etc.   [5] Ps. cxliii. 10.      [6] Acts ix. 6.
[7] Hab. ii. 1.      [8] John ii. 5.

# THIRD DAY.

## Recognizing His Commandments.

'And this is His commandment.'—1 JOHN iii. 23.

WE may be quite sure of three things,—first, that whatever our Lord commands us, He really means us to do;[1] secondly, that whatever He commands us is 'for our good always;'[2] and, thirdly, that whatever He commands us, He is able and willing to enable us to do, for 'all God's biddings are enablings.'[3]

But do we practically recognize all His commandments *as* commandments, and the breach of any one of them as sin?[4] As we read each precept, let us solemnly say to ourselves, 'This is His *commandment;*' and oh, what a touchstone of guilt will it be! How we shall see that what we have been excusing as infirmity and natural weakness which we could not help, and shortcomings with regard to impossible standards, has been all sin, transgression, disobedience, needing to be bitterly repented of, needing nothing less than blood, the precious blood of Christ,[5] for atonement and cleansing,

---

[1] Deut. xii. 32.  [2] Deut. vi. 24.  [3] 2 Cor. ix. 8, xii. 9.
[4] Ps. cxix. 4; Jas. ii. 10. [5] Heb. ix. 22.

needing nothing short of Omnipotence to strengthen us against it. [1]

Perhaps this is the sad secret of many a mourning life among God's children. They are calling sin by other names.[2] They think it is only natural temperament and infirmity, for which they are to claim sympathy, to go on doubting and distrusting their Saviour and their God; yet *'this* is His commandment, That we should believe on the name of His Son Jesus Christ,'[3] and *this*, 'Trust in Him at all times.'[4] They think they are to be tenderly pitied for having such a burden to bear, and such sadness of heart; yet *this* is His commandment, 'Cast thy burden upon the Lord;'[5] and *this*, 'Rejoice in the Lord alway.'[6] They do not think they can exactly help their hearts being so cold that they do not know whether they love Him or not; yet *this* is His commandment, 'Thou shalt love the Lord thy God with all thy heart.'[7] They almost feel as if their state were a rather interesting one.

Yet, oh! dear friend, if the Lord has indeed commanded these things, it is a state of disobedience. If He has said them, He *means* you to do them. Oh, come face to face with His word; do not shrink from the terrible shock of seeing *sin* where you only thought of infirmity. It is by the word that He has spoken that you will be judged,[8] not by man's excusing euphemisms. You are committing sin in doubting Him; you are directly disobedient in not trusting Him, not casting your

---

[1] Isa. xl. 29.   [2] Heb. xii. 1, 2.   [3] 1 John iii. 23.
[4] Ps. lxii. 8.   [5] Ps. lv. 22.   [6] Phil. iv. 4.
[7] Matt. xxii. 37.   [8] John xii. 48.

burden upon Him; not rejoicing alway in Him;
you are a transgressor of His 'first and great commandment'[1] in not loving Him. 'Thou art become
a transgressor of the law,' 'guilty of all.'[2]

Oh! if the Holy Spirit flashes the light which He
only can flash upon these commandments, and
shows you the sins which, child of God though you
are, you have never yet recognized as such, you cannot and will not rest in them, if indeed 'the root
of the matter is found'[3] in you. It will wring from
you an agony cry of 'Lord, have mercy upon me,
and incline my heart to keep *this* law,' as He turns
that terrible and yet merciful light on each. If you
do not yet 'see it quite so strongly,' ask that
blessed Spirit to show you, at any cost, what He
has, sooner or later, to show you. For He will not
show you the sin without the remedy. And never
will the precious blood of Christ have been *so*
precious to you as when, after such an entirely startling revelation of the guilt of your position of disobedience, you come, despairing of yourself, to the
Fountain,[4] and find the cleansing and sanctifying
and overcoming power of the blood of the Lamb[5]

In that power make haste and delay not to keep
His commandments,[6] and, then shall you not be
ashamed when you have respect unto ALL His commandments.[7]

---

[1] Matt. xxii. 38.    [2] Jas. ii. 10, 11.    [3] Job xix. 28.
[4] 1 John i. 9.    [5] Rev. xii. 11.    [6] Ps. cxix. 60.
[7] Ps. cxix. 6.

# FOURTH DAY.

## The Means of Growth.

'Grow in grace, and in the knowledge of our Lord and Saviour Jesus Christ.'—2 PET. iii. 18.

THE very thing we are longing to do, and perhaps mourning over not doing, and perhaps praying every day that we may do, and seeming to get no answer! But when God has annexed·a means to the fulfilment of a command, we cannot expect Him to enable us to fulfil that command if we are not using His means. In this case the means are wrapped in another command: 'Desire the sincere milk of the word, *that ye may grow* thereby.'[1]

Real desire must prove itself by action; it is no use desiring the milk and not drinking it. 'Wherefore criest thou unto Me? speak unto the children of Israel, that they *go forward.*'[2] Let us to-day, and every day henceforth, 'go forward,' and use in faith and honest earnestness this His own great means of growth.

By the word we shall 'grow in grace.' The beginning of grace in our souls was by the same;

[1] 1 Pet. ii. 1.    [2] Ex. xiv. 15.

for it is written, 'Of His own will begat He us
with the word of truth;'[1] 'Being born again, . . .
by the word of God.'[2] At every step it is the same
word which developes the spiritual life. The young
man shall 'cleanse his way' by it. The entrance
of it giveth light and understanding[3] The result
of hiding it in our hearts is, that we 'might not sin
against Thee;'[4] and how often by His word has He
'withheld thee from sinning against Me !'[5] Again
and again we have said, 'Thy word hath quickened
me.'[6] For it comes to us 'not in word only, but
in power and in the Holy Ghost, and in much
assurance.'[7] It is 'able to make thee wise unto
salvation,'[8] and its intended effects of reproof,
correction, instruction in righteousness, rise to what
would seem a climax of growth, 'that the man of
God may be perfect, thoroughly furnished unto *all*
good works.'[9] And yet there is a still more glorious
result of this 'word of God, which effectually
worketh also in you that *believe;*'[10] for by 'His
divine power' 'are given unto us exceeding great
and precious promises, that *by these* ye might be
partakers of the divine nature.'[11] This is indeed
the climax, for what can rise beyond this most
marvellous effect of this blessed means of growth
in grace ! Oh, to use it as He would have us use it,
so that every day we 'may grow thereby' !

By the word we shall also grow in the knowledge
of Christ. The mere surface of this is obvious.

---

[1] Jas. i. 18.  [2] 1 Pet. i. 23.

[3] Ps. cxix. 9; ib. cxix. 130.  [4] Ps. cxix. 11.

[5] Gen. xx. 6.  [6] Ps. cxix. 50.  [7] 1 Thess. i. 5.

[8] 2 Tim. iii. 15.  [9] 2 Tim. iii. 17.  [10] 1 Thess. ii. 13.

[11] 2 Pet. i. 3; ib. i. 4.

For how do we come to know more of any one whom having not seen, we love?[1] is it not by reading and hearing what he has said and written and done? How *are* we to know more of Jesus Christ, if we are not taking the trouble to know more of His word?

He hath said, 'Search the Scriptures; for . . . they are they which testify of Me.'[2] Are we really searching, or only superficially reading, those Old Testament Scriptures of which He spoke? He says they testify of Him, *i.e.* tell us all about Him; are we acting as if we quite believed that?

'Beginning at Moses and all the prophets, He expounded unto them in ALL the Scriptures the things concerning Himself.'[3] Then there are things about Jesus in *all* the Scriptures—not just only in the Psalms and Isaiah, but in every book! How very much there must be for us to find! Let us ask the Holy Spirit to take of *these* things of Jesus and show them unto us,[4] that we may grow in 'the knowledge of the Son of God.'[5]

'The words which I speak unto you, they are spirit, and they are life'[6]—quickening and continually life-giving words. We want to be permeated with them; we want them to dwell in us richly,[7] to be the inspiration of our whole lives, the very music of our spirits, whose melodious overflow may be glory to God and goodwill to man.[8] Jesus Himself has given us this quick and powerful word of God, and our responsibility is tremendous. He has told

---

[1] 1 Pet. i. 8.
[2] John v. 39.
[3] Luke xxiv. 27.
[4] John xvi. 15.
[5] Eph. iv. 13.
[6] John vi. 63.
[7] Col. iii. 16.
[8] Luke ii. 14.

us distinctly what to do as to it; He has said,
'Search!'¹ Now, are we substituting a word of
our own, and merely *reading* them? He did not say,
'Read them,' but '*Search!*'² and it is a most serious
thought for many a comfortable daily *reader* of the
Bible, that, if they are *only* reading and not searching, they are distinctly living in disobedience to
one of His plainest commands. What wonder if
they do not 'grow thereby'!

> Let me then be always growing,
>   Never, never standing still,
> Listening, learning, better knowing
>   Thee, and Thy most blessed will;
> That the Master's eye may trace,
> Day by day, my growth in grace.

---

# FIFTH DAY.

---

# Mental Food.

'Eat ye that which is good.'—ISA. lv. 2.

'SO foolish was I, and ignorant: I was as a beast
before Thee,'³ or this commandment would
not have been needed. Good, wholesome, delicious
food set plentifully before us, and yet we have to be
told to eat that which is good, and to let rubbish
and poison alone! Is it not humiliating?

---

¹ John v. 39.        ² Isa. xxxiv. 16.        ³ Ps. lxiii. 22.

We know too much about feeding on that which is not good, and what profit had we in those things whereof we are now ashamed?[1]  The Lord has had to testify of us, 'He feedeth on ashes,'[2] 'feedeth on wind,'[3] 'feedeth on foolishness.'[4]  Most gracious was His decree, 'They shall eat, and not have enough;'[5] 'Thou shalt eat, but not be satisfied.'[6] He would not *let* us be satisfied.  And now, if we have tasted that the Lord is gracious,[7] we *cannot* be satisfied with the old ashes and wind.

But what about our daily practical obedience to this command?  How much are we going to eat to-day of that which is good, in proportion to that which satisfieth not?  Will it be a question of minutes for the word by which we live,[8] and hours for books which are at best negative as to spiritual nutriment?  What is our present obedience to the parallel command, '*Desire* the sincere milk of the word, that ye may grow thereby'?[9]  What about our appetite for the 'strong meat,'[10] 'the deep things of God'?[11]  If other books contain 'necessary food'[12] mentally, and we are called to use them, so that by study of His works, His providences natural, mental, moral, we may be more meet for the Master's use,[13] do we practically and consciously esteem the words of His mouth *more?*  Can we say, they are 'in my mouth as honey for sweetness'?[14]

But perhaps we are even purposing to eat that which is *not* good.  We may argue that there is no

---

1 Rom. vi. 21.
2 Isa. xliv. 20.
3 Hos. xii. 1.
4 Prov. xv. 14.
5 Hos. iv. 10.
6 Mic. vi. 14.
7 1 Pet. ii. 3.
8 Matt. iv. 4.
9 1 Pet. ii. 2.
10 Heb. v. 12, 14.
11 1 Cor. ii. 10.
12 Job xxiii. 12.
13 2 Tim. ii. 21.
14 Ezek. iii. 3.

harm in certain readings, and that if we don't read
what others do we shall get narrow and lose con-
versational influence, and that people will think
nothing of our opinion if we can't say we have read
such and such books, and so forth.   But all the
time, do we not know, down in our heart of hearts,
that this is all sophistry?[1]   We *know*, though we
do not like to acknowledge, that the books in
question do blunt our spiritual appetite and hinder
our close communion with Jesus ; that the influence
we profess to want is not purely desired ' for Jesus'
sake only,'[2] and to be used ' *all* for Jesus,'—in short,
we *like* the reading, and  we do not want to resist
pleasing ourselves.[3]  And so we deliberately disobey
the command to eat that which is good, excusing
ourselves by pretending that we 'saw that the tree
was good for food,'[4] when the truth was that we
simply saw that it was 'pleasant.'

We are solemnly responsible for the mental in-
fluences under which we place ourselves.  'Take
heed what ye hear'[5] must include 'take heed what
ye read.'  'Lead us not into temptation' is 'vain
repetition'[6] when we walk straight away into it,
hoodwinking our own eyes because we are drawn
away and enticed by our own desires.[7]

Do we feel that we are not strong enough to resist?   'The way of the Lord is strength to the
upright;'[8] and His 'way to escape' is, 'Eat ye
that which is good.'[9]   Perhaps if Eve had fully
availed herself of God's permission, 'Thou mayst

---

[1] Job xiii. 7.
[4] Gen. iii. 6.
[7] Jas. i. 14.
[2] John xii. 9.
[5] Mark iv. 24.
[8] Prov. x. 29.
[3] Rom. xv. 1-3.
[6] Matt. vi. 7, 13.
[9] 1 Cor. x. 13.

freely eat,'[1] she would not have been so ready to disregard His prohibition. If we 'eat in plenty'[2] of 'angels' food,'[3] of course we shall not care about the 'onions and the garlick.'[4] Just fancy wanting *them !* When we are 'satisfied,' of course, there is no craving.[5]

The devil is very fond of persuading us that we have 'no leisure so much as to eat'[6] when it is a question of Bible study. He never says that if we have a novel 'of the earth, earthy, '[7] or a clever magazine of 'modern thought' on hand! He knows better. He wants us not to ' *let* ' our souls delight themselves in fatness.

Jesus, our Wisdom, says, 'Come, eat of *My* bread ; '[8] 'Eat, O friends.'[9] One is utterly ashamed that it should ever be an effort to obey this loving invitation. How weak we are ! But His hand touches us, and He says, 'Arise, and eat.'[10] May He open our eyes to see and rejoice in the provision so close beside us, the feast that He has made for us.

Not only His word, but the happy doing of His will[11] shall be our meat, and we shall ' afterward eat of the holy things, because it is His food.'[12] He will give us to eat of the tree of life and of the hidden manna.[13] And He will give us Himself, the living Bread which came down from heaven, saying, ' He that eateth Me, even he shall live by Me.'[14] Is not this enough ?

---

[1] Gen. ii. 16.   [2] Joel ii. 26.   [3] Ps. lxxviii. 25.
[4] Num. xi. 5.   [5] Jer. xxxi. 14.   [6] Mark vi. 31.
[7] 1 Cor. xv. 47.   [8] Prov. ix. 5.   [9] Cant. v. 1.
[10] 1 Kings xix. 5.   [11] John iv. 34.   [12] Lev. xxii. 7.
[13] Rev. ii. 7, 17.   [14] John vi. 51, 57.

# SIXTH DAY.

## The Transferred Burden.

'If our transgressions and our sins be upon us, and we pine away in them, how should we then live?'—EZEK. xxxiii. 10.

IF they are upon us, how can we live? For 'mine iniquities are as an heavy burden, they are too heavy for me.'[1]  'The burden of them *is* intolerable.'  It is not the sense, but the burden itself which cannot be borne; no one *could* bear his own iniquities without being sunk lower and lower, and at last to hell by it.  It is only not felt when the very elasticity of sin within us keeps us from feeling the weight of the sin upon us; as the very air in our bodies prevents our feeling the otherwise crushing weight of the atmosphere with its tons upon every inch.  Or (thank God for the alternative!) when the whole burden, our absolutely intolerable burden, is known to be laid upon another.

If this burden is upon us, we cannot walk in newness of life,[2] we cannot run in the way of His commandments,[3] we cannot arise and shine.[4]  The

---

[1] Ps. xxxviii. 4.
[3] Ps. cxix. 32.
[2] Rom. vi. 4.
[4] Isa. lx. 1.

burden is ' too heavy ' for these manifestations of
life ; we do but ' pine away ' in our sins, whether
consciously or unconsciously; and the sentence is
upon us, They shall ' consume away for their iniquity.'[1]    For there is no curse so terrible and far-
reaching as, ' He shall bear his iniquity.'[2]

'If ! ' but *is* it ?    It is written, ' The Lord hath
laid on Him the iniquity of us all.'[3]    On Jesus it
has been laid, on Him who alone could bear the
intolerable burden ;[4] therefore it is *not* upon His
justified ones who accept Him as their sinbearer.

This burden is never divided.    He took it *all*,
every item, every detail of it.    The scapegoat bore
' upon him *all* their iniquities.'[5]    Think of every
separate sin, each that has weighed down our conscience, every separate transgression of our most
careless moments, added to the unknown weight of
all the unknown or forgotten sins of our whole life,
and all this laid on Jesus instead of upon us !    The
sins of a *day* are often a burden indeed, but we are
told in another type, ' I have laid upon thee the
*years* of their iniquity.'[6]    Think of the *years* of
our iniquity being upon Jesus !    Multiply this by
the unknown but equally intolerable sin-burdens of
all His people, and remember that ' the Lord hath
laid on Him the iniquity of us *all*,'[7] and then think
what the strength of His enduring love must be
which thus bare ' the sins of *many*.'[8]

Think of His bearing them ' in His own body
on the tree,'[9] in that flesh and blood of which He

---

[1] Ezek. iv. 17.          [2] Lev. v 17.          [3] Isa. liii. 6.
[4] Isa. liii. 11.          [5] Lev. xvi. 22.          [6] Ezek. iv. 5.
[7] Isa. liii. 6.          [8] Heb. ix. 28.          [9] 1 Pet. ii. 24.

took part, with all its sensitiveness and weakness, because He would be made like unto His brethren in all things;[1] and that this bearing was entirely suffering (for He '*suffered* for sins'[2]), and praise the love which has not left 'our sins . . . upon us.'

We cannot lay them upon Him; Jehovah has done that already, and 'His work is perfect:'[3] 'nothing can be put to it, nor anything taken from it.'[4] 'The Lord *hath* laid on Him the iniquity of us all;'[5] 'He hath done this.'[6] We have only to look up and see our Great High Priest bearing the iniquity of our holy things for us;[7] to put it still more simply, we have only to believe that the Lord has really done what He says He has done.[8]

Can we doubt the Father's love to us, when we think what it must have cost Him to lay that crushing weight on His dear Son, sparing Him not,[9] that He might spare us instead?[10] The Son accepted the awful burden, but it was the Father's hand which 'laid it upon' Him.[11] It was death to Him, that there might be life to us. For 'if our transgressions and our sins' were upon us, there could be no answer to the question, 'How should we *then* live?' for we could only 'pine away in them' and die. 'Ye shall die in your sins.'[12] But being 'laid on Him,'[13] how shall we *now* live? 'He died for all, that they which live should not henceforth live unto themselves, but unto Him which died for them and rose again.'[14] Unto Him,[15] by Him,[16]

---

[1] Heb. ii. 14, 17.  [2] 1 Pet. iii. 18.  [3] Deut. xxxii. 4.
[4] Eccles. iii. 14.  [5] Isa. liii. 6.  [6] Ps. xxii. 31.
[7] Ex. xxviii. 38.  [8] Isa. xliv. 23.  [9] Rom. viii. 32.
[10] Mal. iii. 17.  [11] 1 Pet. ii. 24.  [12] John viii. 24.
[13] 2 Cor. v. 15.  [14] Rom. xiv. 8.  [15] Gal. ii. 20.  [16] Phil. i. 21.

in Him,[1] for Him, now; and with Him,[2] where He is, for ever and ever!

> On Thee, the Lord
> My mighty sins hath laid;
> And against Thee Jehovah's sword
> Flashed forth its fiery blade.
> The stroke of justice fell on Thee,
> That it might never fall on me.

## SEVENTH DAY.

## The Recall.

'O Israel, return unto the Lord thy God; for thou hast fallen by thine iniquity.'—Hos. xiv. I.

THANK God that He does not let His children go on comfortably when they wander and fall![3]

Have we not known (God grant we may never again know!) a wretched mental nausea, a sense of discomfort and restlessness, a misgiving that something is wrong, though we can't say what? no actual pain, no acute attack of anything, but a nameless uncomfortableness, most easily described by a negative, that we are *not* ' as in months past.'[4]

[5]If this is the present state of any reader, do let

---

[1] John xvii. 24.   [2] 1 Thess. iv. 17.   [3] Hos. ii. 6.
[5] Job xxix. 2.   [4] Job xv. 11, 12.

me most earnestly and affectionately entreat you not to remain one day—no, not one hour—in this most dangerous state, the beginning of back-sliding, and already a fall from your 'own steadfastness' and your 'first love.'[1] 'Remember from whence thou art fallen;'[2] look unflinchingly at your position, and recognize frankly the difference between to-day, and the past days of closer walking and happy abiding. Do not let yourself drift on, or you 'will revolt more and more' till 'the whole head is sick, and the whole heart faint.'[3] Every day's delay will make your case worse.

Do not shrink from asking Him to show you how and why it is that you have fallen. The 'beautiful crown'[4] which He put 'upon thine head' in 'the time of love,'[5] would not have 'fallen from our head,' but 'that we have sinned.'[6] It is 'by *thine* iniquity' that 'thou art fallen,'[7]—iniquity personal and real, though very likely unguessed by any one, and hidden even from thine own eyes.

Perhaps the knowledge of this is already sent; if so, listen! 'And I said, *after* she had done all these things, Turn thou unto me.'[8] And again, though you may have gone after other 'lovers,' '*yet* return again to me, saith the LORD.'[9] Oh forsake the *thoughts* as well as the way, and return unto the Lord, and he will abundantly pardon.[10] For when 'He showeth them their work and their transgressions,' He also '*commandeth* that they return from iniquity.'[11]

---

[1] 2 Pet. iii. 17.
[2] Rev. ii. 4, 5.
[3] Isa. i. 5.
[4] Ezek. xvi. 12.
[5] Ezek xvi. 8.
[6] Lam. v. 16.
[7] Hos. xiv. 1.
[8] Jer. iii. 7.
[9] Jer. iii. 1.
[10] Isa. lv. 7.
[11] Job xxxvi. 9, 10.

And why? Five infinitely gracious reasons are given. 'Return! . *for* thou hast fallen by thine iniquity;'[1] the very thing which seemed the barrier to return! 'Return!. . .*for* I am merciful, saith the LORD.'[2] 'Return!. . .*for* I have redeemed thee.'[3] 'Return!. . .*for* the Lord hath dealt bountifully with thee.'[4] 'Come, and let us return unto the Lord: *for* He hath torn, and He *will* heal us.'[5] All these gracious words for you! and the Lord Himself waiting that He may be gracious!'[6] Will you keep Him waiting till a more 'convenient season'?[7]

To *whom* are you called to return? Ah! think of *that*—not to a state or position merely; not only 'to thy rest,'[8] but to 'the Lord thy God,'[9] *thy* God, 'our *own* God;'[10] to Him who has betrothed you unto Him for ever;[11] to Him who chose you unto Himself to be His peculiar treasure;[12] to Him who remembers better than you do from whence you have fallen. Hear Him saying, 'I remember thee, the kindness of thy youth, the love of thine espousals.'[13] 'How shall I give thee up?'[14] What pathetic yearning this is over you, even you! Will you not say, 'I will go and return to my first husband; for then was it better with me than now.'[15]

Is intention enough in this matter? Listen again to the arousing words of your Lord, 'If thou *wilt* return, . . . saith the Lord, *return* unto Me;'[16]

---

[1] Hos. xiv. 1.  [2] Jer. iii 12.  [3] Isa. xliv. 22.
[4] Ps. cxvi. 7.  [5] Hos. vi. 1.  [6] Isa. xxx. 18.
[7] Acts xxiv. 25.  [8] Ps. cxvi. 7.  [9] Hos. xiv. 1.
[10] Ps. lxvii. 6.  [11] Hos. ii. 19.  [12] Ps. cxxxv. 4.
[13] Jer. ii. 2.  [14] Hos. xi. 8.  [15] Hos. ii. 7.  [16] Jer iv. 1.

ın other words, ' Now, then, *do* it.'[1] Stay no more at being willing to return, but ' *Return ye* NOW !'[2] It will be harder to-morrow—nay, harder an hour hence than now. He who first caused you to approach,[3] will cause you to return ;[4] so you shall not be left unaided, for ' In Me is thine help '[5] even for returning from self-destruction.[6]

And then—oh, what wealth of promises to the returning one !. what robes and rings and heavenly music ![7] ' If thou return, . . . thou shalt be built up, thou shalt put away iniquity . . . ; then shalt thou have thy delight in the Almighty, and shalt lift up thy face unto God.[8] He shall hear thee, . . . Thou shalt decree a thing, and it shall be established unto thee : the light shall shine upon thy ways.' For He hath said, ' I will heal their backsliding, I will love them freely.'[9]

Return !
O fallen ; yet not lost !
Canst thou forget the life for thee laid down,
The taunts, the scourging, and the thorny crown ?
When o'er thee first my spotless robe I spread
And poured the oil of joy upon thy head,
How did thy wakening heart within thee burn !
Canst thou remember all, and wilt thou not return ?

---

[1] 2 Sam. iii. 18.    [2] Jer. xviii. 11.    [3] Ps. lxv. 4.
[4] Jer. xxx. 3.    [5] Hos. xiii. 9.    [6] Lam. v. 21.
[7] Luke xv. 22, 25.    [8] Job xxii. 23-28.    [9] Hos. xiv. 4.

# EIGHTH DAY.

## The Conditions of Effectual Prayer.

'And all things, whatsoever ye shall ask in prayer, believing, ye shall receive.'—MATT. xxi. 22.

HAVE we not sometimes been tempted to think that here, at least, is a case in which our Lord has not literally and always kept His word? in which we do not get quite so much as the plain English of the promise might lead us to expect? If so, well may He say to us, ' Do ye not therefore err, because ye know not the Scriptures, neither the power of God?'[1] If we had known the Scriptures by searching, we might have known more of the power of God by experience in this matter. For this is no unconditional promise; this marvellous ' whatsoever' depends upon five great conditions; and, if we honestly examine, we shall find that every case of seeming failure in the promise can be accounted for by our own failure in one or more of these.

1. ' Whatsoever ye shall ask *in my name,* that will I do.'[2] Really, not verbally only, in the name of Jesus; asking not in our own name at all; sign-

---

[1] Mark xii. 24.          [2] John xiv. 13; ib. xiv. 6.

ing our petition, as it were, with His name only;[1] coming to the Father by our Advocate, our Representative.[2] Do we always ask thus?

2. '*Believing*, ye shall receive.'[3] The faith-heroes of old 'through faith . . . obtained promises,'[4] and there is no new way of obtaining them. Is it any wonder that, when we stagger at any promise of God through unbelief,[5] we do not receive it? Not that the faith merits the answer, or in any way earns it or works it out, but God has made believing a condition of receiving, and the Giver has a sovereign right to choose His own terms of gift.

3. '*If ye abide in Me, and My words abide in you*, ye shall ask what ye will, and it shall be done unto you.'[6] Ah! here is a deeper secret of asking and *not* having, because we ask amiss.[7] Not, have we come to Christ? but, are we abiding in Him?—not, do we hear His words? but, are they abiding in us? Can we put in this claim to the glorious 'whatsoever'? And, if not, why not? for '*this* is His commandment,' 'Abide in Me.'[8] And this leads us to see the root of our failure in another condition, for,—

4. 'Whatsoever we ask, we receive of Him, *because we keep His commandments, and do those things that are pleasing in His sight.*'[9] Only as we are abiding in Him can we bring forth the fruit of obedience, for without (*i. e.* apart from) Him we can do nothing;[10] only in walking by faith can we

---

1 Phil. ii. 10 (Gr.)    2 I John ii. 1.    3 Matt. xxi. 22.
4 Heb. xi. 33.    5 Rom. iv. 20.    6 John xv. 7.
7 Jas. iv. 3.    8 John xv. 4.
9 I John iii. 22; Ps. lxvi. 18.    10 John xv. 4.

do those things that are pleasing in His sight,[1] for without faith it is impossible to please Him.[2]

5. 'If we ask anything *according to His will*, He heareth us.'[3] When what we ask is founded on a promise or any written evidence of what the will of the Lord is,[4] this is comfortingly clear. But what about petitions which may or may not be according to His will? Surely, then, the condition can only be fulfilled by a complete blending of our own will with His;[5] by His so taking our will, so *undertaking* it and influencing it for us, that we are led to desire and ask the very thing He is purposing to give. *Then*, of course, our prayer is answered; and the very pressure of spirit to pray becomes the pledge and earnest of the answer, for it is the working of His will in us.

Two comforting thoughts arise.

First, the very consciousness of our failure in these great conditions shows us the wonderful kindness and mercy of our King, who has answered so many a prayer in spite of it, according to His own heart, and not according to our fulfilment, giving us 'of His royal bounty'[6] that to which we had forfeited all shadow of claim.

Secondly, that He who knoweth our frame[7] knows also the possibilities of His grace, and would never tantalize us by offering magnificent gifts on impossible conditions. 'Will he give him a stone?'[8] Would an earthly parent? Would *you*? Therefore the very annexing of these intrinsically most blessed

---

[1] 2 Cor. v. 7.  [2] Heb. xi. 6.  [3] 1 John v. 14.
[4] Eph. v. 17.  [5] Phil. ii. 13.  [6] 1 Kings x. 13.
[7] Ps. ciii. 14; Phil. iv. 13.  [8] Luke xi. 11.

conditions implies that His grace *is* sufficient[1] for
their fulfilment, and should lure us on to a blessed
life of faith, abiding in Jesus,[2] walking in obedience
'unto *all* pleasing,'[3] and a will possessed by His
own divine will.

> Thou art coming to a King,
> Large petitions with thee bring;
> For His grace and power are such,
> None can ever ask too much.
>
> NEWTON.

## NINTH DAY.

# The Privilege of Intercession.

'Pray one for another.'—JAS. v. 16.

HERE our divine Master takes up an impulse of
natural affection,[4] raising it to the dignity of a
'royal commandment,'[5] and broadening it to the
measure of His own perpetual intercession.[6] For,
unless a heart has reached the terrible hardening of
being 'without natural affection'[7] as well as 'without God,'[8] it must want to pray for those it loves.
The Lord would sanctify and enlarge this impulse,
making it 'full of the blessing of the Lord.'[9] It is
a plant which He hath planted in the human heart,

---

1 2 Cor. xii. 9.    2 1 John ii. 27.    3 Col. i. 10.
4 Esther i. 19.    5 1 Tim. ii. 1.    6 Heb. vii. 25.
7 Rom. i. 31.    8 Eph. ii. 12.    9 Deut. xxxiii. 23.

and therefore it shall not be rooted up, but He will water and increase it.[1]  What are the indications of His will in the matter, and how far are we following them out?

First, are we asking for each other the special thing annexed to the command?  ' That ye may be healed.'[2]  Prayer for physical healing is clearly included.[3]  How many around us are not spiritually healed! are we definitely asking this for them?  Of how many of His own people is the Lord saying, ' They knew not that I healed them!'[4] Not ' knowing what was done in ' them,[5] they are not witnessing to the power of the Healer; not *seeing*, like the Samaritan, that they were healed, they are not giving Him thanks.[6]  Are we asking that they may realize the healing, so that they may glorify the Healer?[7]

We may be greatly ' helping together by prayer,'[8] by agreement in intercession.[9]  The very fact of having 'agreed'[10] is a great stimulus and reminder. It is the Lord's own indicated way. ' Two of you.'[11] It took two to hold up Moses' hands steadily.[12] When he let down one hand, Amalek prevailed. So Aaron and Hur were both wanted.[13]

Intercession should be definite and detailed. Vagueness is lifelessness.  St. Paul besought the Romans to pray for him, and then told them exactly what he wanted, four definite petitions to be presented for him.[14]  It is a help to reality of inter-

---

1 Matt. xv. 13.  2 Jas. v. 16.  3 Gen. xx. 17.
4 Hos. xi. 3.  5 Mark v. 29, 33.  6 Luke xvii. 15.
7 Ps. ciii. 1–3.  8 2 Cor. i. 11.  9 Dan. ii. 17, 18.
10 Esther iv. 16.  11 Matt. xviii. 19.  12 Eccles. iv. 9.
13 Ex. xvii. 11, 12.  14 Rom. xv. 30, 32.

cession when ministers or other workers who ask our prayers will tell us exactly what they want. General prayers for ' blessing' are apt to become formal.

We must not yield to the idea that, because we are feeble members, doing no great work, our prayers 'won't make much difference.' [1] It may be that this is the very reason why the Lord keeps us in the shade, because He hath need of us [2] (though we feel no better than an ' ass's colt ' [3]) for the work of intercession. Many of us only learn to realize the privilege of being called to this by being called apart from all other work. When this is the case, let us simply and faithfully do it, 'lifting up holy hands, without wrath and doubting,' [4] blessing His name who provides this holy and beautiful service for those who ' *by night* stand in the house of the Lord'. [5] See how wonderfully St. Paul valued the prayers of others. He distinctly expresses this to every Church but one to whom he wrote. Would he have asked their prayers so fervently if he thought it would not 'make much difference ' ?

Intercession is a wonderful help to forgiveness of injuries. See how the personal unkindness of brother and sister stirred up Moses to pray for each ; [6] and how repeatedly the wrong feeling, speaking, and acting of the people against himself was made the occasion of prayer for them [7] Let us avail ourselves of this secret of his meekness. Also it is an immense help to love. Do we not find that the more we pray for any one, the more we love?

---

[1] 1 Cor. xii. 22.  [2] Mark xi. 2, 3.  [3] Job xi. 12.
[4] 1 Tim. ii. 8.  [5] Ps. cxxxiv. 1.
[6] Num. xii. 2, 13; Deut. ix. 18-20.
[7] Num. xiv. 2, 19; ib. xvi. 19, 22 ; ib. xii. 3.

8

Let us intercede ' while we have time.'[1] ' The night cometh, when no man can work.'[2] Those for whom we might be praying to-day-may be beyond the reach of prayer to-morrow. Or our own day of prayer may have passed ; for the only intercession that we have ever heard from the other side was in vain—never granted.[3]

It is considerable practical help if we make our intercession systematic, especially if the Lord gives us many to pray for. If every day has its written list of special names to be remembered, we shall be less likely to forget or drop them. Each several name was engraved on the breastplate of the high-priest, that it might be borne upon his heart continually.[4]

See the two-fold rewards of intercessory prayer.

*First*, blessing for others :

' He shall ask, and He shall give him life for them that sin not unto death.'[5] Compare St. Paul's prayers for the Thessalonians, in his First Epistle, with the exact and abounding answers for which he gives thanks in the Second, after a very short interval.

*Secondly*, blessing for ourselves :

' The Lord turned the captivity of Job, *when* he prayed for his friends.'[6] Something very like a turning of our captivity is granted[7] when, amid oppression and darkness, we pray for our friends. Often it is like a leap into the free sunshine. ' Pray unto the Lord for it ' (the city whither they were

---

1 Gal. vi. 10 (old translation).  2 John ix. 4.  3 Luke xvii. 27-31.
4 Ex. xxviii. 21, 29.  5 1 John v. 16.  6 Job. xlii 10.
7 Ps. cxxvi. 1-3.

carried away), 'for in the peace thereof shall ye have peace.' [1]    Specially true is it in this, that 'he that watereth shall be watered also himself.' [2]

> 'O Saviour Christ, their woes dispel;
> For some are sick, and some are sad,
> And some have never loved Thee well,
> And some have lost the love they had.
>
> And some are pressed with worldly care,
> And some are tired with sinful doubt,
> And some such grievous passions tear
> That only thou canst cast them out.
>
> And some have found the world is vain,
> Yet from the world they break not free;
> And some have friends that give them pain,
> Yet have not sought a friend in Thee.'

HENRY TWELLS.

# TENTH DAY.

# 𝔗𝔯𝔲𝔰𝔱𝔦𝔫𝔤 𝔦𝔫 𝔇𝔞𝔯𝔨𝔫𝔢𝔰𝔰.

'Who is among you that feareth the Lord, that obeyeth the voice of His servant, that walketh in darkness, and hath no light? let him trust in the name of the Lord, and stay himself upon His God.'—ISA. l. 10.

BEFORE we take this peace and strength-giving precept, with its enfolded promise, to ourselves, let us examine ourselves as to the conditions: fear

---

[1] Jer. xxix. 7.       [2] Prov. xi. 25.

of the Lord, and obedience to the voice of His servant. They are very clear. If we are not casting off fear;[1] if we have this 'beginning of wisdom,'[2] this perhaps not sufficiently recognized 'treasure,'[3] the fear of the Lord;[4] and if we have sincerity of purpose about obeying the voice of His servant,[5] and are not persisting in some known and wilful disobedience,[6] which causes a different kind of darkness, the darkness that blindeth our eyes,[7] then we are called to listen to all the comfort of this commandment.

'Let him trust in the name of the Lord.' What name? 'The Lord, the Lord God, merciful and gracious, long-suffering, and abundant in goodness and truth, keeping mercy for thousands, forgiving iniquity and transgression and sin.'[8] What name? 'Wonderful, Counsellor, the Mighty God, the Everlasting Father, the Prince of Peace.'[9] What name? Just this, JESUS![10] But how can we trust in what we do not much consider?[11] Trust needs a very broad and strong foundation for its repose; it cannot poise itself on an inverted pyramid. But if we walk about that foundation, and go round about it, and mark well the bulwarks,[12] we shall put ourselves in the way of realizing what reason we have to trust.[13]

Is it dark now, dear friend? Will you, as a little child, simply do what I ask you this morning? Take this *Name* of the Lord,[14] in all its varied ful-

---

1 Job xv. 4.  2 Ps. cxi. 10.  3 Isa. xxxiii. 6.
4 Ps. cxix. 69.  5 Josh. xxiv. 24.  6 John iii. 20.
7 1 John ii. 11.  8 Ex. xxxiv. 6, 7.  9 Isa. ix. 6.
10 Matt. i. 21.  11 Ps ix. 10; ib. cxix. 55.
12 Ps. xlviii. 12, 13.  13 Prov. xviii. 10.  14 Ps. xx. 7.

ness, 'shut thy door,'[1] and kneel down without hurry. Then, asking first the Spirit's promised help,[2] pray over every separate part of it as so beautifully revealed for our comfort. And as you take up each word in petition, tell the Lord that you *will*, you *do* trust that, even though you cannot see or feel all the preciousness of it.[3]

Trusting in the name of the Lord, the Triune Jehovah—Father, Saviour, Comforter—will lead you on, not perhaps to any great radiance of light as yet, but to staying upon your God; for mark the added pronoun, first only '*the* Lord,' then '*his* God.' Both the trusting and staying may be at first in the dark, but they will not be always in the dark. He that believeth on Him shall not abide in darkness.[4] Unto him 'there ariseth light in the darkness.'[5] But the promises are progressive: we must follow the light as soon as we see it, for 'he that followeth me shall not walk in darkness.'[6]

But, meanwhile, even the trusting and staying shall be blessed, for 'blessed are they that have not seen, and yet have believed.'[7] 'Blessed are all they that put their trust in Him;'[8] and 'all' of course includes you. There may be very much unconscious blessing apart from sensible light and joy.[9] The visible, light-bearing rays of the spectrum are not the whole beam. It is not they which make the plant grow; it is the dark rays with their mysterious, unseen vibrations that bring heat and chemical power.

---

[1] Matt. vi. 6.   [2] Rom. viii. 26; Zech. xii. 10.
[3] Isa. xii. 2; Ps. xci. 2; xxxi. 1; Cant. i. 3.   [4] John xii. 46.
[5] Ps. cxii. 4.   [6] John viii. 12.   [7] John xx. 29.
[8] Ps. ii. 12.   [9] Ps. xxiii. 4.

The first conscious blessing is not linked with even the trust, but with the 'staying'[1] which grows out of it. 'Thou wilt keep him in perfect peace, whose mind is stayed on Thee: because he trusteth in Thee.'[2] Then, again, the staying, and the certainly resulting, because absolutely promised, peace lead on to fuller and more settled trust: 'Trust ye in the Lord for ever.'[3]

How we do love a little child that nestles up to us from its cot in a dark room, and kisses the hand that it cannot see, and pours out all sorts of little confidences which it did not tell in the broad daylight! Do we not fondle it with a special gush of affection? However much we loved the little thing before, we think we love it more than ever! When the Father's little children come to Him in the dark, and simply believe His assurance that He is there, although they cannot see,[4] will He be less loving, less kind and tender?

'I cannot hear Thy voice, Lord,
  But Thou dost hear my cry;
I cling to thine assurance
  That Thou art ever nigh
I know that Thou art faithful;
  I trust, but cannot see
That it is still the right way
  By which Thou leadest me.'

---

1 Jer. xvii. 7.      2 Isa. xxvi. 3.      3 Isa. xxvi. 4.
4 John xx. 29; Ps. xxxiii. 21.

## ELEVENTH DAY.

---

## 𝕱ear 𝕽ot.

'Fear not.'—LUKE xii. 32, etc.

THERE need be no difficulty in distinguishing between the holy and blessed 'fear of the Lord,'[1] which is our 'treasure,' and which is only as the sacred shadow cast by the brightest light of love and joy, and the fear which 'hath torment,'[2] and is cast out by perfect love and simple trust.

> 'Fear Him, ye saints, and you will then
> Have nothing else to fear!'

precisely expresses the distinction.

But it is a very solemn thought how 'verily guilty'[3] we are as to this most absolute command of our King, reiterated by messengers angelic and human, and by His own personal voice, perhaps more often than any other. No wonder that we are left to suffer the fruit of our own thoughts when we do not even see our disobedience, much less cease from it. 'Fear NOT.' There is no qualification, no exception, no modification; it is as plain a com-

---

[1] Isa. xxxiii. 6; Acts ix. 31.      [2] 1 John iv. 18.
[3] Gen. xlii. 21.

mand as, 'Thon shalt *not* steal.'[1]    What excuse
have we for daring to regard it as a less transgression,
or even no transgression at all?    If the heinousness
of a crime might, to human judgment, be measured
by its penalty, what must the true heinousness of
this everyday sin be when God hath said, 'The *fearful* shall have their part in the lake which burneth
with fire and brimstone!'[2]

Why should what seems only a natural infirmity
be catalogued with the blackest sins?    Because, if
we honestly examine it, it is always and only the
fruit of not really believing God's words, not really
trusting His love and wisdom and power.    It is a
bold, 'Yea, hath God said?'[3] to His abundant and
infinitely gracious promises; it is a tacit denial that
He is what He is!    Only let us sincerely and thoroughly trace down every fear to its root, and we
shall (if the Holy Spirit guide our search[4]) be convinced of its sinfulness, and 'by the commandment'
it will 'become exceeding sinful.'[5]  'Let Thy judgments help' us, O Lord,[6] in this matter.

But now for the brighter side!    Would our King
tell us again and again, 'Fear not!' if there were
any reason at all to fear?    Would He say this kind
word again and again, ringing changes as of the
bells of heaven upon it, only to mock us, if He
knew all the time that we could not possibly help
fearing?    Only give half an hour to seeking out the
reasons He gives why we are not to fear, and the
all-inclusive circumstances in which He says we are

---

[1] Ex. xx. 15.    [2] Rev. xxi. 8.
[3] Gen. iii. 10; Luke xix. 21; 2 Sam. vi. 8, 9.    [4] John xvi. 8, 9.
[5] Rom. vii. 13.    [6] Ps. cxix. 175.

not to fear; see how we are to fear nothing, and no one, and never, and nowhere; see how He Himself is in every case the foundation and the grand reason of His command, His presence and His power always behind it; and then shall we hesitate to say, 'I will fear *no* evil; for Thou art with me'?[1] Shall we even fancy there is any answer to those grand and forever unanswered questions, 'The Lord is my light and my salvation; whom shall I fear? the Lord is the strength of my life; of whom shall I be afraid?'[2]

There is a 'Fear not' for every possible case and kind of fear; so that we have never any answer to give when He asks, '*Why* are ye fearful?'[3] but we are 'without excuse.'[4] It is part of His 'holy covenant' that we should 'serve Him without fear.'[5] It is one of His 'precious promises' that 'thou shalt be steadfast, and shalt not fear.'[6] It is one of the blessed results of His reign that His flock 'shall fear no more.'[7] It is no impossible thing, but the simple and natural consequence of really seeking and really trusting the Lord, that He will deliver us not from some, but from '*all*' our fears.[8] He did this for David, will He be less kind to you and me?

The Lord Jesus gives a very tender and gentle expression of the same command when He says, 'Let not your heart be troubled, neither *let* it be afraid.'[9] Ah! we too often *let* our hearts be afraid:

---

[1] Isa. xli. 10, xliii. 1–5; Matt. x. 28; Lam. iii. 57; Rev. i. 17; ib. ii. 10; Isa. li. 12, 13; Gen. xv. 1; Matt. xiv. 27; Isa. xxxv. 4; Ps. xxiii. 4.
[2] Ps. xxvii. 1.     [3] Matt. viii. 26.     [4] Rom. i. 20.
[5] Luke i. 74.     [6] Job xi. 15.     [7] Jer. xxiii. 4.
[8] Ps. xxxiv. 4; Heb. xiii. 8.     [9] John xiv. 27.

we yield without even a parley; a fear arises, and we do not recognize it as an enemy of our King, we just *let* it enter and sit down, instead of unsheathing the sword of the Spirit and attacking it in the power of His might, and in the Name that always conquers. No matter how powerless we feel about it, strength comes with determination to obey.[1] Let us say this morning, *now*, 'I *will* trust and *not* be afraid;'[2] and then let us 'say to them that are of a fearful heart, Be strong, fear not; . . . He will come and save you.'[3]

Is God for me? I fear not, though all against me rise!
When I call on Christ my Saviour, the host of evil flies.
My Friend, the Lord Almighty, and He who loves me—God!
What enemy shall harm me, though coming as a flood?

PAUL GERHARDT.

---

[1] Eph. vi. 17; ib. vi. 10; Ps. xliv. 5; Luke x. 17; Mark iii. 5.
[2] Isa. xii. 2.          [3] Isa. xxxv. 4.

# TWELFTH DAY.

## The Strength=giving Look.

'And the Lord looked upon him, and said, Go in this thy might.'—JUDGES vi. 14.

FOR the might of a look of the Lord is enough for anything ! Only, we must meet His look ; our eyes must be ever toward the Lord,[1] and then we shall not miss it : for He says, ' I will *set* Mine eyes upon them for good.'[2] So, if we are indeed His people, we can never look up to Him without His look of grace and goodness and guidance. meeting ours.

It will not trouble us as it 'troubled the Egyptians'[3] when that mysterious look of the Lord fell upon them 'through the pillar of fire and of the cloud ; ' that *look of judgment* is not for His Israel.

Yet for them there is the solemn *look of searching*, when He ' looketh on the heart.'[4]

For them, too, the *look of expectation*, when He comes to His vineyard and looks ' that it should bring forth grapes ; '[5] when He comes to ' see if the vine flourish, whether the tender grape appear,'

---

[1] Ps. xxv. 15.    [2] Jer. xxiv. 6.    [3] Ex. xiv. 24.
[4] 1 Sam. xvi. 7.    [5] Isa. v. 2.

with the beautiful promise in His hand, ' There will I give thee My loves.' [1]

For them the unspeakable power and tenderness of His *look of recall.* [2] One who, after denial of the faith, had felt the might of that look, said to a lad who stood awed by the manly tears: ' Ah, Willie, it's forgiven sin that breaks a man's heart!' How many a wanderer has been called back even by the record that ' the Lord turned, and looked upon Peter.'

Then the *look of healing and help.* [3] Have we as simple faith as the father who besought Jesus to *look* upon his only son, as if even a look from the dimly recognized Master should be enough? [4] And so it was! the ' word only,' the touch, the look, were enough for health and cure in cases to which this was a terrible climax. [5]

Then the *look of blessing and love.* ' Look down and bless Thy people,' [6] prayed Moses. And what a look of blessing that was when Jesus ' looked round about on them which sat about Him,' and ' stretched forth His hand toward' them, and gave them the right of the nearest and dearest relationships! [7] Oh! let us take time (*make* time, if need be) to ' sit about Him ' [8] and listen to His teaching and meet His look.

And, last of the seven, there is for His people the special *look of strengthening.* [9] There is so much in it. Suppose you are called to take part in some busy and complicated arrangements; it is all new

---

1 Cant. vii. 12.   2 Luke xxii. 61.   3 Mark ix. 24.
4 Luke ix. 38.   5 Matt. viii. 8; Mark v. 28; ib. ix. 20, 21.
6 Deut. xxvi. 15.   7 Mark iii. 34; Matt. xii. 49.
8 Deut. xxxiii. 3; Luke x. 39.   9 Judg. vi. 14.

to you; you are not quite sure you are doing the
right thing in the right way; you hesitate and go
on slowly and uncertainly, with no sense of freedom
and power. All at once you catch the eye of the
one who is leading and organizing![1] The look is
enough; there is direction, approval, confidence,
encouragement, in that one glance, and you work
away altogether differently. Very graciously does
the Master sometimes give this strengthening look—
giving, in a way no one could convey to another,
just what we needed for our special work. We know
that our Lord has looked upon us, and the look has
flashed electric strength into heart and hand; and we
go on our way rejoicing, not at all in feeling any more
able than before, but in the brightness of His power,
saying, 'I will go in the strength of the Lord God.'[2]
And then His own strength is ours, and He says,
'Go in this thy might,' for 'thy God hath commanded thy strength;'[3] and yet we know more
distinctly than ever that it is *His* strength which is
made perfect in *our* weakness.[4] Who is it that shall
have the strengthening look of the Lord? 'To this
man will I look,' saith Jehovah, 'even to him that
is poor and of a contrite spirit.'[5] It was he who
said, 'What is thy servant, that thou shouldest look
upon such a dead dog as I am?' who 'did eat continually at the king's table.'[6]

---

[1] Ps. xxxii. 8.  [2] Ps. xliv. 3; ib. lxxi. 16; ib. lxxxvi. 16.
[3] Ps. lxviii. 28.  [4] Isa. xlv. 4; 2 Cor. xii. 9.
[5] Isa. lxvi. 2.  [6] 2 Sam. ix. 8; ib. ix. 13.

# THIRTEENTH DAY.

---

## All-sided Guidance.

'And guided them on every side.'—2 CHRON. xxxii. 22.

SEE the completeness of Jehovah's guidance! It is so different from human guidance. How seldom we feel that a human counsellor has seen our difficulty from every point of view, balanced all its bearings, and given guidance which will meet all contingencies, and be right not only on one side, but 'on *every* side.' But 'His work is perfect'[1] in this as in all other details; He will guide 'when ye turn to the right hand, *and* when ye turn to the left.'[2] Perhaps we have gone about as Elymas did in his mist and darkness, 'seeking some to lead him by the hand,'[3] putting confidence in earthly guides, and finding again and again that 'it is not in man that walketh to direct his steps,'[4] and getting perplexed with one-sided counsels. Let us to-day put our confidence in His every-sided guidance.

Very often, the very recoil from an error lands us in an opposite one; because others, or we ourselves, have gone too far in one direction, we thenceforth

---

[1] Deut. xxxii. 4.  [2] Isa. xxx. 21.
[3] Acts xiii. 11.  [4] Jer. x. 23.

do not go far enough, or *vice versa*: excess re-acting
in defect, and defect in excess; a received truth
overshadowing its equally valuable complementary
one; the fear of overstepping the boundary line of
the narrow track of truth and right, on the one side,
leading us unconsciously to overstep it on the other
side. But the promise which we should claim is,
that the Holy Spirit would guide us into *all* truth,
' *on every side.*'[1]

How intensely restful is this completeness of guidance! There is nothing outside of God's all-
inclusive promises about it. ' I will direct *all* his
ways.'[2] ' I will direct their work in truth.'[3] Not
only the general course, but ' the *steps* of a good
man are ordered by the Lord;'[4] and what is less
than a single step! Just realize this: every single
little step of this coming day ordered by Jehovah!
And lest you should sigh, ' This is not for me, because I am not good,' He repeats the same assurance still more simply: ' The Lord directeth his
steps.'[5] Now if we really believe these words, *need*
we feel worried because we cannot see the steps
ahead which Jehovah *is* going to direct, if we will
let Him?[6]

*If we will let Him!* Yes, this is no fatalistic
leading. The guidance is conditional. He says, ' I
will guide thee with Mine eye;'[7] but then we must
look up to meet His eye. ' Thou shalt guide me
with Thy counsel;'[8] but then we must listen for and
listen to His counsel. ' He shall direct thy paths;'[9]

---

[1] John xvi. 13.
[2] Isa. xlv. 13.
[3] Isa. lxi. 8.
[4] Ps. xxxvi. 23.
[5] Prov. xvi. 9.
[6] Isa. xlii. 16.
[7] Ps. xxxii. 8.
[8] Ps. lxxiii. 24.
[9] Prov. viii. 34.

but it is when we acknowledge Him in all our ways.[2]
He does not lead us whether or no !

Suppose a little child is going with its father
through an untracked wood. If it walks ever such
a little way apart, it will make many a lost step ; and
though the father will not let it get out of sight and
hearing, will not let it get lost, yet he may let it find
out for itself that going just the other side of this tree
leads it into a hopeless thicket, and stepping just
the other side of this stone leads it into a muddy
place, and the little steps have to be retraced again
and again, till at last it asks the father to hold its
hand, and *puts* and *leaves* its hand in his. Then,
and not till then, there will be *no lost step*, for it is
guided ' on every side.'

Need the little child go on a little longer by itself
first ? Had it not better put its hand into the father's
at once ? Will *you* not do so ' from this time '?[2] from
this morning ? Give up trying to pick your way ;
even if the right paths in which He leads you are
paths that you have not known, say, ' Even there
shall Thy hand lead me.'[3] Let Him teach you *His*
paths,[4] and ask Him to make not your way, but
' *Thy* way straight before my face.'[5] So shall you find
the completeness and the sweetness of His guidance.
For ' the Lord shall guide thee continually,'[6] ' by
the springs of waters shall He guide' thee ;[7] He
shall be the guide of your youth, and carry you
even unto your old age ;[8] He will be your guide
even unto death,[9] and beyond : for one strain of the

---

[1] Prov. iii. 6.     [2] Jer. iii. 4.     [3] Ps. cxxxix. 10.
[4] Ps. xxv. 4.     [5] Ps. v. 8.     [6] Isa. lviii. 11.
[7] Isa. xlix. 19.     [8] Jer. iii. 4; Isa. xlvi. 4.     [9] Ps. xlviii. 14.

song of the victorious ones that stand upon the sea of glass mingled with fire[1] shall be, 'Thou hast guided them in Thy strength unto Thy Holy habitation.'[2]

> 'I know not the way I am going,
>   But well do I know my guide;
> With a childlike trust I give my hand
>   To the Mighty Friend at my side:
>
> And the only thing that I say to Him
>   As He takes it, is: "Hold it fast;
> Suffer me not to lose my way,
>   And lead me home at last."'

---

## FOURTEENTH DAY.

---

# Ruler, because Deliverer.

'Rule thou over us, .        for thou hast delivered us.'— JUDGES viii. 22.

ALTHOUGH the passage in which these words occur cannot be considered a typical one, yet we may perhaps take them as illustrating and epitomizing the desire of every one whom Christ has delivered.

But what about this deliverance which precedes the prayer, 'Rule thou over us'? Is it ours? Do

---

[1] Rev. xv. 2, 3.        [2] Ex. xv. 13.

9

we not know whether He has delivered us or not? It is no doing of ours, for 'we have not wrought any deliverance.'[1] We have only His word about it, but that is indeed enough, in its absolute and unmistakable assurance: 'Jesus, which delivered us from the wrath to come;'[2] 'Who *hath* delivered us from the power of darkness.'[3] This grand deliverance is accomplished, and Jesus Himself proclaims it. Will you doubt His own proclamation of His own act? He has opened the prison doors, and now bids the captives go free, and know that they are free.[4] He has vanquished the foe and broken the bands of his yoke, and now tells you that He giveth you the victory which He has already won. What can He do more? He will do no more, because He has done all; therefore, if you do not accept the deliverance which He *has* wrought, there is no other for you, and 'nothing can be put to it.'[5] Only believe it, and then you will joyfully say, 'He hath delivered my soul in peace from the battle that was against me.'[6]

But you will not stop there. Merely to be 'in peace'[7] is not the end and aim of deliverance. If we are truly delivered, the Deliverer will soon be more to us than even the deliverance, and the gratitude and love will seek expression in obedience. Soldiers are ready to follow the captain who has won the victory anywhere and everywhere; they will not want to be in any other service, least of all in that of his foe.

---

[1] Isa. xxvi. 18.  [2] 1 Thess. i. 10.  [3] Col. i. 13.
[4] Isa. xlii. 7; ib. lxi. 1.  [5] Eccles. iii. 14.  [6] Ps. lv. 18.
[7] Luke i. 74.

We may take this as a test of the reality of our own participation in the deliverance which Christ has wrought for us. If we are saying, ' Rule Thou over us,' it is a sure proof that we may add, ' for Thou hast delivered us; ' for it is *His people* who are willing in the day of His power.[1]

This ruling is indeed the completion of the deliverance. It is not merely that the enemy is conquered and expelled from the stronghold, but that the citadel is occupied by a stronger than he; [2] otherwise the garrison would be left headless and defenceless, and open at any moment to the fatal return of the foe. So the Saviour, who has redeemed our life from destruction,[3] is the Jesus who shall save His people from their sins,[4] who shall cast down imaginations, and bring every thought into captivity to the obedience of Christ.[5] The Deliverer who comes to Zion is He who shall turn away ungodliness from Jacob.[6] If we are not willing for this, we may well doubt whether we have any part or lot in the matter, and fear that we are yet in the bond of iniquity; [7] for Christ will not arrange a partial salvation to meet our partial desire.[8] He will not be our refuge from the penalty of sin, if we do not want Him as our refuge from the power.[9] When the elders of Gilead turned to Jephthah in their distress, that he might lead them to victory over their oppressors, what was his condition? [10]—' If ye bring me home again to fight against the children of Ammon, and

---

[1] Ps. cx. 3.  [2] Luke xi. 22.  [3] Ps. ciii. 4.
[4] Matt. i. 21.  [5] 2 Cor. x. 5.  [6] Isa. lix. 20.
[7] Acts viii. 21 ; ib. viii. 23.  [8] Rom. vi. 1, 22.
[9] Titus ii. 14.  [10] Judg. xi. 4-8.

the Lord deliver them before me, *shall I be your head?*' [1]

Lord Jesus, Thou art exalted to be a Prince and a Saviour,[2] and as such I need Thee and I desire Thee. 'Thou hast delivered my soul from death,'[3] *therefore* I pray Thee to deliver my feet from falling, that I may 'run the way of Thy commandments.'[4] Oh, sit and rule upon Thy throne in my heart;[5] reign there until Thou hast put all enemies under Thy feet![6]

## FIFTEENTH DAY.

## Separation unto

'Seemeth it but a small thing unto you, that the God of Israel hath separated you from the congregation of Israel, to bring you near to himself?'—NUM. xvi. 9.

THE thought of separation, so inseparable from true and growing Christian life,[7] is sometimes invested with an unnecessary sternness, because it is only viewed in one aspect. Young Christians are tempted to think 'separation *from* . . .' a hard thing, because they do not see how it is far more than outweighed by 'separation *unto*.'[8] Let us think a little of this bright and beautiful side of it.

---

[1] Judg. xi. 9.      [2] Acts v. 31.      [3] Ps. lvi. 13.
[4] Ps. cxix. 32.      [5] Zech. vi. 13.      [6] 1 Cor. xv. 25.
[7] John xvii. 16; 1 John ii. 15.      [8] Rom. i. 1.

There is no true separation *from* the things which Jesus calls us to leave,[1] without a corresponding separation *unto* things which are incomparably better.[2] One hardly likes to speak of it as compensation, because the 'unto' is so infinitely more than the 'from;' it is like talking of a royal friendship compensating for dropping a beggar's acquaintance, or the whole Bank of England for a brass farthing, or palace life for 'giving up' workhouse life![3]

First, and chiefly, we are separated unto the Lord Himself.[4] He wants us not only for servants, but for friends;[5] and He makes the friendship a splendid and satisfying reality. He wants to bring us 'near to Himself,' that we may be 'a people near unto Him.'[6] He will not have a half possession in us, and so He says He hath 'severed you from other people,'[7] why? 'that ye should be Mine!' 'chosen unto Himself,' 'His peculiar treasure,'[8] 'separated from among all the people of the earth to be Thine inheritance.'[9] Is it 'a small thing' thus to be the Lord's Nazarite, 'holy unto the Lord all the days of his separation'?[10] is any earthly crown to be compared to 'the consecration (margin, separation) of his God upon his head'?[11]

We are separated also to far happier human friendships than the world knows.[12] There is no isolation intended. 'The Lord is able to give thee much more than this.'[13] Those who separated them-

---

[1] Matt. iv. 19, 20.  [2] Mark x. 29, 30.  [3] Phil. iii. 8; 1 Cor. iii. 21-23.
[4] Num. vi. 2; Ps. iv. 3.  [5] John xv. 15.
[6] Ps. cxlviii. 14.  [7] Lev. xx. 26.  [8] Ps. cxxxv. 4.
[9] 1 Kings viii. 53; Titus ii. 14.  [10] Num. vi. 8.
[11] Num. vi. 7.  [12] *e. g.* 1 Thess. ii. 17-20, iii. 9; 2 John i. 12.
[13] 2 Chron. xxv. 9.

selves *from* the people of the land *unto* the law of God, '*they* clave to their brethren.'[1] That is just it; we may lose 'people,' but we find brethren,'[2] with all the love and pleasure and freedom of intercourse —yes, and even mirth—which that relationship brings. Is not this 'much more' than the society of '*people*'?

But we do not get this, perhaps do not even guess its existence, as long as we try for both.[3] Both means *neither*, in this case; we are conscious of the hollowness of the one, and we are not separated unto, and therefore cannot possibly know the enjoyment of, the other.

Then we are separated unto work, '*the* work whereunto I have called them;'[4] very different kinds, but to every man his own work,[5] and thereby an end of all the gnawing purposelessness, and down-weighing uselessness, and miserable time-killing, and sense of helpless waste of life. *Ennui* is no part of a separated life; there is no room for that wretchedness any more. 'Whose I am, and whom I serve,'[6] fills it up. Some are separated more especially 'to bear the ark of the covenant of the Lord.'[7] Some only to stand before Him, it may be 'by night,'[8] so that 'songs in the night'[9] may ascend to His glory. Some in a thousand ways 'to minister unto Him,' to His poor, to 'His prisoners,'[10] spiritually or temporally; always 'unto Him'[11] in His representatives. But *all* 'to bless in

---

[1] Neh. x. 28, 29.   [2] Mark x. 30; 1 John iii. 14.
[3] Matt. vi. 24; Jas. iv. 4.   [4] Acts xiii. 2.
[5] Mark xiii. 34.   [6] Acts xxvii. 23.   [7] Isa. lii. 11; Deut. x. 8.
[8] Ps. cxxxiv. 1.   [9] Job xxxv. 10.   [10] Ps. lxix. 33
[11] Matt. xxv. 40.

His name;'[1] for praise is the invariable service of separation.

'Ye see your calling;'[2] is it not a high one? 'Seemeth it but a small thing to you?'[3] Seemeth it too stern a thing? Is it not rather a 'better thing' than fallen man could have dreamt of aspiring to?[4] a brighter life than has entered into the natural heart of man even to imagine? Is it for *you?* Listen! 'Be ye separate,' and, what then? '*I* will receive you.'[5] 'This is His commandment'[6] to you, and this is His promise. Will you obey? Then you shall know a little, but every day more and more, of that unspeakable blessing of being 'received' by the Father, until the day when Jesus shall come again and receive you unto Himself[7] for the grand separation of eternity with Him.[8]

'As by the light of opening day
The stars are all concealed,
So earthly pleasures fade away
When Jesus is revealed.'

JOHN NEWTON.

---

[1] 1 Chron. xxiii. 13.    [2] 1 Cor. i. 26; Phil. iii. 14.
[3] Num. xvi. 9.    [4] 1 Cor. ii. 9, 10.    [5] 2 Cor. vi. 17.
[6] 1 John iii. 23.    [7] John xiv. 3.    [8] John xvii. 24.

# SIXTEENTH DAY.

---

## Manifesting the Life of Jesus.

'That the life also of Jesus might be made manifest in our mortal flesh.'—2 COR. iv. 11.

IS not this a 'high' and 'holy' and 'heavenly' calling?[1] Yet 'even hereunto were ye called: because Christ also suffered for us, leaving us an example, that we should follow His steps.'[2] 'Hereunto,' to do just as He would have done, sometimes even just as He did do in like circumstances; to show not our patience, but 'the patience of Jesus Christ,'[3]—not mere human meekness and gentleness, but 'the meekness and gentleness of Christ,'[4] and so on with all the other beautiful and holy qualities which shone in 'the life also of Jesus.' While our 'life is hid with Christ in God,'[5] His life is to be 'manifest in our mortal flesh,'—yes, 'magnified in my body.'[6]

'How shall this be?' First, Jesus Himself must dwell in our hearts by faith,[7] or His life cannot be 'manifest.' He has said He will do so, but it is on conditions which He specifies: 1. Hearing His

---

[1] Phil. iii. 14; 2 Tim. i. 9; Heb. iii. 1.        [2] 1 Pet. ii. 21.
[3] Rev. i. 9.         [4] 2 Cor. x. 1.        [5] Col. iii. 3.
        [6] Phil. i. 20.        [7] Eph. iii. 17.

voice; 2. Opening the door to Him; 3. Loving Him; 4. Keeping His words.[1] Not one of these can we fulfil without His grace, but not one of them will He deny us grace to fulfil, and the real desire to fulfil them is the beginning of that grace. Therefore let us 'open unto Him immediately,' and let Him come in and 'abide with us,'[2] so that henceforth it may be, 'Not I, but Christ liveth in me.'[3]

We want Him to make us vessels meet for this great use;[4] pure and transparent vessels through which His glorious life may shine; so transparent, that, like clear glass, they may be altogether lost sight of in the light which streams through them; so pure, that they may not dim the radiance of His indwelling.

The word 'manifest' is more than mere show ing; it implies a bringing to light, shining forth, and comes from the idea of a torch or lantern. We can only shine as lights in the world by bearing the Light of the world within us.[5] But it is a grand and solemn responsibility. Our Lord Jesus is hidden from the eyes of the world; they do not see Him, they only see us, and our lives are to show them what His life is. What a tremendous trust our Master has given us! Who is sufficient for this thing?[6] It is very real. He, our precious Lord, will be held in more or less esteem this day; His power, His grace, His sweetness will be judged of according to what the outsiders see in our lives. This day it rests

---

[1] Rev. iii. 20; John xiv. 23.  
[2] Luke xii. 36; ib. xxiv. 29.  
[3] Gal. ii 20.  
[4] 2 Tim. ii. 21.  
[5] Phil. ii. 15; John viii. 12.  
[6] 2 Cor. ii. 16.

with us to bring fresh reproach and discredit on His dear name, by caricaturing His life, or so truly to manifest it 'that the name of our Lord Jesus Christ may be glorified in you.'[1]

> Thy life in me be shown!
>   Lord, I would henceforth seek
>   To think and speak
> Thy thoughts, Thy words alone,
> No more my own!

# SEVENTEENTH DAY.

## The Yoke-destroying Anointing.

'The yoke shall be destroyed because of the anointing.'— Isa. x. 27.

THE Assyrian yoke of old was not so real, so tangible, so continually felt a yoke, as that under which many a child of God is writhing; yet they are 'called unto liberty,' even 'the glorious liberty of the children of God.'[2] And if the yoke of sin is felt to be real, the promised destruction of it surely will not be less so. If it is, as we know by sorrowful experience, no imaginary bondage, neither shall the deliverance be imaginary.

---

[1] 2 Thess. i. 12.      [2] Gal. v. 13; Rom. viii. 21.

- You feel the yoke, but *how* shall it be destroyed?

1. Because of the grand anointing of our Lord Jesus Christ by God Himself ' with the Holy Ghost and with power '[1] to proclaim liberty to the captives;[2] the grace and might of the triune Jehovah thus combining in the proclamation of the liberty which Jesus purchased by taking upon Him the form of a slave and becoming obedient to death.[3]

2. ' Because of the anointing ' which we ' have received of Him,'[4] because the precious ointment upon our High Priest's head goes down to the skirts of His garments,[5] shared by His least and lowest members.

Perhaps we stop here and say, ' But I cannot realize that I have received it, because my yoke is heavy upon me.' Then see *how* you shall receive it; there is only one way—not by fresh revelation or special voice from heaven, but simply by faith— ' that ye might receive the promise of the spirit *through faith.*'[6] Give glory to God, and be fully persuaded that what He has promised He is able also to perform;[7] and His ' free Spirit ' will be faithful to His promise, and the yoke, even *your* yoke, ' shall be destroyed because of the anointing.'[8]

All other yokes are sub-included in the yoke of our sins, and this is exactly what Jesus came to save us from; the very first, as it is the all-inclusive New Testament promise, ' Thou shalt call His name Jesus: for He shall save His people from their sins.'[9] Are all His wonderful promises about this

---

[1] Acts x. 38.  [2] Isa. lxi. 1.  [3] Phil. ii. 7, 8.
[4] 1 John ii. 27.  [5] Ps. cxxxiii. 2.  [6] Gal. iii. 14.
[7] Rom. iv. 20, 21.  [8] Ps. li. 12 ; Heb. x. 23.  [9] Matt. i. 21.

mere empty words, with no power or reality in them? Are they the exceptions to His declaration that 'My words shall not pass away'?[1] the only promises which are *not* Yea and Amen in Christ Jesus?[2] Listen! they need no note or comment. 'Sin shall not have dominion over you.' 'Ye were the servants of Sin, but, . . . being made free from sin, ye became the servants of righteousness.'[3] '*Now* being made free from sin,' 'the law of the Spirit of life in Christ Jesus hath made me free from the law of sin and death.'[4] 'Whosoever committeth sin is the servant of sin. . . . If the Son therefore shall make you free, ye shall be free indeed.'[5] Let us look at the context of each (only not quoted for want of space), and, if our experience has nothing answering to all this purpose of His goodness'[6] let us ask Him to show us His own meaning and His own royal intention, and to 'reveal even this unto you'[7] by the unction from the Holy one,[8] who convinces all the more deeply of sin when He convinces also of the practical power of Christ's blood to cleanse from all sin, and of the reality of His present salvation.[9] Do not hug the yoke which He has promised to destroy

'And it shall come to pass in the day that the Lord shall give thee rest from thy sorrow, and from thy fear, and from the hard bondage wherein thou wast made to serve, that thou shalt . . . say, How hath the oppressor ceased!'[10] 'In that day . . . his burden shall be taken away from off thy shoulder.'

---

[1] Matt. xxiv. 35.    [2] 2 Cor. i. 20.    [3] Rom. vi. 14; ib. vi. 17, 18.
[4] Rom. vi. 22; ib. viii. 2.    [5] John viii. 34, 36.
[6] Eph. i. 4.    [7] Phil. iii. 15.    [8] 1 John ii. 20.
[9] John xvi. 8; 1 John i. 7.    [10] Isa. xiv. 3, 4.

But 'that day' may be *this* day! Why not? 'For *now* will I break his yoke from off thee.'[1] 'Where the Spirit of the Lord is, there is liberty;'[2] and He hath said, 'Ask, and ye *shall* receive.'[3] Recognize the anointing by faith, and then 'stand fast therefore in the liberty wherewith Christ *hath* made us free, and be not entangled again with the yoke of bondage;'[4] for 'this is His commandment' Then you shall 'walk at liberty,'[5] and give Him the glad 'offering of a free heart,' rejoicing in His easy yoke,[6] and (shall we not add), 'proclaiming liberty every man to his neighbor.'[7]

> Upon Thy promises I stand,
> Trusting in thee: Thine own right hand
>     Doth keep and comfort me!
> My soul doth triumph in Thy word;
> Thine, Thine be all the praise, dear Lord,
>     As Thine the victory.
>
> Love perfecteth what it begins;
> Thy power doth save me from my sins;
>     Thy grace upholdeth me.
> This life of trust, how glad! how sweet!
> My need and Thy great fullness meet,
>     And I have all in thee.
>
> JEAN S. PIGOTT.

---

[1] Nah. i. 13.   [2] 2 Cor. iii. 17.   [3] Matt. vii. 7.
[4] Gal. v. 1.   [5] Ps. cxix. 45.   [6] Matt. xi. 29.  -
[7] Jer. xxxiv. 15.

## EIGHTEENTH DAY.

___

## Our Works in God's Hand.

'Commit thy works unto the Lord.'—PROV. xvi. 3.

SUPPOSE an angel were sent down to tell us this morning that he was commissioned to take all our work under his charge to-day, that we might just be easy about it, because he would undertake it, and his excellent strength and wisdom[1] would make it all prosper a great deal more than ours, how extremely foolish it would be not to avail ourselves of such superhuman help! What a holiday it would seem, if we accepted the offer, as we went about our business with the angel beside us! what a day of privilege and progress! and how we should thank God for the extraordinary relief His kindness had sent!

Far higher is our privilege this day; not merely permitted, but pressed upon us by royal commandment, 'Commit thy works unto Jehovah!' Yet this is but the third strand of a golden cord which is strong enough (if yielded to) to draw us up out of all the miry clay of the 'pit of noise,'[2] where

___

[1] Ps. ciii. 20.          [2] Ps. xl. 2, margin.

the voices of fear and anxiety and distrust make
such a weary din.   We are to commit the keeping
of our souls to Him ;[1] then we shall be ready for
the command to commit our way unto Him, and
then our works.[2]   Then, having obeyed, we may
exchange the less confident expression, ' Unto God
would I commit my cause,'[3] for the bright
assurance, ' I am persuaded that He is able to keep
that which I *have* committed unto Him.'[4]   *Of
course* He is !

 _ Not an angel, but Jehovah bids us this day commit our works to Him.   It is not approving the
idea, nor thinking about it, nor even asking Him
to take them, that is here commanded, but *committing* them : a definite act of soul, a real transaction
with our Lord.   Suppose you have an interview
with another worker, and, having had a distinct
understanding as to what you wish him to undertake
for you, you verbally and explicitly transfer to him
the management and responsibility of some work.
You are not actually in sight of it, you have no
tangible objects to hand over, you might do it in a
dark room, but the transaction is real.   The burden
of the work is no longer upon you, if only you
have confidence in the one to whom you have committed it.   And if you have the further confidence
that he is considerably more capable than yourself,
and can do it all a great deal better, you are not
only relieved but rejoiced.   Just such a definite
transaction does our Lord bid us make with Him
this morning.   Will you do it ?   Will you not, be-

---

[1] 1 Pet. iv. 19.          [2] Ps. xxxvii. 5.
[3] Job v. 8.              [4] 2 Tim. i. 12.

fore venturing away from your quiet early hour, 'commit thy works' to Him definitely, the special things you have to do to-day, and the unforeseen work which He may add in the course of it?

And then, leave it with Him! You would not have the bad taste to keep on fidgeting about it to the friend who had kindly undertaken your work for you! If we would only apply the commonest rules of human courtesy and confidence to our intercourse with our Divine Master! Leave details and results all and altogether with Him. You see, when you have committed it to Him, your 'works *are* in the hand of God.'[1] Really in His Hand! and where else would you wish them to be? Would you like to have them back in your own? Do you think His grasp is not firm enough, or the hollow of His hand[2] not large enough, to hold your little bits of work quite securely? Even if He tries your faith a little, and you seem to have labored in vain and spent your strength for nought, cannot you trust your 'own Master' enough to add, 'Yet *surely* my judgment is with the Lord, and my work with my God'?[3] Especially as He says, 'Thou art my servant, in whom I *will* be glorified;'[4] by which 'ye *know* that your labor is not in vain in the Lord.'[5]

That for the past work. For the present, 'I will direct their work in truth.'[6] And for all our future work, a singular shining in the eastern horizon: 'Mine elect shall long enjoy the work of their hands.'[7]

---

[1] Eccles. ix. 1.  [2] Isa. xl. 12.  [3] Isa. xlix. 4.
[4] Isa. xlix. 3.  [5] 1 Cor. xv. 58.  [6] Isa. lxi. 8.
[7] Isa. lxv. 22.

Oh to be nothing, nothing!
　　Only to lie at His feet,
A broken and emptied vessel,
　　For the Master's use made meet.
Emptied, that He may fill me,
　　As forth to His service I go;
Broken, that so unhindered
　　His life through me might flow.

Oh to be nothing, nothing!
　　Only as led by His hand;
A messenger at His gateway,
　　Only waiting for His command.
Only an instrument ready
　　His praises to sound at His will;
Willing, should He not require me,
　　In silence to wait on Him still.

G. M. Taylor.

———•———

# NINETEENTH DAY.

———

# The Secret of Fulfilled Desire.

' Delight thyself also in the Lord; and He shall give thee the desires of thy heart.'—Ps. xxxvii. 4.

ONE often hears this promise quoted without its conditional precept; [1] but we have no right to put asunder anything that God has joined together. Every heart has desires, but not even every Christ-

---

[1] Prov. x. 24.

ıan heart delights itself in the Lord. This is the reason of the great wail of unfulfilled desire—the very howl, one might say, which makes a howling wilderness of this fair world.

It stands to reason; if our delight is absolutely and entirely in the Lord, all our desires will be not only 'before Him,'[1] but the whole 'desire of our soul' will be concentrated upon Him,[2] radiating from that centre along the bright rays of His 'good and perfect and acceptable will.'[3] Now, of course, His will must and will be carried out; for 'He doeth according to His will in the army of heaven, and among the inhabitants of the earth: and none can stay His hand.'[4]

So, if we delight truly in the Lord, and thereby have our desires so harmonized with His will that they float out on the same great tide of perfect music, there will be no damper upon their vibrations, but they will be fulfilled for us because His will is fulfilled.[5]

His will is not, as we are tempted practically to think, something quite separate and apart from Himself, so that we may think Him gracious, and yet think His will rather stern; or so that we may love Him, and yet very much dislike His will. His will is the very essence of Himself going forth in force; it is the primary difference between what we know of Jehovah and what the Hindoo imagines of Brahma.

We must not overlook the important word 'also'[6] This points us to a preliminary condition:

---

[1] Ps. lxxiii. 25; ib. xxxviii. 9.    [2] Isa. xxvi. 8, 9; 2 Sam. xxiii. 5. [3] Rom. xii. 2.    [4] Dan. iv. 35.    [5] Eph. v. 17.    [6] Ps. xxxvii. 3.

'Trust in the Lord, and do good.'[1] Trust, evidenced by obedience, is the stepping-stone to delight in the Lord, and the only one. Obedience is the result of trust, and the condition of delight.

Two great cases of this condition of delight are distinctly given us—one spiritual, the other practical.

1. 'If thou return to the Almighty, . . . *then* thou shalt have thy delight in the Almighty.'[2] It is not said to saints, but to repentant sinners[3]—not to the eldest son, but to the returning prodigal.[4] To me, the wanderer, it is offered. To me, the backslider, it is held out. We can never say: 'The Lord does not mean such a one as I to delight in Him; that sort of thing is only meant for those who have always been consistent Christians.' If so, He would not have said, 'If thou *return*.'[5] Without true returning, there cannot be delight in the Lord; but, conversely, if there is no delight, ought we not to 'consider our ways,'[6] lest some 'returning' should be needed?

2. 'If thou turn away thy foot from the Sabbath, from doing thy pleasure on My holy day; and call the Sabbath a delight, the holy of the Lord, honorable; and shalt honor Him, not doing thine own ways, nor finding thine own pleasure, nor speaking thine own words: *Then* shalt thou delight thyself in the Lord.'[7] On our knees before Him let us examine ourselves as to every clause of this great condition. Perhaps *here* we shall find the joints in the

---

[1] Isa. xii. 2, 3.    [2] Job xxii. 23, 26.    [3] Matt. ix. 11, 13.
[4] Luke xv. 2, 32.    [5] Job xv. 11.    [6] Hag. i. 7.
[7] Isa. lviii. 13, 14.

harness, the secret controversy[1] which hinders the realization of delight in the Lord, and therefore of the annexed promise.

A word about the delight itself. There is something so real, and natural, and childlike about it. It is joy realized—joy in flower, bright, growing, alive, beautiful. It is the sparkle of the upspringing fountain in the clear sunlight. This childlike delight is to be in the Lord Himself. It is quite another thing to delight in what He does for us. The Israelites ' delighted themselves in Thy great goodness.[2] Nevertheless they were disobedient, and rebelled.' Not under the shadow of even a God-given gourd,[3] but under His own shadow, may you sit down ' with great delight.'[4] Then all His fruits shall be sweet to your taste; you shall delight in His will, in His comforts, in His commandments, and in His people.[5] You shall desire ' what *His* soul desireth,'[6] and ' He shall give thee the desires of thine Heart.'[7]

> Oh, blessed life!—the heart at rest
>   When all without tumultous seems—
>   That trusts a higher will, and deems
> That higher will, not mine, the best.
>
> Oh, blessed life!—heart, mind, and soul,
>   From self-born aims and wishes free,
>   In all at one with Deity,
> And loyal to the Lord's control.
>
>                     W. T. MATSON.

1 Micah vi. 2.   2 Neh. ix. 25, 26.   3 Jonah iv. 6.
4 Cant. ii. 3.   5 Ps. xl. 8; ib. xciv. 19; ib. cxix. 47; ib. xvi. 3.
6 Job xxiii. 13.   7 Ps. cxlv. 19.

## TWENTIETH DAY.

---

## Taking God at his Word.

'I believe God, that it shall be even as it was told me.'—
ACTS xxvii. 25.

THEN, of course, St. Paul could be calm, and
bright, and confident, 'with a heart at leisure
from itself' to cheer and counsel others. Yet could
any circumstances have been more depressing?—a
miserable and crowded ship, to which our most
wretched steamer would be a palace, exceedingly
tossed with tempest, not a gleam of sun or star for
many days, all reckoning lost, driving wildly on to
certain shipwreck, and the graphic and suggestive
touch of 'long abstinence.'

Whatever this day may bring forth, there can be
nothing like this for us. Yet even the lesser trials
of our own journey may and must be met with the
same simple and sufficient secret of calm, simple
belief in what God has said. It is strange and sur-
prising even to ourselves how absolutely *enough* we
always do find it, just to believe that it shall be
even as God has told us, and 'rest' on His word.[1]

---

Prov. xvi. 3.

The ' it ' may be for us one thing to-day, another
to-morrow, according to the circumstances He
sends; but the ' shall be ' cannot be severed from
it. He has ' told us' so much, that we have only
to recognize our special need, to find at once that
He has already ' told ' us exactly what we want.

Glance at the needs of this day—our weakness,
our openness to temptation, our liability to fall,[1]
our besetting sins, our ignorance, our present or
possible troubles, our longing for Himself, which
includes all other holy longing—seven pressing
realities.[2] Now let us hush our hearts to listen to
the reality of His corresponding replies : ' I will
strengthen thee.'[3] ' Ye shall be able to quench *all*
the fiery darts of the wicked.'[4] 'Able to keep you
from falling'[5] (*Gr.* 'stumbling '). ' He shall save
His people from *their* sins '[6] (*i. e.* just your own
special ones). ' I will instruct thee and teach thee
in the way which thou shalt go.'[7] 'I will not leave
you comfortless.' ' I will come to you.'[8] Can we
read these words—His own words, and say, ' I do
*not* believe God ! ' Even the recoil from such an
expression may help a trembling one to the joyful
and only alternative · ' I believe God, that it shall
be *even as* it was told me.' Not less, not almost as,
but ' even as,' with God's own fullness of meaning
in each word of each promise.

David prayed : 'Do as Thou hast said. . . . For
Thou, O my God, hast *told* Thy servant that Thou
wilt build him an house : *therefore* Thy servant hath

---

[1] 1 Pet. v. 8.   [2] Ps. lxxiii. 22 ; ib. lx. 11 ; ib. lxiii. 1.   [3] Isa. xli. 10.
[4] Eph vi. 16.         [5] Jude 24.         [6] Matt. i. 21.
[7] Ps. xxxii. 8.       [8] John xiv. 18.

found in his heart to pray before Thee.' And because God had 'promised this goodness,' he prayed on confidently: 'Now *therefore* let it please Thee to bless . . . : for Thou blessest, O Lord, and it shall be blessed forever.'[1] Has He not 'told' us of blessings beyond those for which David pleaded, and may we not claim these in the name of Jesus with a childlike, 'Do as Thou hast said'?

The ground of St. Paul's belief was not something, but Some One. Simply, 'I believe *God*'! An earnest worker said the other day, 'Oh, I am so glad it does not say, "I know *what* I have believed," but, "I know *whom* I have believed"!'[2] This belief, of course, includes all His messages, written or spoken. 'If ye will not believe, surely ye shall not be established,'[3] is a word of continual application to the trembling or wavering steps of our daily path. But 'this is His commandment,'[4] 'Believe in the Lord your God, so shall ye be established; believe His prophets, so shall ye prosper.'[5] And then, 'Blessed is she that believed: for there shall be a performance of those things which were *told* her from the Lord.'[6]

'Even *as* it was told me.' 'And *so* it came to pass.'[7]

---

[1] 1 Chron. xvii. 23, 25.   [2] 2 Tim. i. 12.   [3] Isa. vii. 9.   [4] 1 John iii. 23.
[5] 2 Chron. xx. 20.   [6] Luke i. 45.   [7] Acts xxvii. 25, 44.

## TWENTY-FIRST DAY.

———

## Our Commission.

'And let him that heareth say, Come.'—REV. xxii. 17.

'THEY delivered the king's commissions unto the king's lieutenants.'[1] Have some of us thought it would be easier to work for God if a definite commission were delivered to us, so that we could know exactly what we were to do and say[2]—a commission so explicit, that there could be no mistake either in its personal delivery to ourselves or in our execution of it? Then here it is!

To whom is it delivered? Simply to 'him that heareth.' 'The Spirit and the bride say, Come. And let him that heareth say, Come.'[3] Then, if this blessed call has been heard by you, for you is the commission intended, and to you it is given. Not, are you a fit and polished instrument? not, are you a practised worker? not, are you already a trained soldier, and therefore very capable of enlisting others?[4] not, have you a special gift of speech or pen?[5] but simply and solely, have you heard for yourself the one sweet call, 'Come'?[6]

---

[1] Ezra viii. 36.     [2] Josh. i. 16.     [3] Rev. xxii. 17.
[4] 2 Tim. ii. 2, 3.     [5] 1 Cor. xii. 7-11.     [6] Matt. xi. 28.

Now you see that the commission is for you, do you not? But what is it? Can anything be more simple and explicit? You are to 'say, *Come*'*!* That is all; but, in simple obedience to this command of your King, what possibilities of blessing and success, of gladness to you and glory to Him, are enfolded! You are to '*say*, Come.' Are you saying it? Not, are you exercising a general good influence? not, do you try to lead and keep the conversation in profitable channels? not, do you speak about 'good things' or even *about* Christ? not, are you giving time and money to the furtherance of some branch of His work?—you may be doing all this, and yet be distinctly disobeying His command, distinctly faithless and disobedient to your commission. You are missing the present privilege and unspeakable happiness of winning souls, and foregoing the glorious reward annexed to it.[1] For, assuredly, it is those who are literally saying 'Come,' who are really 'turning many to righteousness;'[2] not because they are more gifted, but because God's powerful blessing is given with their obedience to His definite command.

Why should we be at a loss what to say, when He has given us the very word? We have but to transmit the echo of His own call, 'Come unto Me;' 'Come and see;'[3] 'If any man thirst, let him come unto Me and drink.'[4]

Whatever the position of the one to whom we speak, there is always a suitable 'Come.' 'Come thou with us, and we will do thee good.'[5] 'Come

---

[1] Prov. xi. 30.  [2] Dan. xii. 3.  [3] John i. 39, 46.
[4] John vii. 37.  [5] Num. x. 29.

and see Him whom we have found.'[1] 'Come and let us join ourselves to the Lord in a perpetual covenant that shall not be forgotten.'[2] Then, for those who have come, there is still always a 'Come up higher.'[3] 'Come up with me . . . that we may fight against the Canaanite.'[4] 'Come ye, and let us walk in the light of the Lord.'[5] Oh, how such a call may be blessed to a weak-handed and feeble-footed Christian? And still there is a 'come' of special beauty and power for those who have yielded themselves to Him : 'Now ye have consecrated yourselves unto the Lord, come *near*.'[6] And let us not shrink from faithfully echoing with no 'uncertain sound,'[7] 'Come *out* from among them,'[8] remembering that when the heavenly Bridegroom says, 'Come *with* Me,' He adds, '*from* Lebanon . . . *from* the lions' dens.'[9] He who gives the commission *always* gives opportunities of exercising it ; but it is our part faithfully to seek and watch for these, and courage and faith will increase as they widen. The servant who was sent at first only to *say* 'Come' to the bidden guests, was next sent to *bring* them in from a wider range, and then to '*compel* them to come in ' from a wider still.[10]

The commission is laid before you this day ; it is inscribed with your own name, signed by your King's own hand, and sealed by the Spirit, who bears witness with your Spirit that His ' Come ' has ·been heard by you.[11] Do you accept it? or do you refuse it ? There is no third alternative !

---

[1] John i. 46.
[2] Jer. l. 5.
[3] Prov. xxv. 7.
[4] Judg. i. 3.
[5] Isa. ii. 5.
[6] 2 Chron. xxix. 31.
[7] 1 Cor. xiv. 8.
[8] 2 Cor. vi. 17.
[9] Cant. iv. 8.
[10] Luke xiv. 17; ib. xiv. 21; ib. xiv. 23.
[11] Rom. viii. 16.

Ye who hear the blessed call
　　Of the Spirit and the Bride,
Hear the Master's word to all,
　　Your commission and your guide:
'And let him that heareth say,
Come,' to all yet far away.

'Come!' alike to age and youth·
　　Tell them of our Friend above,
Of His beauty and His truth,
　　Preciousness, and grace, and love.
Tell them what you know is true,
Tell them what He is to you.

Brothers, sisters, do not wait,
　　Speak for Him who speaks to you!
Wherefore should you hesitate?
　　This is no great thing to do.
Jesus only bids you say,
'Come!' and will you not obey?

———————◆———————

# TWENTY-SECOND DAY.

———————

# 𝔅𝔢𝔥𝔬𝔩𝔡𝔦𝔫𝔤 𝔞𝔫𝔡 𝔇𝔢𝔠𝔩𝔞𝔯𝔦𝔫𝔤.

'Son of man, behold with thine eyes, and hear with thine ears, and set thine heart upon all that I shall shew thee; for to the intent that I might shew them unto thee art thou brought hither: declare all that thou seest to the house of Israel.'— EZEK. xl. 4.

WHETHER the mysterious Measurer was a created angel or the divine Angel of the Covenant, 'we cannot tell.'[1]  But the message which he here gives to Ezekiel seems to illustrate the work of the Holy Spirit, whose office it is to take both the words and the things of Christ and shew them unto us.[2]

'Eye hath not seen,' yet 'behold with thine eyes;' 'nor ear heard,' yet 'hear with thine ears;' 'neither have entered into the heart of man,'[3] yet 'set thine heart upon all that I shall show thee.' For 'God hath revealed them unto us by His Spirit.'[3]  To Ezekiel should be shown the wonderful temple, with its measurements, its laws, and its mystical services.  To us shall be revealed the things which God hath prepared for them that love Him,[5] and (as if to let the ladder down a step lower) 'for him that waiteth for Him.'[6]  Afterward, he beheld 'the glory of the God of Israel,' and 'he heard Him speaking unto' him.'[7]  And we, by the Spirit, are to behold the glory of the Lord,[8] and to 'hear His voice' calling us by name.[9]

This would seem to be all promise and privilege, rather than commandment; something with which we have nothing at all to do but to wait and see if it comes!  Nay!  'Behold with thine eyes.'  'Go forth and behold'[10] your King!  And when we accept the seemingly impossible command, the Spirit will open our eyes that we may see.  'Hear with thine ears!'[11]  And with (not even after) the obedient inclination of the ear, the still small voice will out-ring not only 'earth's drowsy chime,' but all other voices.  He says: 'They shall hear My

---

[1] Matt. xxi. 27.  [2] John xiv. 26; ib. xvi. 15.  [3] 1 Cor. ii. 9.
[4] 1 Cor. ii. 10.  [5] 1 Cor. ii. 9.  [6] Isa. lxiv. 4.
[7] Ezek. xliii. 1, 2; ib. xliii. 6.  [8] 2 Cor. iii. 18.
[9] John x. 3.  [10] Cant. iii. 11.  [11] Isa. lv. 3.

voice;'[1] 'they shall know in that day that I am He that doth speak.'[2] For the Spirit will unstop the ears of the deaf. When He thus makes us behold and hear, He will finish the work and enable us to 'set' our wandering hearts upon all that He will show us. But the responsibility will still be ours to follow the enabling.

It will act and react. The more we set our hearts the more He will show us; and the more He shows us, the more our hearts will surely there be fixed.

'*All* that I shall shew thee.' What a vista of revelation opens before us! 'He shall take of Mine and shall shew it unto you,'[3]—My love, My grace, My wisdom, My acts, My covenant, My goodness, My glory! He 'will shew thee the truth.'[4] He 'will shew thee great and mighty things, which thou knowest not.'[5] 'He will shew you things to come.'[6] Do we not feel like little children, wondering, in delighted expectation, what it is that we are going to see?

Like little children, too, we have been brought hither, on purpose that He may show us all this. 'Hither,' to the very place, the very point, where we now are. We did not come of ourselves; we were 'brought.' Very likely we should have gone to some other place, and aimed at some other point. But He brought us hither with gracious intent of revelation. It may have been a stiff climb up the 'very high mountain;'[7] but who minds that, if they really believe in the promised view?

---

[1] John x. 16.     [2] Isa. lii. 6.     [3] John xvi. 15.
[4] Ps. xvii. 7; ib. ciii. 7; ib. xxv. 14; Ex. xxxiii. 18, 19; Dan. xi. 2.
[5] Jer. xxxiii. 3.     [6] John xvi. 13.     [7] Ezek. xl. 2.

As commands always lead up to privileges, so privileges again lead on to further commands. Not for ourselves alone are we to 'see' and 'hear.' We are to declare all that we see.[1] When we have seen the house, we are to 'shew the house.'[2] When we have seen the Saviour, we are to make known abroad the saying which was told us concerning Him.[3] When we have seen the King, we are to 'tell it out' that He reigneth. 'Hear with thine ears, and go . . . and speak.'[4] 'What I tell you in darkness, that speak ye in light.'[5]

Do not let us begin quibbling about how much we can tell, or how much we ought to tell. Let us very simply and very humbly bow before this 'His commandment,' and ask Him to enable us to obey it exactly as He means us to obey it, neither losing the spirit in the letter nor ignoring the letter in the spirit.[6]

> Lord, speak to me, that I may speak
> In living echoes of Thy tone;
> As thou hast sought, so let me seek
> Thy erring children, lost and lone.
>
> Oh teach me, Lord, that I may teach
> The precious things Thou dost impart;
> And wing my words that they may reach
> The hidden depths of many a heart.
>
> Oh fill me with Thy fulness, Lord,
> Until my very heart o'erflow,
> In kindling thought and glowing word,
> Thy love to tell, Thy praise to show.

---

[1] 1 John i. 3.  [2] Ezek. xliii. 10.  [3] Luke ii. 17.
[4] Ezek. iii. 10, 11.  [5] Matt. x. 27.  [6] 2 Cor. iv. 13.

# TWENTY-THIRD DAY.

## Telling of the Hand of God.

'Then I told them of the hand of my God which was good upon me; as also the king's words that he had spoken unto me. And they said, Let us rise up and build. So they strengthened their hands for this good work.'—NEH. ii. 18.

'THEN they that feared the Lord spake often one to another.'[1] Yet many hold back from what they call 'talking about religion,' under colour that they fear it too often leads to talking about self. And yet, what about the general conversation which is about 'other things,'[2] not 'the things which are Jesus Christ's'?[3] Are the 'other things' free from self and wholly profitable? Is it 'with grace, seasoned with salt'? Yet this is what we are commanded that our speech should 'always' be.[4]

Let us lay aside this unscriptural notion of 'talking about religion,' which may only be controversy and criticism, and see what our Lord would have us talk about. The sum of our conversation should be, as recorded of Anna, 'She . . . spake of Him.'[5]

---

[1] Mal. iii. 16.  [2] Mark iv. 19.  [3] Phil. ii. 21.
[4] Job. xv. 3; Col. iv. 6.  [5] Luke ii. 38.

Here is our keynote, and what wealth of melody and fulness of harmony spring from it!—the melodies of His word 'in linked sweetness, long drawn out,' for the right hand; the harmonies of His works, in ever-varying marvels, for the left. Why, we have topics for all eternity, much more for our occasional hours and minutes of converse, unfolding more and more as we receive more and more of His fulness!

But there is the point. If we do not want to 'speak of Him,'[1] let us beware of plausibly persuading ourselves that it is because we do not want to speak about ourselves. Let us be honest, and own that the vessel does not overflow because it is not very full of faith and love.[2] Christ said, 'Out of the abundance of the heart the mouth speaketh.'[3] Men say, 'No such thing! one does not speak when one's heart is full!' Yet 'let God be true, but every man a liar,'[4] and let us see whether our unwillingness to speak of Him does not arise from our having nothing to say

Nehemiah had something to tell. 'I told them of the hand of my God which was good upon me.'[5] Nothing about his 'own arm,' but 'Thy right hand and Thine arm,' and what that had done, the wonderful answer to his prayer, and the way made plain before his face.[6] And see how it stirred up his listeners forthwith! They said, 'Let us rise up and build. So they strengthened their hands for this good work.'[7] Have we nothing to tell to those

---

[1] John i. 16.     [2] Eccles. xi. 3.     [3] Matt. xii. 34.
[4] Rom. iii. 4.     [5] Neh. ii. 18.
[6] Ps. xliv. 3; Neh. i. 10; ib. ii. 4, 8.     [7] Neh. ii. 18.

whom we meet this day of what the hand of our
God has done?[1]

David said, 'Come and hear, . . . and I will
declare what He hath done for my soul;'[2] and no
doubt then, as now, the story of His gracious doings
resulted in stimulus and blessing to other souls.
When thus 'confession with the mouth is made,' it
is very, very often 'unto salvation'[3] for the listeners

We must first know and 'consider how great
things He hath done for' us;[4] and then the voice
of Jesus says not only '*Shew*,' but '*Tell* how great
things the Lord hath done for thee,'[5] that thus showing, and thus telling, 'the communication of thy
faith may become *effectual* by the acknowledging
of every good thing which is in you in Christ
Jesus.'[6]

We have also less personal but not less vivid testimony to bear. 'The Lord hath done great things
for us, whereof we are glad,'[7] will put a new song
in many another's mouth,[8] and confirm their faith
in the living God. Thus did Moses, and the result
was not only that Jethro rejoiced for all the goodness which the Lord had done,[9] but that he rose to
the grand confession, '*Now I know* that Jehovah is
greater than all gods.'[10]

It is not to be only a one-sided telling, but a free
and pleasant interchange; for we are distinctly
commanded, '*Talk* ye of all His wondrous works.'
Who can exhaust that '*all*'![11] While we 'talk
together of all these things,'[12] communing together

---

1 Ps. lxxvii. 12.  2 Ps. lxvi. 16.  3 Rom. x. 10.
4 1 Sam. xii. 24.  5 Mark v. 19 ; Luke viii. 39.  6 Philem. 6.
7 Ps. cxxvi. 3.  8 Ps. xl. 3  9 Ex. xviii. 8.
10 Ex. xviii. 11.  11 Ps. cv. 2; ib. lxxvii. 12.  12 Luke xxiv. 14.

II

like the disciples on the Emmaus road, how often does Jesus Himself draw near and go with us! I think He *always* does, only our eyes are not always open to recognize Him. Verily, in keeping of this commandment (and it *is* a commandment), 'there is *great* reward.'[1]

'Make me to understand the way of Thy precepts: so shall I talk of Thy wondrous works.'

Have you not a word for Jesus? not a word to say for Him?
He is listening through the chorus of the burning seraphim!
He is listening; does He hear you speaking of the things of earth,
Only of its passing pleasure, selfish sorrow, empty mirth?
He has spoken words of blessing, pardon, peace, and love to you,
Glorious hopes and gracious comfort, strong and tender, sweet and true;
Does He hear you telling others something of His love untold,
Overflowings of thanksgiving for His mercies manifold?

---

1 Ps. xix. 11; ib. cxix. 27.

## TWENTY-FOURTH DAY.

## Telling of the King's Words.

'Then I told them of . . . the king's words that he had spoken unto me. And they said, Let us rise up and build. So they strengthened their hands for this good work.'—NEH. ii. 18

HOW naturally we should not only treasure, but *tell*, any royal words spoken to ourselves! They would be more to us than any other utterances, and they would ensure the interest of our listeners. How natural for Nehemiah to tell of the king's words which he had spoken unto him, though only an earthly and alien sovereign!

Now, ought it not to be just as natural, delightful, and interesting to tell of the words of our own, our heavenly King, especially when He has commanded, 'He that hath My word, let him speak my word faithfully'?[1] Not that we can ever tell all that passes in the secret audience chamber; nor would it be well that we should try to do so: for 'the secret of the Lord is with them that fear Him.'[2] The King has gifts for us with shining inscriptions which 'no man knoweth saving he that receiveth'[3] them, whispers which cannot resound in words.

---

[1] Jer. xxiii. 28.    [2] Ps. xxv. 14.    [3] Rev. ii. 17; Prov. xvii. 8.

But very much, perhaps most, of His gracious communications to the soul come in the very form which is most easily grasped, remembered, and re- peated — His own written words brought to our remembrance by His good Spirit, and applied to our conscious or unconscious need.[1] Do not let us give our own memories the credit, in- stead of giving Him the praise, when He so kindly sends any of His own words freshly and forcibly into our minds. Have we not often defrauded Him of the glory due unto His name[2] in this matter, by mistaking His voice for our mere obser- vation or recollection?

Now it is these words of the King, spoken to our hearts as they are not spoken to the world, which we may profitably tell others, thus becoming 'the Lord's messenger in the Lord's message,'[3] and spreading the knowledge of His words. Nehemiah did not tell of the king's words which he had spoken unto somebody else, but 'which He had *spoken unto me.*' So, if we would tell the King's words, we must first hear them. Ask that, like Ezekiel, the Spirit may enter into us when He speaks unto us, so that we may hear Him that speaks unto us.[4] 'These words shall be in thine heart;'[5] and then, after that, comes the command: 'Talk of them when thou sittest in thine house, and when thou walkest by the way.'[6]

Watch to see what He will say,[7] and no fear but

---

[1] John xiv. 26; Acts xx. 35.  [2] Ps. xxix. 2.  [3] Hag. i. 13.
[4] Ezek. iii. 10.  [5] Deut. vi. 6.  [6] Deut. vi. 7.
[7] Hab. ii. 1.

that His words will be heard, and that more and more. For it is when He *hath* spoken unto us that we shall be strengthened, and say, 'Let my Lord speak '[1] And then He will say more to us, and show us ' that which is noted in the Scripture of truth.'[2]

It seems a truism to say that this telling of the King's words will be ever so much more useful and resultful than our own words. Yet do we always act upon this? When we try to ' speak a word for Jesus '[3] to a friend, does it not sometimes seem as if we were a little 'ashamed of His words ' ?[4] Is there not sometimes a little shrinking from giving a text? Has it not seemed an easier course to talk about a sermon? If we have visited a cottage, have we not sometimes thought our duty discharged by a little general good advice and kindly sympathy, and not *always* ' told them of the King's words,' which are spirit and life,[5] and which should not have returned void[6]—seed words, by which dead souls might have been born again ; ' sincere milk,' by which babes in Christ might ' grow ' ?[7]

Surely there is no more precious talent entrusted to us,[8] none with which we may trade with more certain success and splendid increase, than these words of our King. What we hear from Him let us commit to others, ' that they may be able to teach others also.'[9] A simple text thus passed on (and who cannot do this !) may be the immediate means of wonderful spiritual help and quickening,

---

[1] Dan. x. 19.  [2] Dan. x. 21.  [3] Jer. xxiii. 28.
[4] Mark viii. 38.  [5] John vi. 63.  [6] Isa. lv. 11.
[7] 1 Pet. i. 23; ib. ii. 2.  [8] Matt. xxv. 16.  [9] 2 Tim. ii. 2.

and '*the* comfort wherewith we ourselves are comforted of God' (not some otherwise concocted
comfort) may comfort many 'which are in any
trouble,'[1] without even one word of man as its
vehicle.

Yes, we have a word for Jesus! Living echoes we will be
Of Thine own sweet words of blessing, of Thy gracious
    'Come to Me.'
Jesus, Master! yes, we love Thee, and to prove our love would
    lay
Fruit of lips which Thou wilt open, at Thy blessed feet to-day.
Many an effort it may cost us, many a heart-beat, many a fear,
But Thou knowest, and will strengthen, and Thy help is always
    near.
Give us grace to follow fully, vanquishing our faithless shame,
Feebly it may be, but truly, witnessing for Thy dear name.

———— ————

## TWENTY-FIFTH DAY.

————

# Evil Speaking

'Speak not evil one of another, brethren.'—JAS. iv. 11.

ONE of the most difficult of 'His commandments,'[2] and yet one which is in a peculiar
degree 'for our good' and personal happiness, as
well as for those around us! The more difficult, the
more need of grace; and the more need, the more
the full supply.[3]

---

[1] 2 Cor. i. 4.    [2] Deut. x. 13.    [3] 2 Cor. xii. 9; Phil. iv. 19.

Well might St. Paul say, 'Put them in mind to speak evil of no man,'[1] for do we not easily fail to keep this in mind? The command is 'exceeding broad;'[2] let us not seek to narrow it, but humbly bow to our Master's distinct orders in all their exactness.

Do we really *wish* to know them fully, that we may obey fully? Then what are they? 'Speak evil of *no* man.'[3] Shall we venture practically to say, 'Yes, Lord, *except* of So-and-so'?

Laying aside *all* evil speakings.'[4] Does not this include the very least?

'Let *all* bitterness, . . . and evil speaking, be put away from you;'[5] then does He give us leave to cherish even one little hidden root of that bitterness from which the evil speaking springs?[6]

'Put away' implies resolute action in the matter,—have we even *tried* to 'put away *all*'?

But this great clause of the 'royal law'[7] is broader still: 'Let none of you *imagine* evil in your hearts against his neighbour.'[8] And the characteristic of that charity, without which we are only 'sounding brass' and 'nothing,' is, that it '*thinketh* no evil.'[9] Is not this the root from which the far-poisoning fruit springs? We have first disobeyed another order: 'Whatsoever things are of good report; . . . think on *these* things.'[10] Instead of that, we 'think' about the bad reports that we may have heard; we develop the unkind

---

[1] Titus iii. 2.  [2] Ps. cxix. 96.  [3] Titus iii. 2.
[4] 1 Pet. ii. 1.  [5] Eph. iv. 31.  [6] Heb. xii. 15.
[7] Jas. ii. 8.  [8] Zech. vii. 10; ib. viii. 17.
[9] 1 Cor. xiii. 1; ib. xiii. 2; ib. xiii. 5.  [10] Phil. iv. 8.

hint into suspicion; and perhaps into accusation, by *thinking* about it, instead of thinking on and think-ing out the probable 'other side' of the case. This thinking has tempted us *not* to 'refrain our tongue;'[1] and thus we have set some one else 'thinking,' and thereby to more speaking evil one of another. At last the little fire has kindled a great matter,[2] and we come ourselves and bring others under the condemnation of taking up 'a reproach against his neighbour,'[3] instead of not enduring nor receiving it (see the striking mar-ginal reading). And what is the just penalty annexed by implication? *Not* to abide in His taber-nacle, *not* to dwell in His holy hill![4]

How very often we speak evil of things which we, more or less, 'understand not'[5]—ah, even of 'things which they *know* not'![6]—instead of obey-ing another part of the royal law, 'Judge nothing before the time, until the Lord come,'[7] when the very person whom we have been condemning shall 'have praise of God!' This often arises from diso-bedience to two other plain commands: 'Debate thy cause with thy neighbour himself, and discover not a secret to another:'[8] and, 'go and tell him his fault between thee and him *alone*.'[9] Yet away we go, and tell somebody else about it instead!

Let us guard against the negative form of evil speaking, generally the most dangerous and cruel, even when the most thoughtless. Absalom was ex-tremely clever in this. Who could quote any actual

---

[1] 1 Pet. iii. 10.  [2] Jas. iii. 5.  [3] Ps. xv. 3.
[4] Ps. xv. 1.  [5] 2 Pet. ii. 12.  [6] Jude 10.
[7] 1 Cor. iii. 5.  [8] Prov. xxv. 9.  [9] Matt. xviii. 15.

evil speaking against his royal father?[1]  Who could charge him with speaking evil of dignities?[2]  And yet by insinuation, by his way of putting things, by his very manner, he wrought a thousand-fold more cruel harm than any amount of speaking out could possibly have done.  Oh to be watchful as to such omissions to speak well, as amount to speaking evil! watchful as to the eloquence of even a hesitation, watchful as to the forcible language of feature and eye!

Of course the question arises: 'But what about cases in which wrong-doing must be spoken of for the sake of truth and justice?'  Clear as crystal are our instructions here: 1. We are to speak 'the truth.'[3]  *The* truth, not such part of it as will best prove our case, and nothing else!  Not what we *suppose* to be the truth. 2. 'In love.'  Does all our testimony stand *this* test? 3. 'In the name of the Lord Jesus.'[4]  Would not this check many a word against another? 4. 'To the glory of God.'[5]  Failure in any one of these four rules brings us in guilty of sin.  Oh may He give us grace to keep our heart with all diligence,[6] and Himself set a watch this day before our mouth, and keep the door of our lips![7]  May we cease to 'reason with unprofitable talk, or with speeches *wherewith we can do no good.'*[8]

Take my lips, and let them be
Filled with messages from Thee.

---

[1] 2 Sam. xv. 3-5.
[4] Col. iii. 17.
[7] Ps. cxli. 3.

[2] 2 Pet. ii. 10.
[5] 1 Cor. x. 31.
[8] Job xv. 4.

[3] Eph. iv. 15.
[6] Prov. iv. 23.

# TWENTY-SIXTH DAY.

## Hindering.

'Lest we should hinder the gospel of Christ.'—I COR. ix. 12.

MANY an active and willing helper in the
Church is too often an unconscious hinderer
of the gospel.   Let us each try to find out how we
may have hindered, that we may do so no more.

A vexation arises, and our expressions of impatience hinder others from taking it patiently.   Disappointment, ailment, or even weather depresses
us; and our look or tone of depression hinders
others from maintaining a cheerful and thankful
spirit.   We let out a fearing or discouraged remark,
and another's hope and zeal is wet-blanketed.
'What man is there that is fearful and faint
hearted? let him go and return unto his house, lest
his brethren's heart faint as well as his heart.'[1]

We *say* an unkind thing,[2] and another is hindered
in learning the holy lesson of charity that *thinketh*
no evil.[3]   We say a provoking thing,[4] and our sister
or brother is hindered in that day's effort to be
meek.   'Make straight paths for *your* feet, lest that
which is lame be turned out of the way.'[5]

---

[1] Deut. xx. 8; Judg. vii. 3.          [2] Jas. iv. 11.
[3] 1 Cor. xiii. 5.          [4] Jas. i. 26.          [5] Heb. xii. 13.

We yield an inch in some doubtful matter, and another is emboldened to take an ell. We do an inexpedient thing, and another improves upon the supposed example, and feels justified in doing an unlawful thing.[1] 'Abstain from all appearance of evil.'[2] 'Let not your good be evil spoken of.'[3]

We miss an opportunity of speaking 'a word for Jesus;' and our pleasant, commonplace talk has checked a half-formed wish for something better, and hindered the light of the glorious gospel from shining into a heart.[4] We do not heed the thoughtful look on some household face just after family prayer or public worship, and our needless chat about 'earthly things'[5] acts the fowls of the air. We make a critical remark about a preacher or writer, and it is brought back by the enemy in swift temptation, at the very moment when a word in season was about to find entrance.[6] 'Them that were entering in, ye hindered.'[7] Oh, terrible condemnation! 'Let not those that seek Thee be confounded for *my* sake.'[8]

We need, too, to be shown whether we are quite unconsciously hindering in even lesser ways; for many have little peculiarities, of which they are hardly or not at all aware, which nevertheless annoy, fidget, depress, or chill those with whom they have much intercourse, and thus hinder the calm reign of peace in their spirits. 'Let not them that wait on Thee, O Lord God of hosts, be ashamed for my sake.'[9]

---

[1] 1 Cor. x. 23; ib. viii. 13.　[2] 1 Thess. v. 22.　[3] Rom. xiv. 16.
[4] 2 Cor. iv. 4.　　　　[5] Phil. iii. 19; Matt. xiii. 4.
[6] Ps. cxix. 130.　[7] Luke xi. 52.　[8] Ps. lxix. 6.　[9] Ps. lxix. 6.

How sadly, too, we may hinder without word or act! For wrong feeling is more infectious than wrong-doing; especially the various phases of ill-temper—gloominess, touchiness, discontent, irritability,—do we not know how catching these are? If the Lord asked us, ' *Wherefore* discourage ye the heart of the children of Israel' in this way, should we not be utterly without excuse?[1] What if he asked each hindered one, ' *Who* did hinder you?'[2] —are our consciences sure that our names would escape mention?

Shall we not watch and pray that this day we may only help and not hinder in the least thing, and that no one may have virtually to say to us, ' Hinder me not'![3] May we never be the helpers of the great hinderer! When ' Satan hindered ' St. Paul, he probably found human agents.[4]

Let us ask that the Lord Jesus would so perfectly tune our spirits to the key-note of His exceeding great love,[5] that all our unconscious influence may breathe only of that love, and help all with whom we come in contact to obey the gospel of our Lord Jesus Christ.[6] ' And let us *consider* one another, to provoke unto love and to good works.'[7]

---

[1] Num. xxxii. 7.    [2] Gal. v. 7.    [3] Gen. xxiv. 56.
[4] 1 Thess. ii. 18.    [5] 2 Cor. iv. 10.    [6] 2 Thess. i. 8.
[7] Heb. x. 24.

## TWENTY-SEVENTH DAY.

---

## Strengthening hands.

'Strengthen ye the weak hands, and confirm the feeble knees.'—ISA. xxxv. 3.

'HE that is not with Me is against Me: and he that gathereth not with Me scattereth.'[1] So it is not enough merely not to hinder; we must help: for not helping generally amounts to hindering. Perhaps we tried yesterday not to be hinderers; to-day let us 'go on to completeness,' and try to be helpers.[2]

'Strengthen ye the weak hands.' Plenty of these around us; for where is one real worker who does not feel his weakness, even in very proportion to what seems to us his strength?[3] It does not the least follow that those who are altogether much stronger than ourselves are not perhaps realizing their weakness much more.[4] We 'should not think of such a thing' as aiming to strengthen their hands, and so very much mutual ministry is left undone. A little child may strengthen the hands of a giant and veteran in the faith, and it is just the giants and

---

[1] Luke xi. 23.  
[2] Heb. vi. 1 (Gr.).  
[3] 2 Cor. xii. 1.  
[4] 1 Cor. ii. 3.

veterans who do *not* say to the more feeble members, ' I have no need of you.' [1]

' David sent to comfort Hanun by the hand of his servants.' [2] St. Paul received the comfort of God by the coming of Titus, his ' own son ' in the faith ; [3] and he seems to have had a great deal of both comfort and joy (which certainly are most strengthening), at second hand, by the ' fervent mind toward ' him of the Corinthians, so that ' exceedingly the more joyed we.' [4]

- Again, those very near us often need strengthening ; are we right if they have practically to look farther for the strengthening which it might be ours to give? There may be a spiritual application of providing specially for those of our own house. [5]

Again, are there not sometimes such very ' weak hands,' [6] that we almost get tired of trying to strengthen them, and feel inclined to think it is no use dealing with such hopeless feebleness? What if our Master did this to us?

How shall we set about it? First, by prayer, as Aaron and Hur held up the hands of Moses. [7] ' Helping together by prayer.' [8] This reaches all. Who knows how much of the weakness of hands, which distresses or even annoys us, may be laid at our door because we talked about it instead of praying about it? Very likely, names will occur to us now ; then take those names at once to the Mighty One, and ask Him this morning to strengthen those weak hands and confirm those feeble knees. [9]

---

[1] 1 Cor. xii. 21, 22.   [2] 2 Sam. x. 2.   [3] 2 Cor. vii. 6; Titus i. 4.
[4] 2 Cor. vii. 7.   [5] 1 Tim. v. 8.   [6] Rom. xv. 1.
[7] Ex. xvii. 12.   [8] 2 Cor. i. 11.   [9] Jas. v. 16.

Secondly, by personal contact. I suppose we never come in contact with one who is really strong in the Lord[1] without being strengthened, whether we feel it or not. But we should not be content with the unconscious influence which it is our singular privilege to radiate. 'Jonathan arose, and went to David in the wood, and strengthened his hand in God.'[2] Arising always implies a little effort. Then make it! What are our orders? 'Comfort ye, comfort ye My people, saith your God.'[3] How are we to do it? 'Speak ye *to the heart* of Jerusalem.'[4] What comes from the heart goes to the heart. '*Speak;*' don't hint and beat about the bush. When the arrow is feathered with love and weighted with wisdom, it must fly straight. What are we to say? 'Say . . . Be strong, fear not; behold, your God will come with vengeance, even God with a recompense; He will come and save you.'[5] 'Cry unto her, that her warfare is accomplished, that her iniquity is pardoned.'[6] Examine these two wonderful messages, and see if they do not actually include everything required for your fulfilment of this commandment. You may amplify them, but that is all. Take with you His words, and then you may say without presumption, 'I would strengthen you with my mouth.'[7]

Before we can really lift up other hands, our own must have been lifted up by His good Spirit,[8] and our own feeble knees must have been confirmed by much bowing at His footstool.[9] 'When *thou* art

---

[1] Eph. vi. 10.  [2] 1 Sam. xxiii. 16.  [3] Isa. xl. 1.
[4] Isa. xl. 2, margin.  [5] Isa. xxxv. 4.  [6] Isa. xl. 2.
[7] Job xvi. 5.  [8] Heb. xii. 12, 13.  [9] Eph. iii. 13, 16.

converted, strengthen thy brethren."[1] 'Uphold *me* with Thy free Spirit. *Then* will I teach.'[2] It is the climax of the grand procession of promises in that magnificent close of the words of Eliphaz. If we acquaint ourselves with God,[3] receive His law, return to Him, and put away iniquity, *then* 'when men are cast down, then thou shalt say, There is lifting up."[4]

May our record on high be : ' Thou hast strength ened the weak hands. Thy words have upholden him that was falling, and thou hast strengthened the feeble knees.'

> Oh lead me, Lord, that I may lead
>   The wandering and the wavering feet;
> Oh feed me, Lord, that I may feed
>   Thy hungering ones with manna sweet.
>
> Oh strengthen me, that while I stand
>   Firm on the Rock, and strong in Thee,
> I may stretch out a loving hand
>   To wrestlers with the troubled sea.

---

1 Luke xxii. 32.  2 Ps. li. 12, 13.
3 Job xxii. 21-29.  4 Job iv. 4.

# TWENTY-EIGHTH DAY.

---

## Seeking to Excel.

'Seek that ye may excel.'—1 COR. XIV. 12.

AN almost startling command; yet it is addressed to '*all* that in *every* place call upon the name of Jesus Christ our Lord,'[1] therefore unmistakably to ourselves.

Very likely our thoughts have been quite different from God's thoughts about it.[2] We have been thinking it was useless to seek to excel, because we saw no likelihood of doing so; that it was presumptuous to think of such a thing; that it was even positively wrong to aim at it; yet, all the time, there the commandment stood, 'Seek that ye may excel!'

For its right fulfilment, there must be one preliminary and one object. The preliminary is, that we must be 'zealous of spiritual gifts.'[3] It is only when we are coveting earnestly the best gifts[4] that the exercise and development of all others comes in its right place; that is, we must be eagerly desiring and heartily striving and using His own means to

---

[1] 1 Cor. i. 2.　　　　[2] Isa. lv. 8.
[3] 1 Cor. xiv. 12.　　　[4] 1 Cor. xii. 31.

12

grow in grace,[1] to receive always more and more of His fulness,[2] more light and love, more faith and power, more, above all, of His Spirit.

Even when this is the case, how often we set some human standard before us, and say: 'Ah! if I only had half as much grace as So-and-so!' Comparing ourselves among ourselves, we are not wise;[3] it is a fruitful source of limitation and hindrance. We are not to aim at 'half as much grace,' nor even *as* much, but at *excelling* the fair self-chosen standard, which after all is so far below the 'exceeding abundantly'[4] which He is able to do for us. Let us give it up, once for all, and strike out into God's more excellent way, and 'seek to excel.'[5] Let us open our mouth wide that He may fill it,[6] asking for such great gifts that His royal bounty may be magnified because of our very poverty;[7] asking for such excellency of power that it may be *seen* to be of Him and not of us;[8] asking that He would so fulfil *all* the good pleasure of His goodness, that the name of our Lord Jesus Christ may be glorified in us.[9]

Then, the one object. 'Seekest thou great things for thyself? seek them not.'[10] But 'seek that ye may excel *to the edifying of the Church.*'

Apart from this, seeking to excel would inevitably become sin. Emulation, ambition, pride, would come in like a flood; envying and strife would follow, 'leading to confusion and every evil work.'[11] 'All things edify not,'—should not this guide the

---

[1] 1 Pet. ii. 2 ; 2 Pet. iii. 18.    [2] John i. 16.    [3] 2 Cor. x. 12.
[4] Eph. iii. 20.    [5] 1 Cor. xii. 31.    [6] Ps. lxxxi. 10.
[7] 2 Cor. ix. 11.    [8] 2 Cor. iv. 7.    [9] 2 Thess. i. 11, 12.
[10] Jer. xlv. 5.    [11] Jas. iii. 16 ; 1 Cor. x. 23.

directions in which we seek to excel? For this end
only let every good gift,[1] spiritual or mental, inward or even outward, be continually cultivated and
carefully used. Let us this day and henceforth aim
at nothing lower.

Perhaps He grants us power to excel in some
seemingly very little things, some little peculiar
gifts which we don't think much of. ' He that is
faithful in that which is *least*,'[2] will be enabled to
use even that for the edifying of some part of the
Church. Those who have no hand in raising the
strong pillars, may yet be called to give a delicate
touch to the lily work which shall crown them.[3]
' To every man his work ;'[4] and in that, even if it is
only running little errands for the skilled workmen,
we may excel to the edifying of the Church.

There are ' diversities of gifts,'[5] but none are
without any. '*Every* man hath his proper gift of
God, one after this manner, and another after
that.'[6] If we think it humble to profess, or are
humble enough really to believe, that we have but
the ' one talent,'[7] that is the more reason why we
should eagerly make the *very* most of it for our
Lord ; for if it is only one, it is not our own, but
' our Lord's money.'

---

[1] Jas. i. 17.   [2] Luke xvi. 10.   [3] 1 Kings vii. 22.
[4] Mark xiii. 34.   [5] 1 Cor. xii. 4.   [6] 1 Cor. vii. 7.
[7] Matt. xxv. 15.

# TWENTY-NINTH DAY.

## What the Will of the Lord is.

'Wherefore be ye not unwise, but understanding what the will of the Lord is.'—EPH. v. 17.

ARE we not apt to connect the thoughts of God's will with efforts to submit to what is not very pleasant to us? Is this *fair*, when all that He Himself tells us of His will should make us love and admire and rejoice in it? Truly our thoughts are not His thoughts[1] about it, or there would not be so many a sigh over that glorious petition, 'Thy will be done.'[2]

Let us see what He says it is, for He hath 'made known unto us the mystery of His will;'[3] and in proportion as we are filled with the knowledge of it, shall we walk worthy of the Lord unto all pleasing.[4]

1. It was the good pleasure of His will to predestinate us unto the adoption of children,[5] that we should be His own 'sons and daughters,' His own 'dear children'[6] And if He had told us no more than this, ought not 'Thy will be done' to peal

---

[1] Isa. lv. 8.    [2] Matt. vi. 10.    [3] Eph. i. 9.
[4] Col. i. 9; ib. i. 10. [5] Eph. i. 5.    [6] 2 Cor. vi. 18; Eph. v. 1.

forth as an 'Amen chorus' from all His adopted ones?

2. It was the will of God our Father that the Lord Jesus Christ should give Himself for our sins, 'that He might deliver us from this present evil world.'[1] Jesus said, 'Lo, I come to do Thy will,[2] O God,' and 'gave Himself for us, that He might redeem us from all iniquity '[3] And day by day He is delivering those who believe that He 'doth deliver,' and 'trust that He will yet deliver;'[4] for *this* is 'the will of the Lord.'

3. By this will we are sanctified.[5] Sanctification is the continual fulfilling of the good pleasure of His goodness in us. It is the making us partakers of His holiness and of the divine nature itself. It is making us like Jesus, so that the life of Jesus may be manifest even in our mortal flesh.[6] It is granting the desire, the thirst of thirsts, of every renewed heart.[7] And '*this* is the will of God, even your sanctification '[8]

4. It is the will of God in Christ Jesus concerning us, that in every thing we should give thanks, 'always for all things.'[9] This implies a life full of cause for praise, and full of power to praise;—can any one describe a brighter ideal? Yet *this* is the will of God concerning *you*.

5. Perishing, failing, dying,—how the very words 'everlasting life '[10] shine out to us in the darkness! a resplendent gift purchased for us by the one transcendent gift of God![11] It includes everlasting

---

[1] Gal. i. 4.  [2] Heb. x. 9.  [3] Titus ii. 14.
[4] 2 Cor. i. 10.  [5] Heb. x. 10.  [6] 2 Cor. iv. 11.
[7] Matt. v. 6.  [8] 1 Thess. iv. 3.  [9] Eph. v. 20.
[10] John iii. 16.  [11] 2 Cor. ix. 15.

salvation, light, joy, love, glory; and it is for *every one* 'which seeth the Son and believeth on Him:' for Jesus says, '*This* is the will of Him that sent Me.'[1]

6. Is not this enough? is there yet a misgiving and a haunting fear lest we should lose this great gift? Again the glorious will of God is our security; for, though our numb hand might let it slip, we are ourselves in the grasp of a Hand which holds us and our eternal life too; for, of all which the Father hath given Him, He 'shall lose nothing,'[2] 'not the least grain shall fall upon the earth,' not you, not I: for '*this* is the Father's will.'[3]

7. Now for the climax; and this time it is the Son, our own Lord Jesus Christ, who tells His Father that He is one with Him, and then, in His own divine name, declares His divine will:[4] 'I *will* that they also whom Thou hast given Me, be with Me where I am.'[5] *This* is the consummation of His will concerning us, that we should be for ever with the Lord![6] Shall we like 'strangers'[7] 'submit to this'? Shall we bow to this? Shall we dare to *sigh* over 'Thy will be done'? Shall we not rather 'submit ourselves wholly to His holy will and pleasure,'[8] bow under the very load of the benefits of His will in deepest adoration and intensest thanksgiving, and *not* wait for 'the happier shore,' but here and now *sing* out of the abundance of a simply believing heart, 'Thy will be done'?[9] For truly it is '*good* will to men;' and may we be so 'trans-

---

1 John vi. 40.　　　2 John vi. 39.　　　3 Amos ix. 9.
4 John xvii. 22.　　　5 John xvii. 24.　　　6 1 Thess. iv. 17.
7 Ps. xviii. 44.　　　8 Ps. lxviii. 19.　　　9 Luke ii. 14.

formed by the renewing of our minds,' that we may
daily and joyfully ' prove what is that good, and
acceptable, and perfect will of God."[1]

> With quivering heart and trembling will
>   The word hath passed thy lips,
> Within the shadow, cold and still,
>   Of some fair joy's eclipse.
> ' Thy will be done!' Thy God hath heard,
> And He will crown that faith-framed word.
>
> Thy prayer shall be fulfilled,—but how?
>   His thoughts are not as thine;
> While thou wouldst only weep and bow,
>   He saith, ' Arise and shine!'
> Thy thoughts were all of grief and night,
> But His of boundless joy and light.
>
> Thy Father reigns supreme above;
>   The glory of His name
> Is Grace and Wisdom, Truth and Love,
>   His will must be the same.
> And thou hast asked all joys in one,
> In whispering forth, ' Thy will be done!'

[1] Rom. xii. 2.

# THIRTIETH DAY

---

## His Last Commandment.

'This do in remembrance of me.'—LUKE XXII. 19.

HIS last commandment! Do we not desire to obey it in its very fullest meaning, to do exactly *what* He meant us to do, and *all* that He meant us to do in it?[1] Let us pray that He may open our eyes to behold wondrous things in it, and enable us to rise through the letter to the spirit.[2]

It is not simply 'This *do*.' We may obey so far month by month or week by week, and yet never once have obeyed our Lord's dying wish or fulfilled His desire. He said, 'This do *in remembrance* of Me.' We cannot remember what we do not know. We must know the Lord Jesus Christ[3] before we can truly remember Him at His table; for He does not say that we are to do it in remembrance of what He said, or even of what He did. That is quite a different thing. We may remember what we have heard or read of Ridley and Latimer, and we might commemorate their martyrdom; but we cannot remember them, because we never knew them,

---

[1] Ps. cxix. 19.        [2] John vi. 63.        [3] Phil. iii. 8.

except as matter of history. But we know the Lord Jesus Christ as we know no man after the flesh.[1] 'We do know that we know Him,'[2] and 'the knowledge of our Lord and Saviour Jesus Christ'[3] is our very life; it is the joy with which no stranger intermeddleth.[4]

Without this personal knowledge of Him, there can be no true remembrance of Him in the Lord's Supper. Let us seek to 'know Him,' so that we may be able to remember Him; then the sweet remembrance of Himself[5] and His exceeding great love will include remembrance of the words and ways of the Lord Jesus;[6] then it will arouse our love into a vivid reality of personal affection; then He will draw nigh to us:[7] for 'Thou meetest Him that rejoiceth and worketh righteousness, those that remember Thee in Thy ways.'[8]

Have we not sometimes gone rather to get something for ourselves than simply to remember Him? and may not this account for some of the disappointment, which is no uncommon experience, that we did not run *exactly* in the way of His commandment?[9] We went to get strengthening and refreshing. We went perhaps vaguely expecting some peculiar manifestation of Himself, some almost sensible consciousness of His presence which is quite outside of His written promise or command. We went expecting something *because* we went, a sort of reward in and for the outward act. We remembered our weakness, and our wants, and our

---

[1] 2 Cor. v. 16.  [2] 1 John ii. 3.  [3] 2 Pet. iii. 18.
[4] Prov. xiv. 10.  [5] Cant. i. 4.  [6] John xiv. 26, xvi. 4.
[7] Lam. iii. 57.  [8] Isa. lxiv. 5.  [9] Ps. cxix. 32.

wishes, and we forgot that He commanded 'one thing'—the remembrance of *Himself.* Shall we not ask the Holy Spirit next time to fix our hearts, so that the whole desire of our soul may be 'to Thy name, and to the remembrance of Thee'?[1]

There was no 'remembrance' in that first celebration of the Lord's Supper, that first solemn evening communion: for He was bodily present as the Master of the feast.[2] The very word was a shadow cast before of the time when He should 'be taken from them.'[3] But now 'the bright light which was in the cloud'[4] shines all along the dim waiting time, revealing 'this same Jesus;'[5] for He whom we specially 'remember' at His table, is with us 'alway,' all the days, 'the same yesterday, to-day, and forever.'[6] He loves us now as He loved us when He prayed for '*all* them which shall believe on Me'[7] in 'the same night in which He was betrayed.'[8] He loves us now as He loved us when He would not come down from the cross to save Himself.[9]

Love is the link between the remembrance and the anticipation; for the two melt into each other, and form one hallowed radiance of present great delight. 'For as often as ye eat this bread, and drink this cup, ye do shew the Lord's death *till He come.*'[10] So perhaps some will be showing it forth, at the very moment when He comes! What a transition of unimaginable blessedness! It is almost too dazzlingly beautiful to think of.

---

[1] Isa. xxvi. 8.    [2] Mark xiv. 17; Matt. xxvi. 20; Luke xxii. 11.
[3] Matt. ix. 15.    [4] Job xxxvii. 21.    [5] Acts i. 11.    [6] Heb. xiii. 8.
[7] John xvii. 20.    [8] 1 Cor. xi. 23.    [9] Mark xv. 30.
[10] 1 Cor. xi. 26.

Luther said: 'I feel as if Jesus Christ died yesterday.' So fresh, so vivid, be our love and thankfulness! But may we add: 'And as if He were coming to-day!' Then our lives would indeed be rich in remembrance and radiant in anticipation,[1] 'looking for that blessed hope, and the glorious appearing of the great God and our Saviour Jesus Christ; who gave Himself for us, that He might redeem us from all iniquity.'[2]

> According to Thy gracious word,
>   In deep humility,
> This will I do, my gracious Lord,
>   I will remember Thee.
>
> Remember Thee, and all Thy pains,
>   And all Thy love to me;
> Yes, while a breath, a pulse remains,
>   Will I remember Thee.
>
> JAMES MONTGOMERY.

# THIRTY-FIRST DAY.

## The Great Reward.

'In keeping of them there is great reward.'—Ps. xix. 11.

NOT, 'Because I keep them I shall have a great reward;' but '*In* keeping of them there *is* great reward.' God Himself wants us to keep them,

---

[1] Ps. cxlv. 7.     [2] Titus ii. 13, 14.

because He loves us. He says : ' O that there were such an heart in them, that they would fear Me, and keep *all My commandments always,* that it might be well with them ' ![1] This reward is an indisputable, though too often not fully recognized, fact of every Christian's experience. That we may have to keep His commandments in the very teeth of trial, loss, opposition, or distress does not touch the matter ;[2] for, nevertheless, not afterward, but *in* the keeping of His words, He takes care to keep His word that there shall be great reward.

If there is not great reward, it only shows that there is not real keeping. The essence of true keeping of God's commandments is love.[3] (See how many times keep and love are joined together in all parts of His word.)[4] Now, if we have only been obeying in mere form and letter, because we were afraid to disobey, this is *not* the heart-obedience which is always crowned with blessings. So, if we cannot quite set to our seal that God is true to this promise,[5] let us be quite sure that it is because we have not fulfilled His condition. And let us now, at once, ask Him to write His laws in our hearts,[6] and so to shed abroad His love in us by the Holy Ghost,[7] that we may begin at once to keep them for very love to our glorious Lawgiver and Mediator.[8] Then we shall know for ourselves that they are not grievous,[9] but that they are ' for our good' always.'[10]

---

1 Deut. v. 29.   2 Matt. xix. 29.   3 John xiv. 24.
4 Ex. xx. 6; Deut. xi. 1 ; John xiv. 15, etc.   5 John iii. 33.
6 Heb. viii. 10.   7 Rom. v. 5.   8 Deut. v. 27.
9 1 John v. 3.   10 Deut. vi. 24.

Yet surely we may appeal to the experience of every one of the King's servants, that, however feeble and imperfect our obedience has been, we do know something about 'great reward,' not *for* it, but *in* it. As in the days of Hezekiah, when the hand of God was to give them one heart to do the commandment of the king, the result was great gladness, great joy, great blessing, and great prosperity, so is it now in the spiritual reign of our King.[1] Not outward and visible reward, though even that He very often adds, far more exceeding; but inward and spiritual reward.

Not in general only, but in minutest particulars. Having pledged Himself to this, He is 'not unrighteous to forget'[2] the least act of Spirit-wrought obedience. Sometimes he puts such wonderful sweetness into the doing of or the refraining from some little thing for His sake, that we wonder what makes us so happy about it, and cannot but be conscious that it is not exactly one's mere natural feeling. Is not this a precious experience of 'great reward,' all the greater because it came through some very little thing?

Let us put together into a bright bit of Bible mosaic the scattered gems which are part of this great present reward, 'the promise of the life that now is,'[3] the hundred-fold which we are to receive ' now in *this* time':[4]—1. *Strength:* ' Therefore shall ye keep all the commandments . . . that ye may be strong;'[5] for ' the way of the Lord is strength to

---

[1] 2 Chron. xxx. 12, 21, 26; ib. xxxi. 10, 21; Job xxxvi. 11.
[2] Heb. vi. 10.      [3] 1 Tim. iv. 8.      [4] Mark x. 30.
[5] Deut. xi. 8.

the upright.'[1] 2. *Safety:* 'Whoso keepeth the commandment shall feel no evil thing,'[1] much less be hurt by it! 3. *Liberty:* 'I will walk at liberty: *for* I seek Thy precepts.'[3] Every commandment kept is a fetter of Satan broken by the grace and might of the 'stronger than he.'[4] 4. *Peace:* ' Great peace have they that love Thy law.'[5] And in proportion as we hearken to His commandments, does our peace flow as a river.[6] Disobedience dries it all up instantly. 5. *Life and Health:* Perhaps more literally than we suppose; for it stands to reason there is less friction and wear and tear even of our nerves and physique when we keep His peacebearing commands to trust and not be afraid,[7] to be without carefulness and anxious thought.[8] 'Let thine heart keep My commandments: for length of days, and long life, and peace, shall they add to thee.'[9] 'It is your life.'[10] 'It shall be health.' [11] 'I know that His commandment is life everlasting.'[12] 6. *Knowledge:* 'If any man will do His will, he shall know of the doctrine.'[13] 'If ye continue in My word, . . . ye shall know the truth.' 7. *Answered Prayers:* 'Whatsoever we ask, we receive of Him, because we keep His commandments.'[14] 8. *Gladness:* Again and again we find this the result of seeking out and keeping the commands of God.[15] 9. *The Father's Love:* ' He that hath My commandments, and keepeth them, he it is that loveth Me: and he that loveth Me shall be

---

[1] Prov. x. 29.  [2] Eccles. viii. 5.  [3] Ps. cxix. 45.  [4] Luke xi. 22.
[5] Ps. cxix. 165.  [6] Isa. xlviii. 18.  [7] Ps. lxii. 8.
[8] 1 Pet. v. 7; 1 Cor. vii. 32; Matt. vi. 25-34.  [9] Prov. iii. 1, 2.
[10] Deut. xxxii. 47.  [11] Prov. iii. 8.  [12] John xii. 50.
[13] John vii. 17.  [14] John viii. 31, 32.  [15] 1 John iii. 22.

loved of My Father.'¹ 10. *The Manifestation of Jesus :* 'And I will love Him, and will manifest Myself unto Him.'² 11. *The indwelling of the Triune God :* 'And we will come unto him, and make our abode with him.'³ 12. *The Witness of the Spirit to this indwelling :* 'He that keepeth His commandments dwelleth in Him, and He in him. And hereby we *know* that He abideth in us, by the Spirit which He hath given us.'⁴

'What shall I more say ?'⁵ *Verily,* in keeping of them there *is* great reward !

---

'Blessed is the man that feareth the Lord, that delighteth greatly in His commandments.'— Ps. cxii. 1.

---

¹ Neh. viii. 14, 17, etc.
² John xiv. 21.
³ John xiv. 23.      ⁴ 1 John iii. 24.      ⁵ Heb. xi. 32.

# ROYAL BOUNTY

OR

## ENING THOUGHTS

FOR

### The King's Guests

13

# FIRST DAY.

## The Royal Bounty.

'And King Solomon gave unto the queen of Sheba all her desire, whatsoever she asked, beside that which Solomon gave her of his royal bounty.'—1 KINGS x. 13

ALL God's goodness to us is humbling. The more He does for us, the more ready we are to say, 'I am not worthy of the least of all the mercies, and of all the truth, which Thou hast shewed unto Thy servant.'[1] The weight of a great answer to prayer seems almost too much for us.[2] The grace of it is 'too wonderful'[3] for us. It throws up in such startling relief the disproportion between our little, poor, feeble cry, and the great shining response of God's heart and hand, that we can only say: 'Who am I, O Lord God, that Thou hast brought me hitherto? Is this the manner of man, O Lord God?'[4]

But it is more humbling still, when we stand face to face with great things which the Lord hath done for us and given us,[5] which we never asked at all,[6] never even thought of asking—royal bounty, with which not even a prayer had to do. It is so hum-

---

[1] Gen. xxxii. 10.    [2] Luke v. 8, 9.    [3] Job xlii. 3. -
[4] 2 Sam. vii. 18.    [5] Ps. cxxvi. 3.    [6] 1 Kings iii. 13.

(191)

bling to get a view of these, that Satan tries to set up a false humility to hinder us from standing still and considering how great things the Lord hath done for us;[1] thus he also contrives to defraud our generous God of the glory due unto His name.[2]

For, of course, we do not praise for what we will not recognize.

Let us try to baffle this device to-day, and give thanks for the overwhelming mercies[3] for which we never asked. 'Blessed be the Lord, who daily loadeth us with benefits.'[4] Just think of them deliberately (they are far too many to think of all in a flash); and how many did we actually ask for? Even that poor little claim was never brought to bear on thousands of them.

[5]To begin at the beginning, we certainly did not ask Him to choose us in Christ Jesus before the world began,[6] and to predestinate us to be conformed to the image of His Son.[7] Was not that 'royal bounty' indeed?

Then, we certainly did not ask Him to call us by His grace;[8] for before that call, we could not have wished, much less asked, for it.[9] Then, who taught us to pray,[10] and put into our entirely corrupt and sinful hearts[11] any thought of asking Him for anything at all?[12] Was not all this 'royal bounty?'

Look back at our early prayers. Has He not more than granted them? did we even know how much He could do for us? did He not answer prayer

---

[1] 1 Sam. xii. 7, 24.　　　[2] Ps.xxix. 2.　　　[3] Isa. lxiii. 7.
[4] Ps. lxviii. 19 ; ib. ciii. 2.　[5] 2 Thess. ii. 13.　[6] Eph. i. 4.
[7] Rom. viii. 29.　　　　[8] 2 Tim. i. 9.　　　[9] Rom. i. 6.
[10] Luke xi. 1.　　　　　[11] Job xxxvii. 19.　[12] Rom. viii. 26.

by opening out new vistas of prayer before us, giving us grace to ask for more grace, faith to plead for more faith?[1] Why, it is *all* 'royal bounty' from beginning to end! And this is going on now, and will go on forever, when He has brought us with gladness and rejoicing into His own palace.[2] Not till then shall we understand about those riches of glory in Christ Jesus,[3] out of which He is even now pouring out the supply of all our need.

The marginal reading is very beautiful; it is, 'that which he gave her *according to the hand* of King Solomon.' We may link this with David's grateful words: '*According to Thine own heart* hast Thou done all these great things;'[4] and again: '.Thou hast dealt well with Thy servant, O Lord, *according to Thy word.*'[5] His hand, His heart, His word—what an immeasurable measure of His bounty! The great *hand* that holds the ocean in its hollow[6] is opened to satisfy our desire,[7] and to go beyond that exceeding abundantly,[8] giving us according to the *heart* that '*so* loved the world,'[9] and according to the *word*[10] which is so deep and full that all the saints that ever drew their hope and joy from it cannot fathom its ever upspringing fountain.

Perhaps nobody knows the Bible well enough to know the full significance of saying, ' Be it unto me *according to Thy word;*'[11] how much less can we imagine what shall be the yet unrevealed royal bounty *according to His heart* of infinite love and

---

1 John i. 16 ; Rom. i. 17 ; Luke xvii. 5.　　2 Ps. xlv. 15.
3 Phil. iv. 19.　　4 2 Sam. vii. 21.　　5 Ps. cxix. 65.
6 Isa. xl. 12.　　7 Ps. cxlv. 16.　　8 Eph. iii. 20.
9 John iii. 16.　　10 John iv. 11, 14.　　11 Luke i. 38.

hand of infinite power! 'What I do thou knowest not now, but thou shalt know hereafter.'[1] 'And ye shall        be satisfied, and praise the name of the Lord your God, that hath dealt wondrously with you.'[2]

> When this passing world is done,
> When has sunk yon glaring sun,
> When we stand with Christ in glory,
> Looking o'er life's finished story,
> Then, Lord, shall I fully know—
> Not till then—how much I owe!
>
> R. M'CHEYNE.

---

[1] John xiii. 7.        Joel ii. 26.

# SECOND DAY.

---

# Tbe Opened Treasure.

'The Lord shall open unto thee His good treasure.'—
DEUT. xxviii. 12.

WHEN the wise men ' opened their treasures,'
they brought out gold and frankincense and
myrrh.[1] When Jehovah opens unto us His good
treasure, we shall see greater things than these.[2]
The context of this rich promise seems to make
' the heaven' the treasure-house; and in its primary
and literal sense, the fertilizing rain is the first outpouring of the opened treasure, soon after expanded
into beautiful details of the ' precious things of
heaven and . . . the precious things of the earth.'[3]
But the spiritual blessings are closely interwoven
with the temporal in the whole passage, and the
faithful Israelites who did not ' look only for transi-
tory promises '[4] may well have claimed the opening
of heavenly treasure through this promise.[5]

What shall He ' open unto thee?' In a word,
the unsearchable riches of Christ.'[6] In Him

---

[1] Matt. ii. 11.  [2] John i. 50.  [3] Deut. xxxiii. 13-16.
[4] Deut. xxviii. 1-14.  [5] Art. vii.  [6] Eph. iii. 8.

'are hid all the treasures of wisdom and knowledge,'[1] but the Lord shall open them unto thee. Riches of goodness, and forbearance, and long-suffering[2] shall be meted out in infinitely gracious proportion to our sins, and provocations, and repeated waywardness; exceeding riches[3] of grace for all our poverty now, and riches in glory[4] enough and to spare for all the needs of glorified capacities though all eternity. 'All are yours' in Him.[5]

Faith is the key to this infinite treasury, and in giving us faith[6] He gives us treasure for treasure. He is ready to make us 'rich in faith,'[7] and then still to 'increase our faith'[8] 'unto all riches of the full assurance of understanding.'[9] Ask for this golden key, and then put it into the Lord's hand, that He may turn it in the lock.

He shall open unto thee the good treasure not only of the living Word, but of the written word.[10] This is indeed 'treasure to be desired,'[11] 'more to be desired than gold;'[12] and when Jehovah the Spirit opens this to us, we shall, we *do*, rejoice 'as one that findeth great spoil.'[13] Christ, the true Wisdom, has said, 'I will fill their treasures,'[14] and 'the chambers shall be filled with all precious and pleasant riches.'[15] So that when He has done this we are 'made treasurers over treasuries,'[16] and may 'bring forth out of' our 'treasure things new and old.'[17]

---

[1] Col. ii. 3.   [2] Rom. ii. 4.   [3] Eph. ii. 7.
[4] Phil. iv. 19.   [5] 1 Cor. iii. 22.   [6] Eph. ii. 8.
[7] Jas. ii. 5.   [8] Luke xvii. 5.   [9] Col. ii. 2.
[10] Luke xxiv. 32.   [11] Prov. xxi. 20.   [12] Ps. xix. 10.
[13] Ps. cxix.162.   [14] Prov. viii. 21.   [15] Prov. xxiv. 4.
[16] Neh. xiii. 13.   [17] Matt. xiii. 52.

It is only with God-given treasure that we can enrich others. When we want to give a word to another, it generally seems to come with more power if, instead of casting about for what we think likely to suit them, we simply hand over to them any treasure word which He has freshly given to ourselves. When He opens to us some shining bit of treasure, let us not forget : ' Freely ye have received, freely *give*.'[1]

Also, let us not stand idly waiting for some further opening of the treasure,[2] but ' let there be *search* made in the king's treasure-house,'[3] ' in the house of the rolls where the treasures were laid-up,'[4] where the ' decrees ' and ' records ' of our King are to be ' found '[5] They are truly 'hidden riches.'[6] Neither must we trust in our own store of spiritual treasures, whether of memory, experience, or even of grace,[7] for we shall soon come under the condemning word, ' O backsliding daughter, that trusted in her treasures ! '[8] No, it is only continual drawing from *His* good treasure that will profit us, even ' the light of the knowledge of the glory of God in the face of Jesus Christ.'[9] And ' we have *this* treasure in earthen vessels, that the excellency of the power may be of God and not of us.'[10]

---

[1] Matt. x. 8.  [2] Prov. ii. 4.  [3] Ezra v. 17.
[4] Ezra vi. 1.  [5] Ezra vi. 2.  [6] Isa. xlv. 3.
[7] Jer. xlviii. 7.  [8] Jer. xlix. 4.  [9] 2 Cor. iv. 6.
[10] 2 Cor. iv. 7.

# THIRD DAY.

## The King's Signature and Seal.

'The writing which is written in the king's name, and sealed with the king's ring, may no man reverse.'—ESTHER viii. 8.

SUCH is the writing which by God's great goodness is the glory of our land and the treasure of our hearts, full of exceeding great and precious promises,[1] of commands not less great and not less precious,[2] and of words of prophecy (which are only words of promise a little farther off) 'more sure' than the testimony of an apostle's senses to the excellent glory and the heavenly voice.[3]

It is written in the King's name. The living Word of God, who came to declare, to manifest, and to glorify the Father,[4] has imprinted His own name upon the same testimony as written by the Spirit, and has given it to us as the 'word of God.'[5]

It is sealed with the King's ring. Sealing is a special work of the Holy Spirit, exercised in different ways;[6] and how clearly has He sealed this great

---

[1] 2 Pet. i. 4.    [2] Ps. cxix. 97.    [3] 2 Pet. i. 17-19.
[4] John i. 1; ib. xvii. 4, 6, 26.    [5] John xvii. 14.
[6] Eph. i. 13, etc.

writing with the King's ring, engraved with His own image and superscription, the convincing token of its being indeed from Himself, and sent forth in unchangeable authority and power !¹

It is a double sealing, without and within²—first, the external and distinctly visible declaration that the writing is 'by the Holy Ghost; '³ and then the all-convincing evidence that it is so by its effectual working⁴ in our own hearts with a power which, we know for ourselves, cannot be less than almighty and therefore divine.⁵

It is thus written in the King's name, and 'sealed with His own signet,'⁶ not only that we may know it to be His, but that we may have the right humbly, yet confidently, to show Him, so to speak, His own name and His own signet as our claim for the fulfilment of all contained therein.⁷    He will never fail to acknowledge them.

This royal writing 'may no man reverse.'    The King Himself cannot reverse it, for He changes not ;⁸ He 'cannot lie,'⁹ 'He cannot deny Himself: '¹⁰ for unchangeable truth is not only an essential attribute, but the very essence of His Deity ¹¹    This one great 'cannot' is the security for all that He 'can' and will do.    And if God 'cannot,' who can ?    All 'the craft and subtilty' of devil or man is powerless against one syllable of this royal writing    'The word of our God shall stand for ever,'¹² and the hoarse recoil of every furious

---

1 John xii. 48.    2 2 Sam. xxiii. 2.    3 Mark xii. 36; 1 Pet. i. 11.
4 1 Thess. ii. 13.    5 Heb. iv. 12.    6 Dan. vi. 17.
7 Gen. xxxviii. 17, 18, 25, 26.    8 Mal. iii. 6.
9 Titus i. 2.    10 2 Tim. ii. 13.    11 John xiv. 6.
12 Isa. xl. 8.

wave that is shattered into foam against this ever-lasting rock only murmurs, ' I *cannot* reverse it.'[1]

And is it not a most blessed and comforting thought that we ourselves cannot reverse it, though this is the quarter from which we are practically most tempted to dread its reversal? For,[2] ' if we believe not, yet He abideth faithful.' All the earth-born or devil-breathed fogs and clouds of doubt, from the fall till this hour, have not been able to touch the splendor of one star that He has set in the unassailable firmament of His eternal truth.

All the promises of God are yea and Amen[3]—where?—' *in Him*,' the Son of God.[4] He holds these stars in His right hand ; He has held the great promise of eternal life for us[5] since God gave it to Him for us before the world began, and every other is subincluded. And it is one of His offices ' to confirm the promises.'[6] Signed, sealed, held, and confirmed thus, should not ' It is written ' be enough for our present ' light, and gladness, and joy, and honour?' "[7]

Another clause of this beautiful verse is too striking to be passed over: ' Write ye also for the Jews, *as it liketh you,* in the king's name, and seal it with the king's ring.'[8] Does not this remind us of another writing of our King: ' If ye abide in me, and my words abide in you, ye shall ask *what ye will,* and it shall be done unto you.' He places His own name and His own signet at the disposal of His ' abiding ' ones, and says :[9]

---

[1] Num. xxiii. 20.  [2] 2 Tim. ii. 13.  [3] 2 Cor. i. 20.
[4] 2 Tim. i. 1.  [5] John x. 28.  [6] Rom. xv. 8.
[7] Esther viii. 16.  [8] Esther viii. 8.  [9] Isa. xlv. 11.

'Ask Me of things to come concerning My sons, and concerning the work of My hands *command ye Me.*'[1] 'Thou shalt also decree a thing, and it shall be established unto thee.' Should not this encourage us in intercession? Perhaps we are saying, like Esther,[2] 'How can I endure to see the destruction of my kindred?' Have we as yet *fully* availed ourselves of 'the King's name,' and 'the King's ring?'

> For He hath given us a changeless writing,
> Royal decrees that light and gladness bring,
> Signed with His name in glorious inditing,
> Sealed on our hearts with His own signet ring.

---

[1] Job xxii. 28.      [2] Esther viii. 6.

# FOURTH DAY.

## The Candour of Christ.

'Come, see a man which told me all things that ever I did:
is not this the Christ?'—JOHN iv. 29.

YES! it is not merely a vague general belief in
Christ as the Teacher who 'will tell *us* all
things'[1] which suffices for heart conviction of 'the
reality of Jesus Christ,' but the individual knowledge of Him as the Searcher who 'told *me* all things
that ever I did.'[2] This was what led the woman of
Samaria to exclaim, 'Is not this the Christ?' this
was to her the irresistible proof of His Messiahship.

What about ourselves? If we know anything of
true intercourse with the Lord Jesus our experience
will not be unlike hers.[3] When He who 'searches
Jerusalem with candles'[4] turns the keen flame of
His eyes upon the dark corners of our hearts, and
flashes their far-reaching, all-revealing beam upon
even the far-off and long-forgotten windings of our
lives; when in His light we see the darkness, and
in His purity we see the sin that has been, or that

---

[1] John iv. 25.      [2] John iv. 29.
[3] Zeph. i. 12.      [4] Rev. ii. 18, 23.

is; when He 'declareth unto man what is his thought,'[1] and then convinces that 'as he thinketh in his heart, so *is* he,'[2] *then* we know for ourselves that He 'with whom we have to do'[3] is 'indeed the Christ.'[4]

He does not merely *show* us; it is something more than that. It is not merely an invisible hand drawing away a veil from hidden scenes, and a light brought to bear upon them, so that we can see them if we will; it is more personal, more terrible, and yet more tender than that. He *tells* us what we have done; and, if we listen, the telling will be very clear, very thorough, very unmistakable.

At first we are tempted not to listen at all; we shrink from the still small voice which tells us such startlingly unwelcome things.

Many feel what one expressed: 'Whenever I *do* think about it, I feel so horribly bad that I don't like to think any more.' Ah, 'if thou hadst known, even thou, at least in this thy day,'[5] that it was not mere 'thinking about it,' but the voice of the Saviour beginning to tell thee what would have cleared the way for 'the things which belong unto thy peace,'[6] what blessing might not the patient and willing listening have brought! Oh, do not stifle the voice, do not fancy it is only uncomfortable thoughts which you will not encourage lest they should make you low-spirited! Instead of that, ask Him to let His voice sound louder and clearer, and believe 'that the goodness of God leadeth thee to

---

[1] Amos iv. 13.  [2] Prov. xxiii. 7.  [3] Heb. iv. 13.
[4] John iv. 42.  [5] Luke xix. 42.  [6] Isa. xlviii. 18.

repentance."[1] Only listen, and He will tell you not only all things that ever *you* did, but all things which He has done for you. He never leaves off in the middle of all He has to tell, unless we wilfully interrupt Him.

Perhaps we have gone through all this, and known the humbling blessedness of being searched and 'told,'[2] and then pardoned and cleansed ;[3] and now again there is something not right. We hardly know what,[4] only there is a misgiving, a dim, vague uneasiness ;[5] we 'really don't know of anything in particular,'[6] and yet there is something unsatisfied and unsatisfactory. There is nothing for it but to come to our Messiah afresh, and ask Him to tell us what we have done, or are doing, which is not in accordance with His will.[7] It will be useless coming if we are not sincerely purposed to let Him tell us what He will, and not merely what we expect ;[8] or if we hush up the first word of an unwelcome whisper, and say, 'Oh, *that* can't have anything to do with it !' or, 'I am all right *there*, at any rate !' We must simply say, 'Master, say on ;'[9] and perhaps He will then show us, as He did Simon,[10] that we have not done Him the true and loving service which some poor despised one has rendered.

Oh, never shrink from the probings of our beloved Physician.[11] Dearer and dearer will the hand become as we yield to it.[12] Sweeter and sweeter will

---

[1] Rom. ii. 4.  [2] Ps. xciv. 12.  [8] Ps. xxxii. 1.
[4] 2 Sam. xxi. 1.  [5] Job xv. 11.  [6] Job x. 2.
[7] Ps. cxxxix. 23 ; Matt. vii. 21.  [8] Job xiii. 22, 23.
[9] Luke vii. 40.  [10] Luke vii. 44, 45, 46.  [11] Matt. ix. 12
[12] Job v. 18.

be the proofs that He is our own *faithful* Friend,
who only wounds that He may perfectly heal.[1]

Only this I know, I tell Him all my doubts, and griefs, and
 fears;
Oh, how patiently He listens, and my drooping soul He
 cheers!
Do you think He ne'er reproves me? What a false friend
 He would be,
If He never, never told me of the sins which He must see!
Do you think that I could love Him half so well, or as I ought,
If He did not tell me plainly of each sinful deed and thought?
No! He is very faithful, and that makes me trust Him more;
For I know that He *does* love me, though He wounds me very
 sore.

ELLEN LAKSHMI GOREH.

---

[1] Prov. xxvii. 6.

14

# FIFTH DAY.

### From Death Unto Life.

'Is passed from death unto life.'—JOHN v. 24.

TWO distinct states with nothing between. No broad space between the two where we may stand, leading to the one or to the other; only a boundary line too fine to balance upon. Not many steps—not even two or three from one to the other, but one step *from* death *unto* life;[1] the foot lifted *from* the hollow crust over the volcanic fire, and set *upon* the Rock of salvation.[2]

How tremendously important to know whether this step is taken; but how clear and simple the test: 'He that heareth My word, and believeth on Him that sent Me, hath everlasting life, and shall not come into condemnation; but is passed from death unto life.' Are you trembling and down-hearted, wanting some very strong consolation for your very weak faith?[3] Lay hold of this.[4] See how the rope is let down low enough to meet the hand which you can scarcely lift.[5]

'He that heareth My word.' Can you say you

---

[1] Acts xxvi. 18.  [2] Ps. xl. 2.  [3] Heb. vi. 18.
[4] 1 Tim. vi. 12.  [5] Heb. xii. 12.

have *not* heard? You have heard His word *as* His word, recognizing it as such, receiving it 'not as the word of men, but as it is in truth, the word of God.'[1] It 'is come unto you,' because it ' is sent ' unto you.[2] The word of Jesus is heard by your innermost self, and you would not be hearing and recognizing it if you were still dead. A marble statue hears not.

'And believeth on Him that sent Me.' 'But that is the very question,' you say; ' if I were sure I believed, I should know I had everlasting life.'[3] Why should you know? Because He says so, and you could not but believe what He says. Then listen now to what He says: ' The father sent the Son to be the Saviour of the world.'[4] Do you *not* believe this? Did the Father *not* send the Son? Did He *not* so love the world?[5] Let the very recoil from such plain English of unbelief show you the sin and folly of doubting any more. You do hear His word, you do believe on the Father who sent the Son to be your Saviour,[6] will you not now believe that Jesus means what He says in threefold assur-ance · ' Hath everlasting life, and shall not come into condemnation; but is passed from death unto life?'[7]

Not ' is passing,' but ' is passed;' a fact whose full blessedness cannot be fully realized here, while we only ' know in part '[8] God's great gift of eternal life,[9] but not affected by varying degrees of realiza-tion.[10]

---

[1] 1 Thess. ii. 13.  [2] Col. i. 6.  [3] John vi. 47.
[4] 1 John iv. 14.  [5] John iii. 16.  [6] John xvi. 9.
[7] John v. 24.  [8] 1 Cor. xiii. 12.  [9] Rom. vi. 23.
[10] 2 Tim. ii. 13.

See your position,—or rather, take His word about it,—and give Him thanks—oh, give Him thanks—for having lifted you in your blindness and helplessness over that solemn boundary line when you could not even step over it. ' Sing        for the Lord hath done it ;'[1] and when you begin to sing and to praise,[2] the Lord's own ambushments of promises will start up before your eyes (*there* all the time, only you did not see them), and the shadowy hosts of fears and doubts shall flee away, and you shall ' *know* ' that you have passed from death unto life.[3]

From death—cold, dark, hopeless, useless, loveless ; the death 'in trespasses and sins ;[4] the death that lives (strange paradox) forever in the lake of fire[5]—unto life with its ever-increasing abundance ;[6] life crowned with light and love ; life upon which only a shadow of death can ever pass, and that only the shadow of the portal of eternal glory ;[7] life in Jesus, life for Jesus, life with Jesus.

This is your position now—made nigh instead of far off ;[8] reconciled to God instead of ' enemies in your mind ; '[9] found instead of lost ;[10] fellow-citizens with the saints instead of strangers and foreigners ;[11] sometimes darkness, but now light in the Lord ;[12] passed from death unto life. And all because Jesus passed from life unto death, even the death of the cross, for you ;[13] because it was the Father's will that He should come as the only re-

---

[1] Isa. xliv. 23.   [2] 2 Chron. xx. 22.   [3] 1 John iii. 14.
[4] Eph. ii. 1.   [5] Rev. xx. 14.   [6] John x. 10
[7] Ps. xxiii. 4.   [8] Eph. ii. 13.   [9] Col. i. 21.
[10] Luke xv. 32.   [11] Eph. ii. 19.   [12] Eph. v. 8.
[13] Phil. ii. 8.

quired 'sacrifice for sin;'[1] and He, our Lord Jesus
Christ, was 'content to do it.'[2]

> There is life for a look at the Crucified One;
> There is life at this moment for thee;
> Then look, sinner—look unto Him, and be saved—
> Unto Him who was nailed to the tree.

> Oh, doubt not thy welcome, since God has declared
> There remaineth no more to be done;
> That once in the end of the world he appeared,
> And completed the work He begun.

> But take, with rejoicing, from Jesus at once,
> The life everlasting He gives:
> And know with assurance, thou never canst die,
> Since Jesus, thy righteousness, lives.

A. M. HULL.

---

[1] Ps. xl. 9, P. B. V.     [2] Ps. xl. 10.

# SIXTH DAY.

---

## Justified.

'And by Him all that believe are justified from all things, from which ye could not be justified by the law of Moses.'— ACTS xiii. 39.

'AND.' For justification does not come first. The robe of righteousness[1] is not put on until the sinner is 'purged from his old sins'[2] So this is God's order—first, 'Through this man is preached unto you the forgiveness of sins;' and then, 'By Him all that believed are justified.'

But 'in Thy sight shall no man living be justified.'[3] 'For not the hearers of the law are just before God, but the doers of the law shall be justified.'[4] But we have *not* 'obeyed the voice of the Lord our God, to walk in His laws, which He set before us.'[5] So 'that no man is justified by the law in the sight of God, it is evident;'[6] for 'by the deeds of the law there shall *no* flesh be justified in His sight.'[7] 'How then can man be justified with God?'[8] 'The law was our schoolmaster to bring

---

[1] Isa. lvi. 10.　　　[2] 2 Pet. i. 9.　　　[3] Ps. cxliii. 2.
[4] Rom. ii. 13.　　　[5] Dan. ix. 10.　　　[6] Gal. iii. 11.
[7] Rom. iii. 20.　　　[8] Job xxv. 4.

us unto Christ, that we might be justified by faith.'[1]

This glorious justification by faith is sevenfold. We are justified, 1. '*By His grace*'[2]—the grace of God the Father, one of whose most wonderful titles is, 'The Justifier of him which believeth in Jesus.'[3] 2. '*By His blood*'[4]—that precious blood which has to do with every stage of our redemption and effectuated salvation ; from the writing of our names ' in the book of life of the Lamb slain from the foundation of the world,'[5] till the chorus of the ' new song '[6] is full in heaven. 3. '*By the Righteousness of One*'(of the One), ' by the obedience of One ; '[7] by which the free gift, the unspeakable gift of eternal life—nay, of Christ Himself to be our life[8]—' came upon all men unto justification of life. 4. '[9]*By the resurrection* of Jesus our Lord, who ' was raised again for our justification,' the grand token that our Substitute had indeed fulfilled all righteousness for us.[10]

' For God released our Surety
To show the work was done.'[11]

5. '*By His knowledge* shall My righteous Servant justify many ; for He shall bear their iniquities '[12] For true faith is founded upon the knowledge of Him, and ' this is life eternal.'[13] 6. *By faith ;* just *only* believing God's word, and accepting God's way about it.[14] 7. *By works ;* because these are the

---

[1] Gal. iii. 24.   [2] Rom. iii. 24.   [3] Rom. iii. 26.
[4] Rom. v. 9.   [5] Rev. xiii. 8.   [6] Rev. v. 9.
[7] Rom. v. 18, 19.   [8] Col. iii. 4.   [9] Rom. iv. 24, 25.
[10] Matt. iii. 15.   [11] John xix. 30.   [12] Isa. liii. 11.
[13] John xvii. 3.   [14] Rom. v. 1.

necessary and inseparable evidence that faith is not mere fancy or talk.[1] We *are* 'justified by faith without the deeds of the law,'[2] the old dead galvanic struggle to do duties and keep outward obligations; but *not* without works, which 'do spring out necessarily from a true and lively faith;' for 'faith without works is *dead*.'[3]

'Therefore, being justified by faith,' what then? 1. 'We have peace with God.'[4] 2. 'We shall be saved from wrath through Him.'[5] 3. We are made heirs of eternal life.[6] 4. We shall be glorified by Him and with Him for ever.[7]

What about my own part and lot in the matter? Whom does God thus justify? and may I hope to be among them? He begins indeed at the lowest depth, so that none may be shut out; for He 'would justify the heathen through faith,'[8] and He 'justifieth the ungodly.'[9] The publican who could only cry, 'God be merciful to me the sinner,'[10] was justified. I can come in here, at all events.

But how shall I be actually and effectually justified *now?* Let God speak and I will listen:[11] 'Even the righteousness of God which is by faith of Jesus Christ unto *all* and upon *all* them that believe:[12] for there is no difference.' 'By Him all that believe *are* justified.'[13] 'I believe in Jesus Christ His only Son our Lord.' Do I? 'Lord, I *believe*.'[14] Then His righteousness is upon me, and I *am* justi-

---

[1] Jas. ii. 24.  
[2] Rom. iii. 28; Gal. ii. 16; ib. v. 4.  
[3] Jas. ii. 26.  
[4] Rom. v. 1.  [5] Rom. v. 9.  
[6] Titus iii. 7.  [7] Rom. viii. 30; John xvii. 22.  
[8] Heb. vii. 25; Gal. iii. 8.  [9] Rom. iv. 5.  [10] Luke xviii. 14.  
[11] Ps. lxxxv. 8.  [12] Rom. iii. 22.  [13] Acts xiii. 39.  
[14] Mark ix. 24.

fied. 'Knowing that a man is not justified by the works of the law, but by the faith of Jesus Christ, even we have believed in Jesus Christ, that we might be justified by the faith of Christ.'[1] And now, ' He is *near* that justifieth me.'[2] 'Who shall lay anything to the charge of God's elect? It is God that justifieth.'[3]

By the grace of God the Father, thou art freely justified,—[4]
Through the great redemption purchased by the blood of Him who died,—[5]
By His life, for thee fulfilling God's command exceeding broad,—[6]
By His glorious resurrection, seal and signet of our God.[7]

Therefore, justified for ever by the faith which He hath given,[8]
Peace, and joy, and hope abounding smooth thy trial-path to heaven:[9]
Unto Him betrothed for ever, who thy life shall crown and bless,[10]
By His name thou shalt be called, Christ, 'The Lord our Righteousness.'[11]

---

[1] Gal. ii. 16.
[2] Isa. l. 8.
[3] Rom. viii. 33.
[4] Rom. iii. 24.
[5] Rom. v. 9.
[6] Rom. x. 4.
[7] Rom. iv. 25.
[8] Rom. v. 1.
[9] Rom. xv. 13.
[10] Hos. ii. 19.
[11] Jer. xxxiii. 16.

# SEVENTH DAY.

---

## The Royal Wine.

'Thy love is better than wine.'—CANT. i, 2.

WINE is the symbol of earthly joy; and who that has had but one sip of the love of Christ does not know this 'royal wine,'[1] this true 'wine of the kingdom,'[2] to be better than the best joy that the world can give! How much more, then, when deeper and fuller draughts are the daily portion, as we 'follow on to know'[3] the love 'which passeth knowledge!'[4] It is the privilege not of a favoured few, but of '*all* saints,' to comprehend something of what is incomprehensible.[5]

1. The breadth, contrasted with the narrowness of earthly love and all its joy. Perhaps it is not so much by looking at His love to all the redeemed ones whom no man can number,[6] that we realize this, as by seeing that the love of Jesus was broad enough to reach and include 'even me.' 'Who loved *me*;'[7] is not that more incomprehensible than that He loved all the saints and angels?

---

[1] Esther i. 7.  [2] John xiv. 27.  [3] Hos. vi. 3.
[4] Eph. iii. 19.  [5] Eph. iii. 18.  [6] Rev. vii. 9.
[7] Gen. xxvii. 38 ; Gal. ii. 20.

2. The length, contrasted with the passing shortness of the longest earthly love and joy. What is the length? 'Unto the end.'[1] And even that is not the full measure, for His immeasurable love is everlasting;[2] and when inconceivable ages have passed, we shall be no nearer 'the end' than now.

3. The depth, contrasted with the shallowness which is always felt, however disguised, in the world's best.[3] Down to the very depth of our fall went that wonderful love of Christ, to the depth of our sin, to the depth of our need, to the depth of those caverns of our own strange inner being which we ourselves cannot fathom, and which only His love can fill.

4. The height, contrasted with the lowness and littleness of all that is represented by the world's wine. This all ends in self, which is like a low vaulted roof, keeping down every possibility of rising; and so the earthly joy can take but a bat-like flight, always checked, always limited, in dusk and darkness. But the love of Christ breaks through the vaulting, and leads us up into the free sky above, expanding to the very throne of Jehovah, and drawing us 'still upward'[4] to the infinite heights of glory. Is there any height beyond, '*As* the Father hath loved Me, *so* have I loved *you*'?[5] These measures (so to speak) of Christ's love are those of the unsearchable perfection of God Himself. 'It is as high as heaven, deeper than hell'[6] (thank God

---

[1] 1 John ii. 17; 1 Cor. vii. 29–31; John xiii. 1.    [2] Jer. xxxi. 3.
[3] Prov. xiv. 13; Eccles. ii. 10, 11; John iv. 13.    [4] Ezek. xli. 7.
[5] John xv. 9.    [6] Job xi. 7–9.

for that word deeper), 'longer than the earth, and broader than the sea.'

For whom is this love? Oh how glad we are that it is not for the worthy and the faithful, so that we must be shut out, but for His own, *though the chief of sinners!*[1] It is 'the love of the Lord toward the children of Israel, who look to other gods, and love flagons of wine.' Has it been so with us, that we have been looking away from Jesus to heart-idols and 'other lords,'[2] and loving some earthly 'flagons of wine'—other love, other pleasures, other joys, ' other things,' which are *not* Jesus Christ's? Then only think of ' the love of the Lord toward' *us!* Well may we say, 'Thy love to me was wonderful,'[3] and own it to be ' better than wine,' ' above my chief joy.'[4] He proved His love to you and me to be ' strong as death;' and when all God's waves and billows went over Him, the many waters could not quench it.[5]

In His love and in His pity He redeemed us; in the same love He bears us and carries us all the day long.[6] He ' loveth at *all* times,'[7] and that includes this present moment; now, while your eye is on this page, His eye of love is looking on you, and the folds of His banner of love are overshadowing you.[8]

Is there even a feeble pulse of love to Him? He meets it with, ' I love them that love Me.'[9] ' I will love him, and will manifest Myself to him.' And

[1] 1 Tim. i. 15.　　[2] Isa. xxvi. 13.　　[3] 2 Sam. i. 26.
[4] Ps. cxxxvii. 6.　　[5] Cant. viii. 6; Ps. xlii. 7; Cant. viii. 7.
[6] Isa. lxiii. 9; ib. xlvi. 4.　[7] Prov. xvii. 17.　　[8] Cant. ii. 4.
[9] Prov. viii. 17.

so surely as the bride says, ' Thy love is better than
wine,' so surely does the heavenly Bridegroom
respond with incomprehensible condescension:
' How fair is *thy* love, my sister, my spouse ! how
much better is *thy* love than wine.'[1]   May this love
of Christ constrain us to live unto Him ' who loved
me and gave Himself for me.'[2]

> O Christ, He is the fountain,
>   The deep, sweet well of love !
> The streams on earth I've tasted,
>   More deep I'll drink above.
> There to an ocean-fulness
>   His mercy doth expand,
> Where glory, glory dwelleth
>   In Immanuel's land.
>
> Oh! I am my Beloved's,
>   And my Beloved is mine !
> He brings a poor vile sinner
>   Into ' His house of wine.'
> I stand upon His merits;
>   I know no safer stand,
> Not e'en where glory dwelleth
>   In Immanuel's land.

A. B. Cousin.

---

[1] Cant. iv. 10.                [2] Gal. ii. 20.

## EIGHTH DAY.

———

## The Gift of Peace.

'My peace I give unto you.'—JOHN xiv. 27.

'PEACE I leave with you' is much; 'My peace I give unto you' is more. The added word tells the fathomless marvel of the gift—'My peace.' Not merely 'peace with God;'[1] Christ has made that by the blood of His cross, and being justified by faith we have it through Him.[2] But after we are thus reconciled, the enmity and the separation being ended, Jesus has a gift for us from His own treasures; and this is its special and wonderful value, that it is *His very own*.[3] How we value a gift which was the giver's own possession! what a special token of intimate friendship we feel it to be! To others we give what we have made or purchased; it is only to very near and dear ones that we give what has been our own personal enjoyment or use. And so Jesus gives us not only peace made and peace purchased, but a share in His very own peace, —divine, eternal, incomprehensible peace,—which dwells in His own heart as God, and which shone

---

[1] Col. i. 20.　　[2] Rom. v. 1.　　[3] Ps. lxviii. 18.

in splendour of calmness through His life as man. No wonder that it ' passeth all understanding.'[1]

But how ? Why does the sap flow from the vine to the branch ? Simply because the branch is joined to the vine.[2] Then the sap flows into it by the very law of its nature. So, being joined to our Lord Jesus by faith, that which is His becomes ours, and flows into us by the very law of our spiritual life. If there were no hindrance, it would indeed flow as a river.[3] Then how earnestly we should seek to have every barrier removed to the inflowing of such a gift ! Let it be our prayer that He would clear the way for it, that He would take away all the unbelief, all the self, all the hidden cloggings of the channel.

Then He will give a sevenfold blessing :[4] ' My peace,' ' My joy,' ' My love,' at once and always, now and for ever ; ' My grace ' and ' My strength ' for all the needs of our pilgrimage ; ' My rest ' and ' My glory ' for all the grand sweet home-life of eternity with Him.

> Thy reign is perfect peace,
>   Not mine, but Thine ;
>   A stream that cannot cease,
> For its fountain is Thy heart.  Oh, depth unknown !
> Thou givest of Thine own,
>   Pouring from Thine, and filling mine.

---

[1] Phil. iv. 7.
[3] Isa. xlviii. 18.
[2] John xv. 5.
[4] John xv. 10, 11.

# NINTH DAY.

---

## The Abiding Joy.

'These things have I spoken unto you, that My joy might remain in you, and that your joy might be full.'—JOHN xv. 11.

WHO that has known anything of joy in the Lord but has asked, 'But will it last?' And why has the question been so often the very beginning of its not lasting? Because we have either asked it of ourselves or of others, and not of the Lord only. His own answers to this continually recurring question are so different from the cautious, chilling, saddening ones which His children so often give. They are absolute, full, reiterated. We little realize how unscriptural we are when we meet His good gift of joy to ourselves or to others with a doubtful, and therefore faithless, '*If* it lasts!'

'To the law and to the testimony,'[1] O happy Christian! there you shall find true and abundant answer to your only shadow on the brightness of the joy. So long as you believe your Lord's word about it, so long it *will* last.[2] So soon as you ask of other counsellors, and believe their word instead,

---

[1] Isa. viii. 20.　　　　[2] Isa. vii. 9.

so soon it will fail. Jesus meets your difficulty explicitly. - He has provided against it by giving the
very reason why He spoke the gracious words of
His last discourse, 'That My joy might *remain* in
you.'[1] Is not this exactly what we were afraid to
hope, what seemed too good to be true, that it
' might *remain*'? And lest we should think that
this abiding joy only meant some moderate measure
of qualified joy, He adds, 'And that your joy may
be *full*,'[2] repeating in the next chapter, and inten-
sifying it in the next. And lest we might think
this was said with reference only to an exceptional
case, He inspired His beloved disciple to echo the
words in his *general* epistle : ' That your joy may
be full,' and ' the anointing which ye have received
of Him abideth in you.'

*Never* in His word are we told anything contra-
dicting or explaining away this precious and reiterated promise. All through we are brightly pointed
not merely to hope of permanence, but to increase.
' The meek shall increase (not merely shall keep up)
their joy in the Lord.'[3] There are mingled
promises and commands as to growth and increase
in grace, knowledge, love, strength, and peace, and
does not increase of these imply and ensure joy?[4]
Is joy to be the *only* fruit of the Spirit of which it
may not be said that it ' sprang up and *increased*'?[5]

When it is suggested that we ' cannot ' (some even
say, ' must not') ' expect to be always joyful,' remember that ' it is written,' ' Rejoice in the Lord '

[1] John xv. 11.        [2] John xvi. 24.        [3] Isa. xxix. 19.
[4] 2 Pet. iii. 18 ; Col. i. 10 ; 1 Thess. iii. 12 ; iv. 10 ; Isa. xl. 29 ; ib. lx. 7 ;
Gal. v. 22.        -        [5] Mark iv. 8.

15

(not 'sometimes,' but) '*alway*.'[1]  'As sorrowful, yet *alway* rejoicing.'[2]  When we are told that 'it would not even be good for us,' remember that 'it is written again,' 'The joy of the Lord is your strength.'  Perhaps in that word 'of' lies the whole secret of lasting joy; for it is more than even 'joy *in* the Lord:' it is His own joy flowing into the soul that is joined to Himself, which alone can 're-main' in us, not even our joy in Him.  'That they might have *My* joy fulfilled in themselves.'[3]  Let us, then, seek not the stream, but the fountain; not primarily the joy, but that real and living union with Jesus by which His joy becomes ours

Let us not, either for ourselves or others, acquiesce in disobedience to any of His commandments.  See how absolute they are!  'Serve the Lord with gladness;'[4] 'Rejoice in the Lord, ye righteous,'[5] and many others.  Turn to the terribly distinct condemnation, 'Because thou servedst not the Lord thy God with joyfulness, and with gladness of heart,

therefore shalt thou serve thine enemies,

and He shall put a yoke of iron on thy neck until He have destroyed thee.'[6]

No one need be cast down because they cannot *yet* tell of abiding joy, or because others cannot tell of it.  Thank God, our experience is not the measure of His promises; they are all yea and Amen in Christ Jesus,[7] and our varying, short-falling experience touches neither their faithfulness nor their fulness.  Forget the things which are behind, and

---

1 Phil. iv. 4.  2 2 Cor vi. 10.  3 John xvii. 13.
4 Ps. c. 2.  5 Ps. xcvii. 12.  6 Deut. xxviii. 47, 48.
7 2 Cor. i. 20.

press on to firmer grasp and fuller reception of
Christ and His joy.[1]  Then it shall be always
'praise . . . more and more,' 'more grace,' 'grace
for grace,'[2] 'from strength to strength,'[3]—yes, even
'from glory to glory.'[4]  Then you shall indeed
'hold fast the confidence and the *rejoicing* of the
hope firm unto the end.'[5]

May I earnestly ask every reader who is saying,
'Will it last?' to seek 'out of the book of the Lord'
for themselves; taking a concordance, and looking
out, under the words, Joy, Rejoice, Gladness, etc.,
the overwhelming reiterations of promises and commands which can leave them in no doubt as to
God's answer.

---

[1] Phil. iii. 13.  [2] Jas. iv. 6.  [3] Ps. lxxxiv. 7.
[4] 2 Cor. iii. 18.  [5] Heb. iii. 6.

# TENTH DAY.

---

## The Sure Afterward.

'Now no chastening for the present seemeth to be joyous,
but grievous: nevertheless, afterward it yieldeth the peaceable
fruit of righteousness unto them which are exercised thereby.'
—HEB. xii. 11.

THERE are some promises which we are apt to
reserve for great occasions, and thus lose the
continual comfort of them. Perhaps we read this
one with a sigh, and say : ' How beautiful this is for
those whom the Lord is really chastening ! I almost think I should not mind that, if such a promise might then be mine. But the things that try me
are only little things that turn up every day to
trouble and depress me.' Well, now, does the
Lord specify what degree of trouble, or what kind
of trouble, is great enough to make up a claim to
the promise? And if He does not, why should
you? He only defines it as ' not joyous, but grievous.' Perhaps there have been a dozen different
things to-day which were ' not joyous, but grievous ' ·
to you. And though you feel ashamed of feeling
them so much, and hardly like to own to their having been so trying, and would not think of dignify-

ing them as 'chastening,' yet, if they come under
the Lord's definition, He not only knows all about
them, but they were, every one of them, chasten=
ings from His hand; neither to be despised and
called 'just nothing,' when all the while they *did*
'grieve' you; nor to be wearied of; because they
are working out blessing to you and glory to Him.
Every one of them has been an unrecognized token
of His love and interest in you; for 'whom the
Lord loveth, He chasteneth.'[1]

Next, do not let us reserve this promise for chas-
tenings in the aggregate. Notice the singular pronoun, 'Nevertheless, afterward IT yieldeth,' not
'*they* yield.' Does not this indicate that every
separate chastening has its own special 'afterward'?
We think of trials as intended to do us good in the
long-run, and in a general sort of way; but the
Lord says of each one, '*It* yieldeth.' Apply this to
'the present.' The particular annoyance which
befell you this morning; the vexatious words which
met your ear and 'grieved' your spirit; the dis=
appointment which was His appointment for to-
day; the slight but hindering ailment; the presence of some one who is 'a grief of mind' to you;
whatever this day seemeth not joyous, but grievous,
is linked in 'the good pleasure of His goodness,'[2]
with a corresponding afterward of 'peaceable
fruit;' the very seed from which, if you only do
not choke it, this shall spring and ripen.

If we set ourselves to watch the Lord's dealings
with us, we shall often be able to detect a most beau-

---

[1] Heb. xii. 6.          [2] 2 Thess. i. 11.

tiful correspondence and proportion between each individual 'chastening' and its own resulting 'afterward.' The habit of thus watching and expecting will be very comforting, and a great help to quiet trust when some new chastening is sent : for then we shall simply consider it as the herald and earn-I est of a new 'afterward.'

Lastly, do not let us reserve this promise for some far future time. The Lord did not say '*a long while* afterward,' and do not let us gratuitously insert it. It rather implies that, as soon as the chastening is over, the peaceable fruit shall appear 'unto the glory and praise of God.'[1] So let us look out for the 'afterward' as soon as the pressure is past. This immediate expectation will bring its own blessing if we can say, 'My expectation is from Him,'[2] and not from any fruit-bearing qualities of our own ; for only 'from Me is thy fruit found.'[3] Fruit from Him will also be fruit unto Him.

> What shall Thine afterward be, O Lord?
> I wonder, and wait to see
> (While to thy chastening hand I bow)
> What peaceable fruit may be ripening now,
> Ripening fast for Thee !

---

[1] Phil. i. 11.    [2] Ps. lxii. 5.    [3] Hos. xiv. 8.

# ELEVENTH DAY.

---

# No Hurt.

'Nothing shall by any means hurt you.'—LUKE x. 19.

IS not this one of those very strong promises which we are apt to think are worded a little *too* strongly, and off which we 'take a great discount'? Now, instead of daring a 'Yea, hath God said'?[1] let us just take *all* the comfort and rest and gladness of it for ourselves. Let us believe every word, just as our beloved Master uttered it to the simple-hearted seventy who were so surprised to find His name so much more powerful than they expected.

Nothing! If He said 'nothing,' have we any right to add, 'Yes, but *except*  '?  Nothing can hurt those who are joined to Christ, 'for with me thou shalt be in safeguard,'[2] unless anything could be found which should separate us from Him. And 'who shall separate us?'[3]  Earthly tribulations, even the most terrible, shall not do it, for 'in all these things we are more than conquerors through Him that loved us.'[4]  Yet a farther reaching and,

---

[1] Gen. iii. 1.
[2] 1 Sam. xxii. 23.
[3] Rom. viii. 35.
[4] Rom. viii. 37.

indeed, entirely exhaustive list is given, none of which, 'nor *any* other creature, shall be able to separate us.' Let us take everything that possibly could hurt us to that list, and see for ourselves if it is not included, and then rejoice in the conclusion, based and built upon Christ's bare word, but buttressed and battlemented by this splendid utterance of His inspired apostle that it is indeed so—' *nothing* shall by any means hurt you.'

But He who knows our little faith never gives an isolated promise. He leaves us no chance of overlooking or misunderstanding any one, except by wilful neglect, because it is always confirmed in other parts of His word. So He has given the same strong consolation in other terms. 'The Lord shall preserve thee from *all* evil' (do you believe *that?*). 'There shall *no* evil happen to the just.'[1] 'In seven (troubles) there shall no evil touch thee '[2] Then see how He individualized it to Shadrach, Meshach, and Abednego, even *in* the burning fiery furnace, 'They have no hurt;' to Daniel among the lions, 'They have not hurt me;' to St. Paul among turbulent men with a care-nought governor, 'No man shall set on thee to hurt thee.'[3] We are not likely to be more exposed to 'hurt' than these, and we have the same God, 'who keepeth His promise for ever.'[4] He is the 'wall of fire round about [5] us; and what fortification so impenetrable— nay, so unapproachable ! And 'He that toucheth you toucheth the apple of His eye'[6]—the very least touch is felt by the Lord, who loves us and is

---

[1] Prov. xii. 21.   [2] Job v. 19.   [3] Acts xviii. 10.
[4] Ps. cxlvi. 6.   [5] Zech. ii. 5.   [6] Zech. ii. 8.

mighty to save! Well may He say, 'And who is he that will harm you?'

'Nothing shall by *any* means hurt you,' for 'no weapon that is formed against thee shall prosper;'[1] man's curse shall be turned into God's blessing. Jehovah Himself, watering His vineyard every moment, says: 'Lest any hurt it, I will keep it night and day.'[2] Again, the promise, with a solemn condition, takes an even stronger form· 'Whoso keepeth the commandment shall *feel* no evil thing.'[3]

Is not all this enough? It might well be, but His wonderful love has yet more to say—not only that nothing shall hurt us, but that all things work together for our good;[4] not merely *shall* work, but actually *are* working. All things, if it *means* all things, must include exactly those very things, whatever they may be, which you and I are tempted to think will hurt us, or, at least, *may* hurt us. Now will we this evening trust our own ideas, or Christ's word? One or other must be mistaken. Which is it? Christ, my own Master, my Lord and my God, has given a promise which meets every fear; therefore, 'I will both lay me down in peace, and sleep: for Thou, Lord, only makest me to dwell in safety,'[5] and 'nothing shall by any means hurt' me.

---

[1] Isa. liv. 17.      [2] Isa. xxvii. 3.      [3] Eccles. viii. 5.
[4] Rom. viii. 28.    [5] Ps. iv. 8.

## TWELFTH DAY.

---

## The Putting Forth of the Sheep.

'When He putteth forth His own sheep, He goeth before them.'—JOHN x. 4.

WHAT gives the Alpine climber confidence in wild, lonely, difficult passes or ascents, when he has 'not passed this way heretofore'?[1] It is that his guide has been there before; and also that in every present step over unknown and possibly treacherous ice or snow, his guide 'goeth before.'[2]

It is to Christ's 'own sheep' that this promise applies; simply those who believe and hear His voice. It is when *He* putteth them forth that it comes true; not when they put themselves forth, or when they let a 'stranger'[3] lure them forth, or such traitors as self-cowardice or impatience drive them forth.

Sometimes it is a literal putting forth. We have been in a sheltered nook of the fold, and we are sent to live where it is windier and wilder. The

---

[1] Josh. iii. 4.      [2] Isa. xlv. 2.      [3] John x. 26, 27; ib. x. 3.

home nest is stirred up,[1] and we have to go (it may
be only for a few days, it may be for years, it may
be for the rest of our lives) into less congenial sur-
roundings, to live with fresh people, or in a different position, or in a new neighborhood. We do
not put ourselves forth, we would rather stay; but
it has to be. But Jesus 'goeth before.' He prepares
the earthly as well as the heavenly places for us.
He will be there when we get to the new place.
He went in the way before to search us out a place
to pitch our tents in[2] (and perhaps we were forgetting that they were tents and not palaces).[3] If we
wilfully persisted in staying where we were when
He said, ' Arise and depart, for this is not your
rest,'[4] we should find that Presence was gone which
only could cause us to rest. He is not *sending* us
forth away from Him, but only *putting* us forth
with His own gentle hand, saying, ' Rise up, My
love, and come away,'[5] ' Come with Me.'

Sometimes it is putting forth into service. We
had such a nice little quiet shady corner in the
vineyard, down among the tender grapes, with such
easy little weedings and waterings to attend to.
And then the Master comes and draws us out into
the thick of the work, and puts us into a part of
the field where we never should have thought of going, and puts larger tools into our hands, that we
may do more at a stroke. And we know we are
not sufficient for these things,[6] and the very tools
seem too heavy for us, and the glare too dazzling,
and the vines too tall. Ah ! but would we really go

---

[1] Deut. xxii. 11.  [2] Deut. i. 33.  [3] Heb. xiii. 14.
[4] Micah ii. 10.  [5] Cant. ii. 10: ib. iv. 8.  [6] 2 Cor. ii. 16.

back? He would not be in the old shady corner
with us now; for when He put us forth He went
before us, and it is only by close following that we
can abide with Him. Without Him we could do
nothing if we perversely and fearfully ran back to
our old work. With Him, 'through Christ which
strengtheneth' us, we 'can do all things' in the
new work. Not our power, but His presence will
carry us through.[1]

Sometimes it is putting forth into the rough places
of suffering, whether from temptation, pain, 'or any
adversity.' Not one step here but Jesus has gone
before us; and He still goeth before us, often so
very close before us, that even by the still waters[2]
we never seemed so near Him. 'He Himself hath
suffered, being tempted.'[3] How strangely comforting to remember that He has passed even *that* way
before us! 'The things which *He* suffered' include
and cover, and stretch wide on every side beyond,
all possible 'sufferings of this present time.'[4] It is
in patient suffering, rather than in doing, that we
are specially called 'to follow His steps.'[5] 'The
footsteps of Thine anointed have lain through reproach,' and 'the reproach of Thy servants' is no
light part of 'the fellowship of His sufferings.'
How specially tender the Master's hand is when it
is laid upon us to put us forth into *any* path of suffering! How specially precious, then, to know that
it is indeed His own doing!

Sooner or later, perhaps again and again, He puts
forth His own sheep into a position of greater sep-

---

[1] Zech. iv. 6.    [2] Ps. xxiii. 2.    [3] Heb. ii. 18.
[4] Rom. viii. 18.    [5] 1 Pet. ii. 21.

aration—forth from an outer into an inner circle, always nearer and nearer to the great Centre. Let us watch very sensitively for such leading. Every hesitation to yield to His gentle separation from the world results in heart separation from Him. When He thus goeth before, shall we risk being left behind?

He will put forth His own sheep at last into the path which none of them shall ever tread alone, because He trod it alone. 'Yea, though I walk through the valley of the shadow of death, I will fear no evil: for Thou art with me.'[1] Our 'Joshua, he shall go over before thee, as the Lord hath said.'[2] Jesus knows every single step of that valley; and when His people enter it, they will surely find that 'their King shall pass before them;'[3] and the Comforter will say, 'He it is that doth go before thee.'[4]

## THIRTEENTH DAY.

## Safe Stepping.

'Thy foot shall not stumble.'—PROV. iii. 23.

MANY a Christian says: 'I shall be kept from falling at last; but, of course, I shall stumble continually by the way.' But 'have ye not read

---

[1] Ps. xxiii. 4.
[2] Deut. xxxi. 3.
[3] Micah ii. 13.
[4] Deut. xxxi. 8.

this Scripture,' ' Thy foot shall *not* stumble '?[1] And
if we have only once read it, ought not the 'of
course' to be put over on the other side? for 'hath
He spoken, and shall He not make it good?'[2]
'And the Scripture *cannot* be broken.'[3]

' But as a matter of fact we do stumble, and
though he riseth up again, yet even the just man
falleth seven times.'[4]  Of course we do; and this
is entirely accounted for by the other ' of course.'
God gives us a promise, and, instead of humbly
saying, ' Be it unto me according to Thy word,'[5]
we either altogether overlook or deliberately refuse
to believe it ; and then, ' of course,' we get no fulfilment of it.  The measure of the promise is God's
faithfulness ; the measure of its realization is our
faith.  Perhaps we have not even cried, ' Help Thou
mine unbelief' as to this promise, much less said,
' Lord, I believe.'[6]

It does not stand alone; it is reiterated and varied.
He knew our constant, momentary need of it.  He
knew that without it we *must* stumble, and fall too ;
that we have not the least power to take one step without a stumble—or, rather, that we have no power to.
take one single onward step at all.  And He knew
that Satan's surest device to make us stumble would
be to make us believe that ' it can't be helped.'
We have thought that, if we have not said it.

But 'what saith the Scripture?'[7]  'When thou
runnest' (the likeliest pace for a slip), ' thou shalt
not stumble.'[8]  ' He will not suffer thy foot to be

---

[1] Mark xii. 10.      [2] Num. xxiii. 19.      [3] John x. 35.
[4] Prov. xxiv. 16.    [5] Luke i. 38.         [6] Mark ix. 24.
[7] Rom. iv. 3.        [8] Prov. iv. 12.

moved.'[1] 'He will keep the feet of His saints.'[2]
'He led them . . . that they should not stumble.'[3]
*Can* we say, 'Yea, hath God said?'[4] to all this?
Leave that to Satan; it is no comment for God's
children to make upon His precious promises. If
we do not use the power of faith, we find the neu-
tralizing power of unbelief.

'But how *can* I keep from stumbling?' You
cannot keep from stumbling at all; but He is 'able
to keep you from falling,'[5] which in the Greek is
strongly and distinctly 'without *stumbling*.' The
least confidence in, or expectation from, yourself
not only leads to inevitable stumbling, but is itself
a grievous fall. But again we are met with the very
promise we need to escape this snare: 'For the
Lord shall be thy confidence, and shall keep thy
foot from being taken.'[6]

'Still, *how* shall I be kept?' Jesus Himself has
answered: 'If any man walk in the day, he stum-
bleth *not*, because he seeth the light of this world.'[7]
'Walk in the light,' 'looking unto Jesus,' and so
shall we be 'kept by the power of God through
faith.'

We tell a little child to look where it steps and
pick its way; but Christ's little children are to do
just the opposite: they are to look away to Him.
'Let thine eyes look,' not down, but 'right on, and
let thine eyelids look straight before thee.'[8] Why?
Because 'He it is that doth go before thee,'[9] and it

---

[1] Ps. cxxi. 3.  [2] 1 Sam. ii. 9.  [3] Isa. lxiii. 13.
[4] Gen. iii. 1.  [5] Jude 24.  [6] Prov. iii. 26.
[7] John xi. 9.  [8] Prov. iv. 25.  [9] Deut. xxxi. 8.

is on Him, the Light of the world, that the gaze must be fixed.

'Having therefore these promises, dearly be-loved,'[1] let us use them. Let us turn them into prayers of faith. 'Hold up my goings in Thy paths, that my footsteps slip *not*'[2] (did David add the whisper, 'But nevertheless, of course, they *will* slip'?). 'Hold Thou me up, and I *shall* be safe.' 'When I said, My foot slippeth; Thy mercy, O. Lord, *held* me up' (not '*picked* me up').[3]

Then comes the New Testament echo· 'Yea, he shall be holden up: for God is able to make him stand.'[4] But take 'all the counsel of God;'[5] for this, too, is needed: 'And thou standest by faith. Be not high-minded, but fear.'

Now if these promises are worth the paper they are written on, ought we not to believe and accept and give thanks for them, and go on our way re-joicing, claiming His promise not once for all, not for to-morrow, but always for the *next* step of the way? 'Thy foot shall *not* stumble!' Jesus is now 'upholding all things by the word of His power;'[6] shall our unbelief make us the exception? Shall we not rather say, 'Uphold *me*, according to Thy word'?[7]

Look away to Jesus,
Look away from all!
Then we shall not stumble,
Then we need not fall.

---

[1] 2 Cor. vii. 1.  [2] Ps. xvii. 5.  [3] Ps. cxix. 117; ib. xciv. 18.
[4] Rom. xiv. 4.  [5] Acts xx. 27.  [6] Heb. i. 3.
[7] Ps. cxix. 116.

# FOURTEENTH DAY.

---

## Thine.

'I am Thine.'—Ps. cxix. 94.

THIS is a wonderful stone for the sling of faith. It will slay any Goliath of temptation, if we only sling it out boldly and determinately at him.

When self tempts us (and we know how often that is), let it be met with 'not your own,'[1] and then look straight away to Jesus with 'I am *Thine.*'

If the world tries some lure, old or new, remember the words of the Lord Jesus, how He said :[2] 'If ye were of the world, the world would love his own ;[3] . . . but I have chosen you out of the world ; '[4] and lest the world should claim us as 'his own,' look away to Jesus, and say, 'I am *Thine.*'

Is it sin, subtle and strong and secret, that claims our obedience? Acknowledge that ' ye *were* the servants of sin ; ' but now, ' being made free from sin, ye became the servants of righteousness,'[5] and conquer with the faith-shout, ' I am *Thine !* '

Is it a terrible hand-to-hand fight with Satan himself, making a desperate effort to reassert his old power? Tell the prince of this world that he hath *nothing* in Jesus,[6] and that you are ' in Him that is

---

[1] 1 Cor. vi. 19.
[4] John xvii. 16.
[2] Acts xx. 35.
[5] Rom. vi. 17, 18.
[3] John xv. 19.
[6] John xiv. 30.

16

true,"[1] a member of His body, His very own ; and see if he is not forced to flee at the sound of your confident 'I am Thine!'

But after all, 'I am Thine' is only an echo, varying in clearness according to faith's atmosphere and our nearness to the original voice. Yes, it is only the echo of 'Thou art Mine,'[2] falling in its mighty music on the responsive, because Spirit-prepared, heart. This note of heavenly music never originated with any earthly rock. It is only when God sends forth the Spirit of His Son in our hearts that we cry, 'Abba, Father.'[3] It was when the anointed but not yet openly crowned king had gone out to meet Amasai, and the Spirit came upon him, that he said, 'Thine are we, David.' Therefore do not overlook the Voice, in the gladness of the echo. Listen, and you will hear it falling from the mysterious heights of high-priestly intercession · 'They are Thine. And all Mine are Thine, and Thine are Mine.'[4]

This is no vague and general belonging to Christ, but full of specific realities of relationship. 'I am Thine' means, 'Truly I am Thy servant.'[5] I am one of Thy 'dear children.'[6] I am Thy chosen soldier.[7] I am Thy ransomed one.[8] I am Thy 'own sheep.' I am Thy witness. I am Thy friend.[9] And all these are but amens to His own condescending declarations. He says we are all these, and we have only to say, 'Yes, Lord, so I am.' Why should we ever contradict Him ?

---

[1] 1 John v. 20.  [2] Isa. xliii. 1.  [3] Rom. viii. 15.
[4] John xvii. 9, 10.  [5] Ps. cxvi. 16.  [6] Eph. v. 1.
[7] 2 Tim. ii. 4.  [8] Isa. xxxv. 10.  [9] John x. 4.

In deeper humility and stronger faith let us listen further to the voice of our Beloved, as He breathes names of incomprehensible condescension and love. Shall we contradict Him *here*, in the tenderest out- flow of His divine affection, and say, 'Not so, Lord'? Shall we not rather adoringly listen, and let Him say even to us in our depths of utter un- worthiness, 'My sister, My spouse,' 'My love, My dove, My undefiled,' answering only with a won- dering, yet unquestioning, 'I *am* Thine,' 'I am all that Thou choosest to say that I am'?

The echo may vary and falter (though it is nothing short of atrocious ingratitude and unbelief when it does), but the Voice never varies or falters. He does not say, 'Thou art Mine' to-day, and reverse or weaken it to-morrow. We are 'a people unto Thee *for ever*,' and why grieve His love by doubt- ing His word, and giving way to a very fidget of faithlessness? Love that is everlasting *cannot* be ephemeral; it *is* everlasting, and what can we say more?

The more we by faith and experience realize that we are His own in life and death, the more willing we shall be that He should do what He will with His own, and the more sure we shall be that He will do the very best with it, and make the very most of it. May we increasingly find the strength and rest of this our God-given claim upon God. 'I am Thine, save me!'[1] And 'He will save, He will rejoice over thee with joy; He will rest in His love.'[2]

---

[1] Ps. cxix. 94.     [2] Zeph. iii. 17.

‘Not your own!’ but His ye are,
  Who hath paid a price untold
For your life, exceeding far
  All earth’s store of gems and gold.
With the precious blood of Christ,
Ransom-treasure all unpriced,
Full redemption is procured,
Full salvation is assured.

‘Not your own!’ but His by right,
  His peculiar treasure now,
Fair and precious in His sight,
  Purchased jewels for His brow.
He will keep what thus He sought,
Safely guard the dearly bought,
Cherish that which He did choose,
Always love and never lose.

---

## FIFTEENTH DAY.

# Unto Thee for Ever.

‘What one nation in the earth is like Thy people, even like
Israel, whom God went to redeem for a people to Himself,
and to make Him a name, and to do for you great things and
terrible, for Thy land, before Thy people, which Thou re-
deemedst to Thee from Egypt, from the nations and their
gods? For Thou hast confirmed to Thyself Thy people
Israel to be a people unto Thee for ever: and Thou, Lord,
art become their God.’—2 SAM. vii. 23, 24.

ONE thought, containing three thoughts, seems
    to pervade this epitome of the history of God's
people. The one thought is ‘Unto Thee!’ The

three thoughts contained in it are—Redeemed, Separated, Confirmed unto Thee

Let us take them in order. 1. God 'went to redeem' His people. It was no easy sitting still, no costless fiat : 'Thou *wentest forth* for the salvation of Thy people, even for salvation with Thine anointed.'[1] These 'goings forth have been from of old, from the days of eternity,'[2] and we have seen by faith these 'goings of my God, my King.'[3]

It was not only to purchase them out of bondage and death, as one might buy a captive thrush on a winter evening, and let it loose into the hungry cold, and think no more about it ; it was to redeem them unto Himself, to be His own portion and inheritance and treasure and delight, to be a 'people near unto Him,' to be the objects on which all His divine love might be poured out, to be the very opportunity of His joy.

His glory and our good were inseparably joined in it. He did it 'to make Him a name ; ' and we may reverently say, that even the very Name which is above every name[4] could not have been the crown of the exaltation of the Son of God but for this.

He also did it because He would 'do *for you* great things and terrible,'—great things in mercy, 'terrible things in righteousness,'—bringing all His sublimely balanced attributes to bear on His great work 'for *you*.' '*Before* His people,' that we might see, and know, and believe, and praise.

2. This redemption to Himself necessarily involved separation 'from Egypt, from the nations

---

[1] Hab. iii. 13.
[2] Micah v. 2, margin.
[3] Ps. lxviii. 24.
[4] Phil. ii. 9.

and their gods.' We cannot have the 'to' without
the 'from,' any more than we could go to the equa-
tor and not come away from the arctic regions.
And the test and proof of the 'to Thee' lies in the
'from Egypt' But what do we want with Egypt?
what is there to attract us to the house of bondage and
its old taskmasters? Did we not have enough of
them? and shall we not gratefully accept redemption 'from the nations,' '*out of*' them, from the
tyranny of ' the customs of the people,' ' from our
vain conversation,'[1] and say henceforth, ' Thy people shall be my people' ?[2] 'What have *I* to do any
more with idols,'[3] when God Himself has redeemed
me 'from their gods' ? Yes, *has* redeemed me, for
He says so. 'Sing, O ye heavens; for the Lord
hath done it !' He 'gave Himself for us, that He
might redeem us from all iniquity.'[4]

3. How magnificently God seals all His transac-
tions ! So He has not only redeemed and separated us unto Himself, but 'Thou hast *confirmed to
Thyself* Thy people Israel.' He, not we. His
hands laid the foundation, and His hands shall also
finish it. He stablisheth us in Christ, and He
'hath also sealed us.' He 'shall also confirm you
to the end ;'[5] your life shall be one great Confirmation Day of continual defending and strengthening
and blessing ; He avouching you this day and every
day to be His peculiar people, ' as He hath promised,' and establishing you an holy people unto
Himself, and you avouching the Lord to be your
God and to walk in His ways.

---

[1] 1 Pet. i. 18.   [2] Ruth i. 16.   [3] Hos. xiv. 8.
[4] Titus ii. 14.   [5] 1 Cor. i. 8.

Not ' this day, only 'for we are confirmed to Him
' to be a people unto Thee for ever.'   ' Thine for
ever ! '   ' For I know that whatsoever God doeth,
it shall be for ever ; '[1] so, having done this, it must
be ' for ever ! '   Fling this at the enemy when he
tempts you to doubt your complete and eternal
redemption—' Unto Thee for ever ! ' when he tempts
you to regret or tamper with your separation—
' Unto Thee for ever ! ' when he tempts you to quiver
about your confirmation ' to the end '—' Unto Thee
*for ever !* '

For ' the Lord is faithful.'[2]   ' And now, O Lord
God, the word that Thou hast spoken . . . establish it for ever, and do as Thou hast said.'[3]

> In full and glad surrender,
> I give myself to Thee,
> Thine utterly and only,
> And evermore to be.
> O Son of God, who lovest me,
> I will be Thine alone,
> And all I have and all I am
> Shall henceforth be Thine own.

---

[1] Eccles. iii. 14.          [2] 2 Thess. iii. 3.          [3] 2 Sam. vii. 25.

## SIXTEENTH DAY.

---

## Captive Thoughts.

'Bringing into captivity every thought to the obedience of Christ.'—2 COR. x. 5.

ARE there any tyrants more harassing than our own thoughts? Control of deeds and words seems a small thing in comparison; but have we not been apt to fancy that we really can't help our thoughts? Instead of our dominating them, they have dominated us; and we have not expected, nor even thought it possible, to be set free from the manifold tyranny of vain thoughts, and still less of wandering thoughts. Yet, all the time, *here* has been God's word about this hopeless, helpless mat ter, only *where* has been our faith?

It is very strong language that the inspiring Spirit uses here—not 'thoughts' in general, but definitely, and with no room for distressing exceptions, '*every* thought.'[1] Must it not be glorious rest to have *every* thought of day and night brought into sweet, quiet, complete captivity to Jesus, entirely 'obedient to the faith,'[2] to His holy and loving influence, to His beautiful and perfect law? We should not have dared to hope or dream of such a rest unto our souls; we should not have guessed it included in that prom-

---

[1] Ps. xciv. 19.  [2] Acts vi. 7.

ise to those who take the yoke of Christ upon them ; and if we could find one text stating that it was not any part of God's infinitely gracious purposes for us, we should only say, ' Of course, for it stands to reason it could not be ! '

To reason, perhaps, but not to faith ; for words cannot be plainer than these in which St. Paul sets forth this marvellous privilege not of himself personally, but of all God's children, if they are only willing and simply believing in the matter. For while ' the riches of His glory in Christ Jesus '[1] is the measure of the fulness of His promises, ' accord ing to your faith '[2] is the appointed measure of their reception and benefit by ourselves. ' Lord, increase *our* faith. '[3]

But there is an order in their effectual working, and we must not begin at the wrong end. Before this triumph-leading of every thought can take place, there is the ' casting down imaginations, '[4] or, as in the more correct margin, ' reasonings.' As long as we are reasoning about a promise, we never know its reality. It is not God's way. It is the humble who hear thereof and are glad.[5] Have we not found it so? Did we *ever* receive the powerful fulfilment of *any* promise so long as we argued and reasoned, whether with our own hearts or with others, and said, ' How can these things be ? '[6] Has it not always been, that we had to lay down our arms and accept God's thought and God's way instead of our own ideas, and be willing that He should ' speak the word only,' and believe it as little children believe

---

[1] Phil. iv. 19.   [2] Matt. ix 29.   [3] Luke xvii. 5.
[4] 2 Cor. x. 5.   [5] Ps. xxxiv. 2.   [6] John iii. 9.

our promises? Then, *never* till then, the promise
and the privilege became ours not only in potential-
ity but in actuality. Now, how is it that we do not
*yet* understand, and apply the same principle to
every promise or privilege which as yet we see only
afar off? It is the old way and the only way:
'Who through faith . . . obtain promises.'[1]

It is a solemn thought that the alternative of 'the
obedience of Christ'[2] is disobedience. Thoughts
that are not brought into the one are in the other;
for 'the thought of foolishness is *sin*,'[3] nothing less
or lighter; and when the Holy Spirit 'declareth
unto man what is his thought,' unsuspected sin and
unrecognized guilt come terribly to light. But 'how
long shall thy vain thoughts lodge within thee?'[4]
The Conqueror, the always triumphing Saviour,
stands at the door and knocks; shall we not 'open
unto Him *immediately*,' and *now* cast down the
reasonings which hinder His present triumph, and
yield up to Him 'who alone *can* order them' the
unruly will and affections, and deliver into His victorious hands the unmanageable thought-garrison
(reserving no private slaves, who would quickly
again become our masters), and then let Him dwell
in our hearts by faith as absolute Captain of our
salvation?[5] Then He will garrison our hearts with
the peace of God which passeth all understanding.[6]

Let every thought
Be captive brought,
Lord Jesus Christ, to Thine own sweet obedience;

---

[1] Heb. xi. 33.     [2] 2 Cor. x. 6.     [3] Prov. xxiv. 9.
[4] Jer. iv. 17.     [5] Heb. ii. 10.     [6] Phil. iv. 7.

That I may know,
In ebbless flow,
The perfect peace of full and pure allegiance.

---•---

## SEVENTEENTH DAY.

---

# The Imagination of the Thoughts of the Heart.

'Keep this for ever in the imagination of the thoughts of the heart of Thy people, and prepare (margin, stablish) their heart unto Thee.'—I Chron. xxix. 18.

THE words are probably more familiar to us in another connection: 'And God saw that every imagination of the thoughts of his heart was only evil continually.'[1] There is Satan's work through the fall; now let us look at God's work through the redemption that is in Christ Jesus.[2]

What was to be kept for ever in the imagination of the thoughts of the heart? Something that God had put there; for you cannot keep a thing in any place till it is first put there. The people had responded to the appeal of their king, 'Who then is willing to consecrate his service this day unto the Lord?'[3] As the expression of this service, they had offered willingly and rejoicingly to the Lord. What they had offered was all His own: 'Of thine

---

[1] Gen. vi. 5.     [2] Rom. iii. 24.     [3] 1 Chron. xxix. 5.

own have we given Thee."[1] And David acknowl-
edges that it was all of Him that they were enabled
(margin, obtained strength) 'to offer so willingly
after this sort.' Was all this consecration and joy
to be a thing of a day? Nay! in his grand inspired
prayer, David, foreshadowing the Royal Intercessor,
by whom alone we 'offer up spiritual sacrifices,'
prays, 'O Lord God, keep this *for ever* in the imagination of the thoughts of the heart of Thy people.'

Now, does not this precisely meet the fear, the
desire, and the need of our souls? I may have
yielded myself unto God to-day, I may have sincerely presented myself a living sacrifice to Him[2]
to-day, but what about to-morrow? My heart is so
treacherous, I dare not trust it, I cannot even know
it. Who that has consecrated himself to the Lord
has not had some such thought! In too many instances, the thought is brooded over till it grows into
doubt of His power; and then, of course, we begin
to sink, for only by faith do we stand or walk in the
bright path of consecration. Doubt indulged soon
becomes doubt realized.

He who by His free grace and mighty power put
it into our hearts must be equally willing and able
to keep it there. If He can keep it there for one
day,—nay, for one hour,—He can keep it—how
long? Two days? A whole year? What saith
the Scripture? '*For Ever.*' Yes, but He only; not
ourselves. We cannot 'keep' it one minute. The
more totally we distrust our own ability to put or to

---

[1] 1 Chron. xxix. 14.    [2] Rom. vi. 13; ib. xii. 1.

keep any right thing whatever in our minds, the more we shall see that we may and must totally trust His power.

There is real comfort in knowing that *every* imagination of the thoughts of the natural heart is *only* evil continually, because this shows how really He is working in us when we find Him putting and keeping holy things in our minds. We may be quite sure no Godward thought comes natural to us ; but His new covenant is : ' I will put My laws into their mind, and write them in their hearts.'[1]

The words are very remarkable and far-reaching. We feel that they go to the very depths, that it is our *whole* mental being which is to be thus pervaded with the incense of consecration ; not that it is to be kept only in some inner recess of the heart, and not equally so in the mental consciousness. ' Keep this for ever in the *imagination*,' so that the mind (margin, imagination) may be stayed on Thee, and the keeping in perfect peace may result [2] Just the very thing that seems most curbless, the mental lightning that seems too quick for us ! The flashing wings that used to bear us too swiftly whither we would not, shall be folded over the golden purpose of consecration. ' In the imagination of the *thoughts*.' ' Bringing into captivity every thought to the obedience of Christ.' And then the peace of God enters in to garrison the heart and *thoughts* (for it is the same word, here translated ' mind '). ' In the imagination of the thoughts of the *heart*,' the very central self, the inner citadel of the soul.

---

[1] Heb. viii. 8-10.   [2] Isa. xxvi. 3.

*That* shall be 'established with grace,' stablished unblameable in holiness, 'fixed' so that it shall sing and give praise; for Thou, Lord, 'hast heard the desire of the humble: Thou wilt establish their heart.'

We rejoice in His omniscience; for, because 'the Lord searcheth all hearts, and understandeth all the imaginations of the thoughts,'[1] we are fully persuaded that what He has promised He is able also to perform [2]

> 'Only for Jesus!' Lord, keep it for ever
>   Sealed on the heart and engraved on the life;
> Pulse of all gladness, and nerve of endeavour,
>   Secret of rest, and the strength of our strife.

———•———

## EIGHTEENTH DAY.

———

# The Everlasting Service.

'And he shall serve him for ever.'—Ex. xxi. 6.

A PROMISE only differenced from a threat by one thing, love! But that makes all the difference.

To those who are still 'enemies in their minds,'[3] the prospect of serving for ever would be anything but pleasant. But when the enmity is slain by the

---

[1] 1 Chron. xxviii. 9.　　[2] Rom. iv. 21.　　[3] Col. i. 21.

cross of Christ,[1] and all things are become new,[2] and the love of Christ constraineth,[3] then it is among the brightest of our many bright anticipations, and everlasting joy and everlasting service become almost synonymous.

Rest is sweet, but service (in proportion to our love) is sweeter still. Those who have served much here cannot but anticipate the fuller and more perfect service above. Those who have to do little more than 'stand and wait' here, will perhaps revel even more than others in the new experience of active service, coming at once, as it were, into its full delight.

The Hebrew servant had trial of his master's service for six years, and in the seventh he might go out free if he would. But then, ' if the servant shall plainly say' (plainly, avowedly, no mistake about it), 'I love my master, . . . I *will* not go out free,' then, publicly and legally, he was sealed to his service 'for ever.' It all depended on the love. He would say, ' I will not go away from thee;'[4] because he loveth thee and thine house, because he is well with thee.'

How this meets our case, dear fellow-servants! We do not want to 'go away from' Jesus, because we love Him ; and we love His house too,—not only, ' the house of God' with which so much of our service is connected, but ' His own house,' the 'spiritual house,' 'the blessed company of all faithful people.'

And are we not ' well ' with Him? Where else

---

1 Eph. ii. 16.        2 2 Cor. v. 17.
3 2 Cor. v. 14.        4 Deut. xv. 16.

so well? where else anything but *ill?* Has He not
dealt well with His servants?[1] What a chorus it
would be if we all spoke out, and said, 'I love my
Master, and it hath been well for me with Him'!
Why *don't* we speak out, and let people know what
a Master He is, and what a happy service His is?
Who is to speak out, if *we* have not a word to say
about it! Let us stand up for Jesus and His service,
every one of us!

Perhaps, when we do speak out, we shall realize
the joy of this promise as never before. It was not
till the servant had owned his love, and given up
'the rest of his time in the flesh,' and had his ear
bored, that the word was spoken, 'He shall serve
him for ever;'[2] and it is only the loving and consecrated heart that leaps up for joy at the heavenly
prospect: 'And His servants shall serve Him.'[3]

Think about it a little. What will it be to be
able at last to express not only all the love we now
feel, but all the perfected love of infinitely enlarged
capability of loving in the equally perfected service
of equally enlarged capability of serving?—able to
show Jesus a love which would burst our hearts if
poured into them now! Able to put all the new
rapture of praise into living action for Him! Able
to go on serving Him day and night,[4] without any
weariness in it, and never a hateful shadow of
weariness of it; without any interruptions; without
any mistakes at all; without any thinking how much
better some one else could have done it, or how
much better we ought to have done it; above all,

---

1 Ps. cxix. 65.       2 Ex. xxi. 6.
3 Rev. xxii. 3.       4 Rev. vii. 15.

without the least mixture of sin in motive or deed—pure, perfect service of Him whom we love and see face to face! What *can* be more joyful?

We are not told much about it, we could not understand it now; the secrets of this wonderful service will only be told when we are brought to His house above, and see what are the heavenly 'good works which God hath before ordained' (margin, *prepared*) for us.

How full of surprises the new service will be!—new powers, new and entirely congenial fellow-workers, new spheres, new ministries; only two things not new, if our earthly service has been true,—no new power, and no new end and aim, but the same, even His power and His glory! Then shall come the full accomplishment of the Messianic prophecy: 'A seed *shall* serve Him;'[1] and still we shall say (only I think we shall *sing* it), 'Thine is the kingdom, and the power, and the glory, for ever. Amen.'[2] 'Whose I am and whom I serve' *for ever!*[3]

> My Lord hath met my longing
>   With word of golden tone,
> That I shall serve for ever
>   Himself, Himself alone.
> 'Shall serve him,'—and 'for ever!'
>   Oh hope most sure, most fair!
> The perfect love outpouring,
>   In perfect service there!

---

[1] Ps. xxii. 30.      [2] Matt. vi. 13.      [3] Acts xxvii. 23.

17

# NINETEENTH DAY.

---

## Most Blessed for Ever.

'Thou hast made him most blessed for ever, Thou hast made him exceeding glad with Thy countenance.'—Ps. xxi. 6.

PROBABLY every one who reads this has at least one of those golden links to heaven which God's own hand has forged from our earthly treasures. It may be that the very nearest and dearest that had been given are now taken away. And how often 'no relation, only a dear friend' is an 'only' of heart-crushing emphasis!

Human comfort goes for very little in this; but let us lay our hearts open to the comfort wherewith we are comforted of God[1] Himself about it.

There is not much directly to ourselves; He knew that the truest and sweetest comfort would come by looking not at our loss, but at their gain.

Whatever this gain is, it is all His own actual and immediate doing. '*Thou* hast made him' (read here the name of the very one for whom we are mourning) 'most blessed.'

'Most!' How shall we reach that thought? Make a shining stairway of every bright beatitude in the Bible, blessed upon blessed, within and also far beyond our own experience. And when we

---

[1] 2 Cor. i. 4.

have built them up till they reach unto heaven, still this ' *most* blessed ' is beyond, out of our sight, in the unapproachable glory of God Himself. It will always be 'most,' for it is ' for ever '—everlasting light without a shadow, everlasting songs without a minor.

No more death, neither sorrow nor crying, neither shall there be any more pain.[1] 'And the inhabitant shall not say, I am sick.'[2] No more sunsets, no more days of mourning. The troubling of the wicked and the voice of the oppressor ceased for ever.[3] No more memory of troubles ; no more tears. No more anything that defileth ! All this only the negative side of our dear one's present blessedness

Then, the rest for the weary one, the keeping of the sabbath that remaineth, and yet the service free and perfect and perpetual. The crowns of life, of righteousness, and of glory. The great reward in heaven, full of love-surprise to the consciously unprofitable servant. The far more exceeding weight of glory[4] borne by some to whom the grasshopper had been a burden.[5]

The scene of all the blessedness,—the better country, the continuing city, the King's palace, the Father's house, the prepared mansions (perhaps full of contrasts to the past pilgrimage)—all summed up in the transcendent simplicity and sublimity of His words, ' That where I am, *there* ye may be also.'

The music ! What will all the harps of heaven

---

[1] Rev. xxi. 4.  [2] Isa. xxxiii. 24.  [3] Job iii. 17, 18.
[4] 2 Cor. iv. 17.  [5] Eccles. xii. 5.

be to the thrill of the One Voice, saying, ' Come, ye blessed of my Father ! '[1] and, ' Well done, good and faithful servant, enter thou into the joy of thy Lord.'[2] Our dear ones *have heard that !* and that one word of the King must have made them *most* blessed for ever.

But more yet. ' Thou hast made him exceeding glad with thy countenance.' ' Hast,' for it is done. At this moment they *are* exceeding glad, and the certainty of it stills every quiver of our selfish love. The glory and joy of our Lord Christ are revealed to them, and they are ' glad also with exceeding joy,'[3] rejoicing together with Jesus.

How can they help reflecting His Divine joy when they see it no longer by faith and afar off, but visibly, actually ' face to face ! '[4] nay, more, ' eye to eye,' that very closest approach of tenderest intercourse too deep for words. They see Him ' as He is ; ' in all His beauty and love and glory ; through no veil, no glass, no tear-mist.

The prayer for them, ' The Lord lift up His coun tenance upon thee,'[5] is altogether fulfilled, and they are ' full of joy with Thy countenance.' And *every* other prayer we ever prayed for them is fulfilled exceeding abundantly, above all we asked or thought. We may not pray any more for them, because God has not left one possibility of blessedness unbestowed.

> ' Breaking the narrow prayers that may
> Befit your narrow hearts, away
> In His broad, loving will.'
> —*E. B. Browning.*

---

[1] Matt. xxv. 34.   [2] Matt. xxv. 21, 23.   [3] Luke xv. 6.
[4] 1 Cor. xiii. 12.   [5] Num. vi. 26.

God Himself, their exceeding joy, has done and
is doing His very best for them. ' Even so, Father!'[1]

> For I know
> That they who are not lost, but gone before,
> Are only waiting till I come; for death
> Has only parted us a little while,
> And has not severed e'en the finest strand
> In the eternal cable of our love :
> The very strain has twined it closer still,
> And added strength. The music of their lives
> Is nowise stilled, but blended so with songs
> Around the throne of God, that our poor ears
> No longer hear it

## TWENTIETH DAY.

# Do Thou for Me.

'Do Thou for Me.'—Ps. cix. 21.

THE Psalmist does not say what he wanted God
to do for him. He leaves it open. So this
most restful prayer is left open for all perplexed
hearts to appropriate ' according to their several ne-
cessities.' And so we leave it open for God to fill
up in His own way.

Only a trusting heart can pray this prayer at all:

---

[1] Matt. xi. 26.

the very utterance of it is an act of faith. We
could not ask any one whom we did not know inti-
mately and trust implicitly to ' do ' for us, without
even suggesting what.

Only a self-emptied heart can pray it. It is when
we have come to the end of our own resources, or
rather, come to see that we never had any at all,
that we are willing to accept the fact that we can
' do nothing,' and to let God do everything for us.

Only a loving heart can pray it. For nobody
likes another to take them and their affairs in hand,
and ' do ' for them, unless that other is cordially
loved. We might submit to it, but we should not
like it, and certainly should not seek it.

So, if we have caught at this little prayer as being
just what we want, just what it seems a real rest to
say, I think it shows that we do trust in Him and
not in ourselves, and that we do love Him really and
truly. There is sure to be a preface to this prayer.
' Neither know *we* what to do.'[1] Perhaps we have
been shrinking from being brought to this. Rather
let us give thanks for it. It is the step down from
the drifting wreck on to the ladder still hanging at
the side. Will another step be down into the dark
water? Go on, a little lower still, fear not! The
next is, ' We know not what we should pray for.'[2]
Now we have reached the lowest step. What next?
' Do Thou for me.' This is the step into the captain's boat. Now He will cut loose from the wreck
of our efforts, ladder and all will be left behind, and
we have nothing to do but to ' sit still ' and let Him

---

[1] 2 Chron. xx. 12.                    [2] Rom. viii. 26.

take us to our 'desired haven,' probably steering quite a different course from anything we should have thought best. Not seldom '*immediately* the ship is at the land whither' we went.

What may we, from His own word, expect in answer to this wide petition?

1. 'What His soul desireth, even that He doeth.'[1] Contrast this with our constantly felt inability to do a hundredth part of what we desire to do for those we love. Think of what God's desires must be for us, whom He so loves, that He spared not His own Son.[2] '*That* He doeth!'

2. 'He performeth the thing that is appointed for me.'[3] This is wonderfully inclusive; one should read over all the epistles to get a view of the things present and future, seen and unseen, the grace and the glory that He has appointed for us. It includes also all the 'good works which God hath before ordained, that we should walk in them.' It will not be our performance of them, but His; for He 'worketh in you to will and to do,'[4] and 'Thou also hast wrought all our works in us.'[5]

3. The beautiful old translation says, He 'shall perform the cause which I have in hand.'[6] Does not that make it very real to us to-day? Just the very thing that 'I have in hand,' my own particular bit of work to-day—this cause that I cannot manage, this thing that I undertook in miscalculation of my own powers, *this* is what I may ask Him to do 'for

---

[1] Job xxiii. 13.
[4] Phil. ii. 13.
[2] Rom. viii. 32.
[5] Isa. xxvi. 12.
[3] Job xxiii. 14.
[6] Ps. lvii. 2.

me,' and rest assured that He will perform it. 'The wise and their works are in the hand of God!'

4. He 'performeth all things for me.'[1] Does He mean as much as this? Well, He has caused it to be written for us 'that we might have hope;'[2] and what more do we want? Then *let* Him do it. *Let* Him perform all things for us.

Not some things, but *all* things; or the very things which we think there is no particular need for Him to perform will be all failures—wood, hay, and stubble to be burnt up. One by one let us claim this wonderful word; 'the thing of a day in his day,' 'as the matter shall require,' being always brought to Him with the God-given petition, 'Do Thou for me.'

Do not wait to feel very much 'oppressed' before you say, 'O Lord, undertake for me.'[3] Far better say that at first than at last, as we have too often done! Bring the prayer in one hand, and the promises in the other, joining them in the faith-clasp of 'Do as Thou hast said!'[4] And put both the hands into the hand of Him whom the Father heareth always, saying, 'Do Thou for me, O Lord God, for Thy name's sake,' for the sake of Jehovah-Jesus, the mighty God, the everlasting Father, yet the Saviour of sinners.

---

[1] Ps. lvii. 2.
[2] Rom. xv. 4.
[3] Isa. xxxviii. 14.
[4] 2 Sam. vii. 2.

## TWENTY-FIRST DAY.

---

## Marvellously Helped.

'Marvellously helped.'—2 CHRON. xxvi. 15.

UZZIAH seems to have been the type of a variously busy and successful man. He had all sorts of irons in the fire. So many energetic interests and tastes, with both faculty and opportunity for developing them, must have made his life much more agreeable and lively than most royal careers. His architecture and his agriculture, his war organizations and his engineering, spread his name far abroad. For 'as long as he sought the Lord, God made him to prosper.' Yet the end of his story is a strange contrast—a leper, dwelling in a several house, and cut off from the house of the Lord.

Where was the turning-point? Probably in the words, 'He strengthened *himself* exceedingly' It had been God's help and strength before, and he had risen very high. Then he thought he was strong, and he was brought fearfully low.

'Marvellously helped *till* he was strong' Then who would not be always weak, that they might be always 'marvellously helped!'

'Marvellously!' For is it not wonderful that God should help us at all? Have we not wondered hundreds of times at the singular help He has given? If we have not, what ungrateful blindness! For He has been giving it ever since we were helpless babies. 'Through Thee have I been holden up ever since I was born.'[1] How much of His help has been forgotten or altogether unnoticed.

The very little things, the microscopical helpings, often seem most marvellous of all, when we consider that it was Jehovah Himself who stooped to the tiny need of a moment. And the greater matters prove themselves to be the Lord's doing, just because they are so marvellous in our eyes.

Why should we fear being brought to some depth of perplexity and trouble when we know He will be true to His name, and be 'our Help,' so that we shall be even 'men wondered at' because so marvellously helped!

It is not a mere expression. The Bible always means what it says; and so the help to Uzziah, and the same help with which God makes us to prosper, is literally 'marvellous.' We do wonder at it, or ought to wonder at it. Wonder is one of the God-given faculties which distinguish us from the beasts that perish. And He gives us grand scope for its happy exercise not merely in His works in general, but in His dealings with us in particular. But wonder is always founded upon observation. We do not wonder at that which we do not observe. So, if we have not wondered very much at the help He has given us, it is because we have not noticed, nor considered very much, how great things He hath done for us.

---

[1] Ps. lxxi. 6, P. B. V.

Let us turn our special attention to it each day. We are wanting help of all kinds all day long ; now just observe how He gives it ! Even if nothing the least unusual happens, the *opened* and *watching* eye will see that the whole day is one sweet story of marvellous help. And perhaps the greatest marvel will be, that He has helped us to *see* His help after very much practical blindness to it. And then the marvelling will rise into praising 'the name of the Lord your God, that hath dealt wondrously with you.'[1]

The times of marvellous help are times of danger. 'When thou hast eaten and art full, . . . and all that thou hast is multiplied,' 'beware lest' '*then* thy heart be lifted up.'[2] '*When* he was strong, his heart was lifted up to his destruction.'[3] Unclasp the ivy from the elm, and it is prostrate at once. Thank God, if He keeps us realizing, amidst the busiest work, and the pleasantest success, that we have no power *at all* of ourselves to help ourselves ! Then there will be nothing to hinder His 'continual help.' As long as we say quite unreservedly, 'My help cometh from the Lord,'[4] the help will come. As long as we are saying, 'Thou art my help,' 'He *is* our help,' 'a very present help.' Then we shall not 'be holpen with a *little* help,' which is too often all we really expect from our omnipotent Helper, just because we do not feel that we have '*no* might.' Peter was a good swimmer, but he did not say, 'Lord, help me to swim ! ' He said, 'Lord, *save* me ! '[5] and so the Master's help

---

[1] Joel ii. 26.    [2] Deut. viii. 11–14.    [3] 2 Chron. xxvi. 16.
[4] Ps. cxxi. 2.    [5] Matt. xiv. 30, 31.

was instant and complete. 'Most gladly therefore will I rather glory in my infirmities, that the power of Christ may rest upon me.'[1]

> The Lord *hath* done great things for thee!
>   All through the fleeted days
> Jehovah hath dealt wondrously;
>   Lift up thy heart and praise!
> For greater things thine eyes shall see,
>   Child of His loving choice!
> The Lord *will* do great things for thee;
>   Fear not, be glad, rejoice!

---

# TWENTY-SECOND DAY.

---

## Thou Understandest.

'Thou understandest my thought.'—Ps. cxxxix. 2.

WHO does not know what it is to be misunderstood? Perhaps no one ever is always and perfectly understood, because so few Christians are like their Master in having the spirit of '*quick* understanding.'[2] But this does not make it the less trying to you; and you do not feel able to say with St. Paul, 'With me it is a very small thing.'[3] But this precious Word, which meets every need, gives you a stepping-stone which is quite enough to ena-

---

[1] 2 Cor. xii. 9.     [2] Isa. xi. 3.     [3] 1 Cor. iv. 3.

ble you to reach that brave position, if you will
only stand on it. '*Thou* understandest my thought.'

Even if others 'daily mistake' your words, He
understands your thought, and is not this infinitely
better? He Himself, your ever-loving, ever-pres-
ent Father, understands. He understands perfectly
just what and just when others do not. Not your
actions merely, but your thought—the central self
which no words can reveal to others. 'All my desire is before Thee.'[1] He understands how you desired to do the right thing when others thought you
did the wrong thing. He understands how His
poor weak child wants to please Him, and secretly
mourns over grieving Him. ' Thou understandest '
seems to go even a step further than the great comfort of ' Thou knowest ' ' His understanding is
infinite.'[2]

Perhaps you cannot even understand yourself,
saying, ' How can a man then understand his own
way?'[3] Even this He meets, for ' He declareth
unto man what is His thought.'[4] But are you
willing to let Him do this? He may show you
that those who have, as you suppose, misunderstood you, may have guessed right after all. He
may show you that your desire was not so honest,
your motives not so single as you fancied; that
there was self-will where you only recognized resolution, sin where you only recognized infirmity or
mistake. *Let* Him search, let Him ' declare ' it
unto you. For then He will declare another mes-

---

1 Ps. xxxviii. 9.                    2 Ps. cxlvii. 5.
3 Prov. xx. 24.                      4 Amos iv. 13.

sage to you: 'The blood of Jesus Christ His Son cleanseth us from all sin.'[1]

Then, when all is clear between Him and you, 'nothing between' (and let that '*when*' be '*now!*'), how sweet you will find it in the light of His forgiveness, and the new strength of His cleansing, to look up and say, '*Thou* understandest!' and wait patiently for Him to let you be understood or misunderstood, just as He will, even as Jesus did. For who was ever so misunderstood as He?

Almighty God, unto whom all hearts be open, all desires known, and from whom no secrets are hid; Cleanse the thoughts of our hearts by the inspiration of Thy Holy Spirit, that we may perfectly love Thee, and worthily magnify Thy holy name, through Christ our Lord. Amen.

———•———

## TWENTY-THIRD DAY.

——

## The Proof of His Purpose.

'No man can come unto me, except it were given him of my Father.'—JOHN vi. 65.

PERHAPS we have hardly counted this as any part of the royal comfort of our King. And yet it is full of 'strong consolation.'[2]

---

[1] 1 John i. 7.  [2] Heb. vi. 18.

If some of us were asked, 'How do you know you have everlasting life?' we might say, 'Because God has promised it.'[1] But how do you know He has promised it to you? And then if we answered, not conventionally, nor what we think we ought to say, but honestly what we think, we might say, 'Because I have believed and have come to Jesus.'[2] And this looks like resting our hope of salvation upon something that we have done, upon the fact of our having consciously believed and consciously 'come.' And then, of course, any whirlwind of doubt will raise dust enough to obscure that fact and all the comfort of it.

Yet there is grand comfort not in it, but in the glorious chain of which even this little human link is first forged and then held by Jehovah's own hand. Apart from this, it is worth nothing at all.

Do not shrink from the words; do not dare to explain them away; the Faithful and True Witness spoke them, the Holy Ghost has recorded them for ever: 'No man *can* come unto Me, except it were given unto him of My Father.'[3] There it stands; reiterated and strengthened instead of softened, because many even of His disciples murmured at it. So our coming to Jesus was not of ourselves; it was the gift of God[4]

How did the gift operate? Not by driving, but by drawing. 'No man can come to Me, except the Father which hath sent Me, draw him.'[5] Here comes in the great 'Whosoever *will*.'[6] For unless

---

[1] 1 John ii. 25.　　[2] John iii. 16.　　[3] John vi. 60-66.
[4] Eph. ii. 8.　　[5] John vi. 44.　　[6] Rev. xxii. 17.

and until the Father drew us, no mortal born of
Adam ever wanted to come to Jesus. There was
nothing else for it; He *had* to draw us, or we never
should have thought of wishing to come; nay, we
should have gone on distinctly willing *not* to come,
remaining aliens and enemies. Oh, the terrible
depth of depravity revealed by that keen sword-
word, 'Ye *will not* come to Me that ye might have
life.'[1] Settle it, then, that you never wanted to
come till He drew you, and praise Him for thus
beginning at the very beginning with you. You
were not ready for the 'whosoever will' before.
But no one ever had a glimmer of a *will* to come,
but that shining 'whosoever'[2] flashed its world-wide
splendour for their opening eyes.

By your will, now being wrought upon more and
more by His Spirit, the Father drew you, 'with
cords of a man, with bands of love.'[3] Just examine
now,—was it not so? was it with anything *but* loving-kindness that He drew you? Remember the
way by which He led you;[4] it may have been
hedged with thorns, but was it not 'paved with
love?' were not the very stones laid 'with fair
colours?'[5] Can you help seeing 'the loving-kind-
nesses of the Lord' all along? and what were they
lavished for, but to draw you?

That being acknowledged, what next? Loving-
kindness is the fruit and expression and absolute
proof of everlasting love. There is no escape from
this magnificent conclusion,—'Yea, I have loved
thee' (personally *thee*) 'with an everlasting love,'

---

[1] John v. 40.     [2] John iii. 15, 16.     [3] Hos. xi. 4.
[4] Deut. viii. 2     [5] Isa. liv. 11.

for '*therefore* with loving-kindness have I drawn thee' (personally *thee*).[1]  The coming was personal and individual; it may have been 'in the press,'[2] but we had nothing to do with the rest of the throng; we know in ourselves that we, you and I, individually, have come.  That personal coming was because of God the Father's personal drawing. I do not know how He drew you, you do not know how He drew me; but without it most certainly neither you nor I ever could have come, because we never *would* have come   This personal drawing by personal loving-kindness was because of personal and individual everlasting love.  Coming only be-- cause drawn, drawn only because loved !  Here we reach, and rest on, the firm foundation of the elect- ing love of God in Christ, proved by His drawing, resulting in our coming !  When we know that this sun is shining in the heaven of heavens, should we be watching every flicker of our little farthing candle of faith ?

> From no less fountain such a stream could flow,
>     No other root could yield so fair a flower ·
> Had He not loved, He had not drawn us so;
>     Had He not drawn, we had nor will nor power
> To rise, to come,—the Saviour had passed by
> Where we in blindness sat without one care or cry.

---

[1] Jer. xxxi. 3.                    [2] Mark v. 27.

18

## TWENTY-FOURTH DAY.

---

# The Garnering of the Least Grain.

'I will sift the house of Israel among all nations, like as corn is sifted in a sieve, yet shall not the least grain fall upon the earth.'—AMOS ix. 9.

THERE is double comfort here, as to *others* and as to *ourselves*.

As to others,—have not some of us had a scarcely detected notion, as if to some extent the salvation of others depended upon our efforts? Of course, we never put it in so many words; but has there not been something of a feeling that if we tried very hard to win a soul we should succeed, and if we did not try quite enough it would get lost? And this has made our service anxious and burdensome.

But what says Christ? 'All that the Father giveth Me shall come to Me.'[1] They shall come, for the Father will draw them, and Jesus will attract them, and the Holy Spirit will lead them. And the purpose precedes the promise, even as the promise precedes the call, and the call precedes the coming. Thus God first planned and proposed the ark for the salvation of Noah from the flood. Then He said, 'Thou *shalt come* into the ark.'[2] Long after

---

[1] John vi. 37.      [2] Gen. vi. 13, 16; ib. ver. 18.

that, when all things were ready, He said, ' Come thou and all thy house into the ark.'[1]   And then Noah went in ; and then ' the Lord shut him in.'[2]

Now let us, in our work, practically trust our Lord as to His purposes, promises, and calls ; quite satisfied that He ' will work, and who shall let it ? '[3] that He will not accidentally miss anybody, or lose anything of all that the Father hath given Him, for this is the Father's own will.[4]

It may seem a great trial of trust very often, but who is it that we have to trust thus unquestioningly and quietly?   Jesus Christ !   Cannot we trust Him whom the Father trusted with the tremendous work of redemption ?   Shall He not do right?   Cannot we trust the Good Shepherd about His own sheep? Why should it actually seem harder to trust Him about His own affairs than about our own ?   ' Trust in Him at *all* times,'[5] includes the time when we almost fancy the salvation of a dear one depends on our little bits of prayers and efforts.   Not that this trust will tend to easy-going idleness.   It never does this when it is real.   The deepest trust leads to the most powerful action.   It is the silencing oil that makes the machine obey the motive power with greatest readiness and result.

· Then the comfort for ourselves.   Satan has de sired to have us, that he may sift us as wheat ;[6] but the Lord Himself keeps the sieve in His own hand, and pledges His word that not the least grain shall fall on the earth.[7]

---

[1] Gen. vii. 1.       [2] Gen. vii. 7, 16.       [8] Isa. xliii. 13.
[4] John vi. 39.       [5] Ps. lxii. 8.       [6] Luke xxii. 31.
[7] Amos ix. 9.

We are so glad of that word, 'not the *least;*' not even me, though less than the least of all saints,[1] though feeling as if my only claim upon Christ Jesus is that I am the chief of sinners.[2]

'Not the least grain;' for He says, 'Ye shall be gathered one by one.' Think of His hand gathering you separately and individually out of His million-sheaved harvest; gathering you, one by one always, into His garner, even in that tremendous day of sifting, when He shall thoroughly purge His floor.[3] You may feel a little overlooked sometimes now; only one among so very many, and perhaps not first nor even second in anybody's love, or care, or interest, but He is watching His 'least grains' all the time. A flock of sheep look most uninterestingly alike and hopelessly undistinguishable to us, but a good shepherd knows every one quite well. Yes, the Good Shepherd calleth His own sheep by name here,[4] and 'in Zion every one of them appeareth before God.'[5]

For as He said at first, 'All that the Father giveth Me *shall come* to Me;'[6] so He says they '*shall come* from the east and west'[7] to receive the eternal welcome to the great feast of His kingdom; His '.sons *shall come* from far,'[8] 'they *shall come* up with acceptance;' till every one (and that means you and I) has heard His own 'Come, ye blessed of My Father,'[9] and has come into the fulness of all that He has prepared for us.

---

1 Eph. iii. 8.  2 1 Tim. i. 15.  3 Matt. iii. 12.
4 John x. 3.  5 Ps. lxxxiv. 7.  6 John vi. 37.
7 Matt. viii. 11.  8 Isa. lx. 4, 7.  9 Matt. xxv. 34.

Our Saviour and our King,
Enthroned and crowned above,
Shall with exceeding gladness bring
The children of His love.

All that the Father gave
His glory shall behold
Not one whom Jesus came to save
Is missing from His fold.

---

# TWENTY-FIFTH DAY.

---

# Vindication.

'And they shall know.'—EZEK. vi. 10; xxxvi. 38, etc.

'IF they only knew!' How often we say or think
this when 'they' misunderstand and misjudge
a person, a position, or an action, just because
'they' do not know what we know! How we chafe
against their speaking evil of things which they
know not, and most of all when 'they' speak
wrongly or unworthily of a person whom we know
much better than 'they' do! Ah! if they only
knew!

This grieving sense of the injustice of ignorance
rises to a feeling which needs much tempering of
faith and patience when we see our God Himself
misunderstood and misjudged. Oh, how they 'daily
mistake' His words and His character, and how it

*does* pain us ! How we do want them to know what He is, even so far as we are privileged to know Him ! How every word which shows they do not know His exceeding great love and absolute goodness, and the sublime balancing of all His attributes, jars upon us and distresses us, and causes a quick up-glance of His little children who have *known* the Father, and an involuntary closer nestling of their hand in His, as if they wanted to give Him fresh assurance of their love and confidence, just because these others do *not* know Him !

What an added grandeur it gives to our anticipations of the day when every eye shall see Him, that He, our Father, will be *known* at last to be what He is, and that Jesus, our Lord and Master, will be seen in His own glory, and can never, never be misunderstood any more? One revels in the thought of this great and eternal vindication of Him whom we love ; His ways, His works, His word all justified, and Himself revealed to the silenced universe, henceforth only to receive honour and glory and blessing ! It seems as if we should almost forget our own share in the glory and joy of His coming in this transcendent satisfaction

'And they *shall* know ! ' It is one of the shining threads that run all through the Bible, a supply indeed for the heart's desire of those who delight in the Lord. It is never long out of sight, judgments and mercies being alike sent for this great purpose, that men may know that Jehovah is Most High over all the earth. For this the waters of the Red Sea receded and returned again ; for this Jordan was dried up ; for this Goliath was delivered into David's hand; for this 185,000 of the Assyrians were smitten by God's angel; and many more instances. Throughout Ezekiel it seems the very keyword, recurring seventy-five times as the divine reason of divine doings, that they may ' know that I am the Lord '[1] Is there not a peculiar solace in this?

His word, too, shall be vindicated, for ' ye shall *know* that I the Lord have spoken it.'[2]

His ways shall be vindicated, for ' ye shall *know* that I have not done without cause all that I have done in it.'[3]  ' Thou *shalt* know hereafter.'[4]

His house shall be vindicated, for He will answer the prayers ascending from it, ' that they may *know* that thy name is called upon this house.'

And He will not leave His own children out of the great vindication; for ' the hand of the Lord shall be known toward His servants.'[5]  ' All that see them shall acknowledge them, that they are the seed which the Lord hath blessed.'[6]  More than that, the whole world shall ' *know* that Thou hast loved them as Thou hast loved Me,'[7] and ' I will make them . . . to know that I have loved thee.'[8] Is not this superabounding compensation for any tiny share we may now have in the world-wide misunderstanding of our Father's wisdom and our Saviour's love?

' And they shall know,' is not only for those who do not know at all; for ' at that day *ye* shall know that I am in My Father, and ye in Me, and I in you,'—revelations of the mysteries of Godhead and

---

[1] Ezek. xv. 7, etc.   [2] Ezek. xvii. 21.   [3] Ezek. xiv. 23.
[4] John xiii. 7.   [5] Isa. lxvi. 14.   [6] Isa. lxi. 9.
[7] John xvii. 23.   [8] Rev. iii. 9.

of the ineffable union of Christ with His people, which have not yet entered into our hearts to conceive. 'Then shall *we* know (if we follow on to know) the Lord.'[1] 'For now I know in part; but then shall I know even as also I am known.'[2]

Oh! the joy to see Thee reigning,
Thee, my own belovèd Lord!
Every tongue Thy name confessing,
Worship, honour, glory, blessing,
Brought to Thee with glad accord!
Thee, my Master and my Friend,
Vindicated and enthroned,
Unto earth's remotest end,
Glorified, adored, and owned!

# TWENTY-SIXTH DAY.

## Wakeful Hours.

'Thou holdest mine eyes waking.'—Ps. lxxvii. 4.

IF we could always say, night after night, 'I will both lay me down in peace and sleep,'[3] receiving in full measure the Lord's quiet gift to His beloved, we should not learn the disguised sweetness of this special word for the wakeful ones. When the wearisome nights come, it is hushing to know that they are appointed. But this is something

---

[1] Hos. vi. 3.     [2] 1 Cor. xiii. 12.     [3] Ps. iv. 8.

nearer and closer-bringing, something individual and personal ; not only an appointment, but an act of our Father : 'Thou *holdest* mine eyes waking.'[1] It is *not* that He is merely not giving us sleep; it is not a denial, but a different dealing. Every moment that the tired eyes are sleepless, it is because our Father is holding them waking. It seems so natural to say, 'How I wish I could go to sleep!' Yet even that restless wish may be soothed by the happy confidence in our Father's hand, which will not relax its 'hold' upon the weary eyelids until the right moment has come to let them fall in slumber.

Ah! but we say, 'It is not only *wish*, I really *want* sleep.' Well; wanting it is one thing, and needing it is another. For He is pledged to supply 'all our *need*, not all our *notions*' And if He holds our eyes waking, we may rest assured that, so long as He does so, it is not sleep but wakefulness that is our true need.

Now, if we first simply submit ourselves to the appointed wakefulness, instead of getting fidgeted because we cannot go to sleep, the resting in His will, even in this little thing, will bring a certain blessing. And the perfect learning of this little page in the great lesson-book of our Father's will, will make others easier and clearer.

Then, let us remember that He does nothing without a purpose, and that no dealing is meant to be resultless. So it is well to pray that we may make the most of the wakeful hours, that they may

---

[1] Ps. xxiii. 14.

be no more wasted ones than if we were up and dressed. They are His hours, for 'the night also is Thine.'[1] It will cost no more mental effort (nor so much) to ask Him to let them be holy hours, filled with His calming presence, than to let the mind run upon the thousand 'other things' which seem to find even busier entrance during the night.

> 'With thoughts of Christ and things divine
> Fill up this foolish heart of mine.'

It is an opportunity for proving the real power of the Holy Spirit to be greater than that of the Tempter. And He will without fail exert it, when sought for Christ's sake. He will teach us to commune with our own heart upon our bed, or perhaps simply to 'be still,'[2] which is, after all, the hardest and yet the sweetest lesson. He will bring to our remembrance many a word that Jesus has said, and even 'the night shall be light about'[3] us in the serene radiance of such rememberings. He will so apply the word of God that the promise shall be fulfilled: 'When thou awakest, it shall talk with thee.'[4] He will tune the silent hours, and give songs in the night, which shall blend in the Father's ear with the unheard melodies of angels.

Can we say, 'With my soul have I desired Thee in the night'?[5] and, 'By night on my bed I sought Him whom my soul loveth'?[6] Then he will fulfil that desire; the very wakefulness should be recognized as His direct dealing, and we may say,

---

[1] Ps. lxxiv. 16.  [2] Ps. iv. 4.  [3] Ps. cxxxix. 11.
[4] Prov. vi. 22.  [5] Isa. xxvi. 9.  [6] Cant. iii. 1, 4.

' Thou hast visited me in the night.'[1]   It is not an
angel that comes to you as to Elijah, and arouses
you from slumber, but the Lord of angels.   He
watches while you sleep, and when you are awake
you are still with Him who died for you, that
whether you wake or sleep, both literally and figura-
tively, you should live together with Him.

-------•-------

## TWENTY-SEVENTH DAY.

------

## Midnight Rememberings.

' When I remember Thee upon my bed.'—Ps. lxiii. 6.

MEMORY is never so busy as in the quiet time
while we are waiting for sleep ; and never,
perhaps, are we more tempted to useless recollec·
tions and idle reveries than ' in the night watches.'
Perhaps we have regretfully struggled against them ;
perhaps yielded to effortless indulgence in them,
and thought we could not help it, and were hardly
responsible for ' vain thoughts ' at such times.   But
here is full help and bright hope.   This night let
us ' remember Thee.'   We can only remember
what we already know ; oh praise Him then, that
we have material for memory !
    There is enough for all the wakeful nights of a

------

1 Ps. xvii. 3.

lifetime in the one word 'Thee.' It leads us
straight to 'His own self;' dwelling on that one
word, faith, hope, and love, wake up and feed and
grow. Then the holy remembrance, wrought by
His Spirit, widens. For 'we will remember the
*name* of the Lord our God,'[1] in its sweet and manifold revelations. 'I will remember the *years*' and
'the *works* of the Lord.' 'Surely I will remember
Thy *wonders* of old.'[2] Most of all 'we will remember Thy *love*,' the everlasting love of our
Father, the 'exceeding great love of our Master
and only Saviour,' the gracious, touching love of
our Comforter. And the remembrance of all this
love will include that of its grand act and proof,
'Thou shalt remember that . . . Jehovah thy God
redeemed thee.'[3]

Perhaps we know what it is to feel peculiarly
weary-hearted and dispirited 'on our beds.' But
when we say, 'O my God, my soul is cast down
within me;' let us add at once, '*Therefore* will I
remember Thee.'[4]

And what then? what comes of thus remembering Him? 'My soul' (yes, your soul) 'shall be
satisfied as with marrow and fatness, and my mouth
shall praise Thee with joyful lips: *when* I remember Thee upon my bed, and meditate on Thee in
the night watches.'[5] What can be a sweeter, fuller
promise than this!—our heart's desire fulfilled in
abundant satisfaction and joyful power of praise!
Yet there is a promise sweeter and more thrilling
still to the loving, longing heart. 'Thou meetest

---

[1] Ps. xx. 7.  [2] Ps. lxxvii. 10, 11.  [3] Deut. xv. 15.
[4] Ps. xlii. 6.  [5] Ps. lxiii. 5, 6.

. . . those that remember Thee in Thy ways.'[1]
And so, this very night, as you put away the profit-
less musings and memories, and remember Him
upon your bed, He will keep His word and meet
you. The darkness shall be verily the shadow of
His wing, for your feeble, yet Spirit-given remembrance, shall be met by His real and actual presence, for ' hath He said and shall He not do it?'[2]
Let us pray that this night ' the desire of our soul '
may be ' to Thy name, and to *the remembrance of
Thee.*'[3]

## TWENTY-EIGHTH DAY.

# Ube Bright Side of Growing Older.

' And thine age shall be clearer than the noonday; thou
shalt shine forth, thou shalt be as the morning.'—JOB xi. 17.

I SUPPOSE nobody ever did naturally like the
idea of getting older, after they had at least
' left school.' There is a sense of oppression and
depression about it. The irresistible, inevitable
onward march of moments and years without the
possibility of one instant's pause—a march that,
even while on the uphill side of life, is leading to
the downhill side—casts an autumn-like shadow
over even many a spring-birthday ; for perhaps this

---

1 Isa. lxiv. 5.          2 Num. xxiii. 19.          3 Isa. xxvi. 8.

is never more vividly felt than when one is only passing from May to June,—sometimes earlier still. But
how surely the Bible gives us the bright side of
everything! In this case it gives three bright sides
of a fact, which, without it, could not help being
gloomy.

First, it opens the sure prospect of *increasing
brightness* to those who have begun to walk in the
light. Even if the sun of our life has reached the
apparent zenith, and we have known a very noonday of mental and spiritual being, it is no poetic
'western shadows' that are to lengthen upon our
way, but 'our age is to be *clearer* than the noonday.'[1] How suggestive that word is! The light,
though intenser and nearer, shall dazzle less; 'in
Thy light shall we *see* light,'[2] be able to bear much
more of it, see it more clearly, see all else by it
more clearly, reflect it more clearly. We should
have said, 'At evening-time there shall be shadow;'
God says, 'At evening-time there shall be light'[3]

Also we are not to look for a very dismal after-
noon of life with only some final sunset glow; for
He says it 'shineth more and more unto the perfect
day;'[4] and 'more and more' leaves no dark inter-
vals; we are to expect a continually brightening
path. 'The future is one vista of brightness and
blessedness' to those who are willing only 'to walk
in the light.' Just think, when you are seven, or
ten, or twenty years older, that will only mean
seven, or ten, or twenty years' more experience of
His love and faithfulness, more light of the knowl-

---

[1] Job xi. 17.    [2] Ps. xxxvi. 9.    [3] Zech. xiv. 7.    [4] Prov. iv. 18.

edge of the glory of God in the face of Jesus Christ; and *still* the 'more and more unto the *per- fect* day,'[1] will be opening out before us! We are 'confident of this very thing!'[2]

The second bright side is *increasing fruitfulness.* Do not let us confuse between works and fruit. Many a saint in the land of Beulah is not able to *do* anything at all, and yet is bringing forth fruit unto God beyond the busiest workers. So that even when we come to the days when 'the strong men shall bow themselves,'[3] there may be more pleasant fruits for our Master, riper and fuller and sweeter, than ever before. For 'they shall still bring forth fruit in old age;'[4] and the man that simply 'trusteth in the Lord' 'shall not be careful in the year of drought, neither shall cease from yielding fruit.'[5]

Some of the fruits of the Spirit seem to be espe- cially and peculiarly characteristic of sanctified older years; and do we not want to bring them *all* forth? Look at the splendid ripeness of Abraham's 'faith' in his old age; the grandeur of Moses' 'meekness,' when he went up the mountain alone to die; the mellowness of St. Paul's 'joy' in his later epistles; and the wonderful 'gentleness' of St. John, which makes us almost forget his early character of 'a son of thunder,' wanting to call down God's lightnings of wrath. And 'the same Spirit' is given to us, that we too may bring forth 'fruit that may abound,'[6] and always 'more fruit.'[7]

The third bright side is brightest of all: '*Even*

---

[1] Prov. iv. 18.    [2] Phil. i. 6.    [3] Eccles. xii. 3.    [4] Ps. xcii. 14.
[5] Jer. xvii. 7, 8.    [6] Phil. iv. 17.    [7] John xv. 2.

*to your old age, I am He;*[1] always the same
Jehovah-Jesus; with us 'all the days,' bearing and
carrying us 'all the days;' reiterating His promise
—'even to hoar hairs will I carry you ; even
I will carry and will deliver you,'[2] just as He carried the lambs in His bosom.[3] For we shall always
be His little children, and 'doubtless'[4] He will
always be our Father. The rush of years cannot
touch this!

> Fear not the westering shadows,
>   O Children of the Day!
> For brighter still and brighter,
>   Shall be your homeward way.
> Resplendent as the morning,
>   With fuller glow and power,
> And clearer than the noonday,
>   Shall be your evening hour.

---

# TWENTY-NINTH DAY.

---

# The Earnests of More and More.

'He hath given you the former rain moderately, and He
will cause to come down for you the rain, the former rain,
and the latter rain in the first month.'—JOEL ii. 23.

GOD keeps writing a commentary on His Word
in the volume of our own experience. That

---

[1] Isa. xlvi. 4.
[3] Isa. xl. 11.
[2] Isa. lxiii. 9; ib. xlvi. 4.
[4] Isa. lxiii. 16.

is, in so far as we put that volume into His hands,
and do not think to fill it with our own scribble.
We are not to undervalue or neglect this commentary, but to use it as John Newton did, when
he wrote—

'His love in time past forbids me to think
He'll leave me at last in trouble to sink;
Each sweet Ebenezer I have in review
Confirms His good pleasure to help me quite through.'

The keywords of what the Spirit writes in it are,
'He hath,' and therefore 'He will.'  Every record
of love bears the great signatures, 'I am the Lord,
I change not;'[1] 'Jesus Christ, the same yesterday,
*and* to-day, *and* for ever.'[2]  Every Hitherto of
grace and help is a Henceforth of more grace and
more help.  Every experience of the realities of
faith widens the horizon of the possibilities of faith.
Every realized promise is the stepping-stone to one
yet unrealized.

This principle (and it is a very delightful one)
of arguing from what God has done for us to what
He will do for us, comes up perpetually in all parts
of His word.  If He *hath* given us the former rain,
it is the pledge and proof that 'He *will* cause to
come down for us the rain, the former rain, *and* the
latter rain;'[3] the blessing already given shall be
continued or repeated, and a fuller future one shall
be certainly added.  Manoah's wife argued well:
'If the Lord were pleased to kill us, He would not
. . . have showed us all these things, nor told us
such things as these.'[4]  Oh consider *what* things

---

[1] Mal. iii. 6.    [2] Heb. xiii. 8.    [3] Joel ii. 26.    [4] Judges xiii. 23.

19

the Lord has shown and told you and me! are they not abounding proofs of His purposes towards us? David made frequent use of the thought, arguing from the less to the greater: 'The Lord that delivered me out of the paw of the lion and out of the paw of the bear, He will deliver me out of the hand of this Philistine.'[1] St. Paul gives a close parallel, rising from temporal to spiritual deliverance: 'I was delivered out of the mouth of the lion. And the Lord shall deliver me from *every* evil work.'[2]

'Who delivered us from so great a death and doth deliver; in whom we trust that He will yet deliver us.'[3]

'The Lord *hath* heard the voice of my supplication; the Lord *will* receive my prayer.'[4] 'The Lord *hath* dealt bountifully with me,' comes first; then follows, 'Deal bountifully with Thy servant;' and then, 'Thou *shalt* deal bountifully with me.' 'The Lord *hath* done great things for us, whereof we are glad,'[5] leads us on to the prophecy, 'Be glad and rejoice, for the Lord *will* do great things.'[6]

The same argument is used in prayer. 'Pardon, I beseech Thee, the iniquity of Thy people, . . . as Thou *hast* forgiven this people, from Egypt even until now.'[7] 'Thou *hast* delivered my soul from death; *wilt Thou not* deliver my feet from falling?'[8] So in the lovely typical request of Achsah to her father, 'Give me a blessing; for thou *hast* given me a south land; give me also springs of water.'[9]

---

[1] 1 Sam. xvii. 37.  [2] 2 Tim. iv. 17, 18.  [3] 2 Cor. i. 10.
[4] Ps. vi. 9.  [5] Ps. cxxvi. 3.  [6] Joel ii. 21.
[7] Num. xiv. 19.  [8] Ps. lvi. 13.  [9] Judges i. 15.

Turn now to the basis of such expressions of trust and petition 'He that spared not His own Son,' —there is the entirely incontrovertible fact of what He hath done : ' shall He with Him also freely give us all things,'[1]—there is the inspired conclusion of what He will do. ' Having loved His own which were in the world, He loved them unto the end.'[2] ' He which *hath* begun a good work in you *will* perform it until the day of Jesus Christ.'[3] For how true is the type,-both as to each individual temple of the Holy Ghost, and ' all the building that groweth unto an holy temple in the Lord :'[4]—' The hands of Zerubbabel have laid the foundation of this house, his hands shall also finish it,'[5]—' His own house, whose house are we.'[6] Our Lord Jesus Christ endorses it in the very amen of His great prayer : ' I *have* declared unto them Thy name, and *will* declare it.'[7] Only let us simply receive and believe what He shows us and tells us, and then to every Nathanael who comes to Him, He will say, ' Because I said unto thee, I saw thee under the fig-tree, believest thou ? thou shalt see greater things than these.'[8] Then we shall have, personally and indeed, ' showers of blessing.'[9]

> Unto him that hath Thou givest
> Ever more abundantly ;
> Lord, I live because Thou livest,
> *Therefore* give more life to me,
> Therefore speed me in the race,
> Therefore let me grow in grace.

---

[1] Rom. viii. 32.  [2] John xiii. 1.  [3] Phil. i. 6.
[4] Eph. ii. 21.  [5] Zech. iv. 9.  [6] Heb. iii. 6.
[7] John xvii. 26.  [8] John i. 50.  [9] Ezek. xxxiv. 26.

## THIRTIETH DAY.

---

# The Perpetual Presence

'Lo, I am with you alway.'—MATT. xxviii. 20.

SOME of us think and say a good deal about 'a sense of His presence;' sometimes rejoicing in it, sometimes going mourning all the day long because we have it not; praying for it, and not always seeming to receive what we ask; measuring our own position, and sometimes even that of others, by it; now on the heights, now in the depths about it. And all this April-like gleam and gloom instead of steady summer glow, because we are turning our attention upon the *sense* of His presence, instead of the changeless *reality* of it!

All our trouble and disappointment about it is met by His own simple word, and vanishes in the simple faith that grasps it. For if Jesus says simply and absolutely, 'Lo, I *am* with you *alway*,' what have we to do with feeling or 'sense' about it? We have only to *believe* it, and to *recollect* it. And it is only by thus believing and recollecting that we can realize it.

It comes practically to this: Are you a disciple of the Lord Jesus at all? If so, He says to you, 'I am with you *alway*.' That overflows all the regrets of the past and all the possibilities of the future, and most certainly includes the present.

Therefore, at this very moment, as surely as your eyes rest on this page, so surely is the Lord Jesus with you. 'I *am*,' is neither 'I was,' nor 'I will be' It is always abreast of our lives, always encompassing us with salvation. It is a splendid perpetual '*Now*.' It always means 'I am with you *now*,' or it would cease to be 'I am' and 'alway.'

Is it not too bad to turn round upon that gracious presence, the Lord Jesus Christ's own personal presence here and now, and, without one note of faith or whisper of thanksgiving, say, 'Yes, but I don't realize it!' Then it is, after all, not the presence, but the realization that you are seeking—the shadow, not the substance! Honestly, it is so! For you have such absolute assurance of the reality, put into the very plainest words of promise that divine love could devise, that you dare not make Him a liar and say, 'No! He is *not* with me!' All you *can* say is, 'I don't feel a *sense* of His presence.' Well, then, be ashamed of doubting your beloved Master's faithfulness, and 'never open thy mouth any more'[1] in His presence about it. For those doubting, desponding words were said *in His presence*. He was *there, with* you, while you said or thought them. What must He have thought of them!

As the first hindrance to realization is not believing His promise, so the second is not *recollecting* it, not 'keeping it in memory.'[2] If we were always recollecting, we should be always realizing. But we go forth from faith to forgetfulness, and there

---

[1] Ezek. xvi. 63.          [2] 1 Cor. xv. 2.

seems no help for it.  Neither is there, in ourselves.
But ' in Me is thine help.'[1]  Jesus Himself had provided against this before He gave the promise.  He
said that the Holy Spirit should bring all things to
our remembrance.[2]  It is no use laying the blame
on our poor memories, when the Almighty Spirit is
sent that He may strengthen them.  Let us make
real use of this promise, and we shall certainly find
it sufficient for the need it meets.  He can, and He
will, give us that holy and blessed recollectedness,
which can make us dwell in an atmosphere of remembrance of His presence and promises, through
which all other things may pass and move without
removing it.

Unbelief and forgetfulness are the only shadows
which can come between us and His presence ;
though, when they have once made the separation,
there is room for all others.  Otherwise, though all
the shadows of earth fell around, none could fall
between ; and their very darkness could only in-
tensify the brightness of the pavilion in which we
dwell, the Secret of His Presence.  They could not
touch what one has called ' the unutterable joy of
shadowless communion.'

What shall we say to our Lord to-night?  He
says, ' I *am* with you alway.'  Shall we not put
away all the captious contradictoriness of quota-
tions of our imperfect and double-fettered experience, and say to Him, lovingly, confidingly, and
gratefully, ' Thou *art* with me ! '[3]

---

[1] Hos. xiii. 9.  [2] John xiv. 26.  [3] Ps. xxiii. 4.

' I am with thee ! '   He hath said it,
In His truth and tender grace !
Sealed the promise, grandly spoken,
With how many a mighty token
Of His love and faithfulness !

' I am with thee ! '   With thee always
All the nights and ' all the days ; '
Never failing, never frowning,
With His loving-kindness crowning,
Tuning all thy life to praise.

---

## THIRTY-FIRST DAY.

---

# Ube Fame=excelling Reality.

' Thou exceedest the fame that I heard.'—2 CHRON. ix. 6.

THOU ! Lord Jesus ! for whom have I in heaven but Thee ? and there is none upon earth that I desire beside Thee.[1]   Thou ! who hast loved me and washed me from my sins in Thine own blood. Thou ! who hast given Thyself for me.   Thou ! who hast redeemed me, called me, drawn me, waited for me.   Thou ! who hast given me Thy Holy Spirit to testify of Thee.   Thou ! whose life is mine, and with whom my life is entwined, so that nothing shall separate or entwine it.   '*Thou exceedest the fame that I heard !* '

---

[1] Ps. lxxiii. 25.

Yet I heard a great fame of Thee. They told me Thou wert gracious. They told me as much as they could put into words. And they said, ' Come and see '[1] I tried to come, but I could not see. My eyes were holden,[2] though Thou wast ' not far.'[3] Then I heard what Thou wast to others, and I knew that Thou wast the same Lord. But now I believe, not because of their saying, for I have heard Thee myself, and know that Thou art indeed the Christ, the Saviour of the world—my Saviour Thee, 'whom l shall see for myself,'[4] I now know for myself; my Lord and my God.[5]

I did not understand how there could be satisfaction here and now. It seemed necessarily future, in the very nature of things. It seemed, in spite of Thy promises, that the soul could never be filled with anything but heaven. But Thou fillest, Thou satisfiest it.

> Now it wonderingly rejoiceth,
>   Finds in Thee unearthly bliss,
> Rests in Thy divine perfection,
>   And is satisfied with this.
>
> Altogether fair and lovely,
>   Evermore the same to me ;
> Precious, infinite Lord Jesus,
>   *I am satisfied with Thee !*'
>
> —*Jean S. Pigott.*

For Thou *exceedest* the fame that I heard. I find in Thee more than I heard, more than I expected,

---

1 John i. 46.     2 Luke xxiv. 16.     3 Acts xvii. 27.
4 Job xix. 27.     5 John xx. 28.

'more than all.' The excellency of the knowledge of Thee, Christ Jesus my Lord, not only includes all other treasures of wisdom and knowledge, but outshines them all. Every other fame that I heard has had some touch of disappointment; imagination could always flash beyond reality, even if actual expectation, quieted by experience, had kept within the mark. But 'now I see'[1] that Thou exceedest all that God-given mental powers can reach; every glimpse is but an opening vista, all the music is but a prelude; what I know of Thee only magnifies the yet unknown. All the God-implanted craving for something beyond, all the instinct for the infinite, is met, responded to, satisfied in Thee. There is no part of my being but finds its full scope and its true sphere in Thee.

Thou exceedest all that I heard in every respect. No one could tell me what Thy pardoning love, Thy patience, Thy long-suffering would be to me. No one could tell me how Thy strength, Thy grace, Thy marvellous help would fit into the least as well as the greatest of my continual needs. No one could tell me what grace was poured into Thy lips for me.[2] Thou art *All* to *each* of Thy children; a complete and all excelling Christ to every one, as if it were only for each one. Thy secret is with each.[3] Thou givest the white stone and the new name which no man knoweth saving he that receiveth it.[4] And if Thou exceedest all that I heard, now and here amid the shadows and the veils, how

---

[1] John ix. 25.    [2] Ps. xlv. 2.
[3] Ps. xxv. 14.    [4] Rev. ii. 17.

far more exceeding will be Thy unshadowed and
unveiled glory! Lord Jesus, I bless Thee for Thy
promised eternity. For I shall need it all to praise
Thee, that Thou exceedest the fame that I heard!

# THE ROYAL INVITATION

OR

# DAILY THOUGHTS

OF

# Coming to Christ

# FIRST DAY.

---

## The Giver of the Invitation.

'Come unto ME.'—MATT. xi. 28.

THIS is the Royal Invitation. For it is given by the King of kings. We are so familiar with the words, that we fail to realize them. May the Holy Spirit open our ear that we may hear the voice of our King in them,[1] and that they may reach our souls with imperative power.[2] Then, 'they shall know in that day that I am He that doth speak.'[3]

'Lord, to whom shall we go?'[4] Not 'to *what* shall we go.' For the human heart within us craves a personal, living rest and refuge. No doctrines, however true; no systems, however perfect; nothing mental, moral, or spiritual, will do as the answer to this question of every soul that is not absolutely dead in trespasses and sins.[5] As surely as you and I are persons, individualities, real separate existences, so surely must we have a Person, no less real and individual, to whom to go in our more or less conscious need of salvation. And so

---

[1] John x 27.　　　[2] 1 Thess. i. 5.　　　[3] Isa. lii. 6.
[4] John vi. 68.　　　[5] Eph. ii. 1.

(297)

the great word of Invitation, Royal and Divine,
is given to us, ' Come unto ME I '

' Unto *Me.*'    Just think what that one word
means ! Seek out all the great and wonderful
titles of Christ for yourself, and write after each
one—' And *He* says, Come unto *Me !* ' Unto
Me, ' the mighty God,'[1] nothing less than that !
' Mighty to save '[2] and ' ready to save me.'[3]

Then seek out all the exquisitely winning
beauties of the character and words and ways of
Him who went about doing good,[4] till you ' have
heard Him and observed Him '[5] all through those
years of patient and perfect ministry, and recollect
all the time that it is *He* who says to you, ' Come
unto *Me !* '[6] Unto Him, the man Christ Jesus,[7]
full of compassion, and tender yet royal grace.

Then look at the great central scene of the
universe,—the central moment not of a world's
history only, but of eternity ;—look at the Saviour,
who His own self bare our sins in His own body
on the tree,[8] bowing His bleeding head under that
awful burden,[9] because His faithfulness was unto
the death,[10] and His love was strong as death ![11]
' Behold your God,'[12] and ' Behold the Man,'[13]
who loved you and gave Himself for you ;[14] hear
His own touching call, ' I said, Behold Me, behold
Me ! '[15] Look away from all the ' other things,'
look at the Crucified One, and, as you gaze, remember that *He* says, ' Come unto Me ! '

---

[1] Isa. ix. 6.      [2] Isa. lxiii. 1.      [3] Isa. xxxviii. 20.
[4] Acts x. 38.      [5] Hos. xiv. 8.      [6] Matt. xx. 28
[7] 1 Tim ii. 5.      [8] 1 Pet. ii. 24.      [9] Isa. liii. 6.
[10] John xiii. 1.      [11] Cant. viii. 6.      [12] Isa. xl. 9.
[13] John xix. 5.      [14] Gal. ii. 20.      [15] Isa. lxv. 1.

Is it nothing to you, all ye that pass by,[1] that both from the depth of sorrow and from the height of glory this Royal Invitation comes to you?

For it is the call not only of Jesus Crucified, but of Jesus Reigning and Jesus Coming. 'See that ye refuse not Him that speaketh,'[2] for He is coming to judge the quick and the dead.[3] He is reigning now, and there are no neutrals in His kingdom.[4] All are either willing and loyal subjects, or actual rebels,— those who have obeyed the King's call, and come, and those who have 'made light of it,'[5] and *not* come.

Which are you?

Think of the day when the great white throne is set,[6] and when the Son of man shall come in His glory;[7] when all will be gathered before Him, and He shall separate them one from another,[8] and know that it is 'this same Jesus'[9] who now says to you, 'Come unto *Me!*'

> Just as I am—without one plea,
> But that Thy blood was shed for me,
> And that Thou bidd'st me come to Thee,
> O Lamb of God, I come! 

---

[1] Lam. i. 12.    [2] Heb. xii. 25.    [3] Acts x. 42.
[4] Luke xi. 23.    [5] Matt. xxii. 5.    [6] Rev. xx. 11.
[7] Matt. xxv. 31.    [8] Matt. xxv. 32.    [9] Acts i. 11.

## SECOND DAY.

———

# What is ' Coming ' ?

' *Come* unto Me.'—MATT. xi. 28.

'BUT what is " coming " ? '
   One's very familiarity with the terms used
to express spiritual things, seems to have a ten-
dency to make one feel mystified about them.
And their very simplicity makes one suspicious,
as it were, that there must be some mysterious and
mystical meaning behind them,[1] because they
sound *too* easy and plain to have such great
import. ' Come ' means ' come,'—just that ! and
not some occult process of mental effort.

   What would you understand by it, if you heard
it to-day for the first time, never having had any
doubts or suppositions or previous notions whatever about it ? What does a little child understand by it ? It is positively too simple to be
made plainer by any amount of explanation. If
you could see the Lord Jesus standing there, right
before you, and you heard Him say, ' Come ! '[2]
would you say, ' What does " come " mean ? ' And
if the room were dark, so that you could only hear

---

1 1 Cor. ii. 14.            2 Matt. xiv. 29.

and not see, would it make any difference? Would you not turn instantly towards the 'Glorious Voice'?[1] Would you not, in heart, and will, and intention, instantaneously obey it?[2]—that is, if you *believed* it to be Himself[3] For 'he that cometh to God must believe that He is.'[4] The coming so hinges on that, as to be really the same thing. The moment you really believed, you would really come; and the moment you really come, you really believe. Now the Lord Jesus is as truly and actually 'nigh thee'[5] as if you could see Him. And He as truly and actually says 'Come' to you as if you heard Him. Fear not, believe only,[6] and *let* yourself come to Him straight away! 'Take with you words, and turn to the Lord: say unto Him, Take away all iniquity, and receive us graciously.'[7] And know that His answer is, 'Him that cometh to Me I will in no wise cast out.'[8]

Do you still feel unaccountably puzzled about it? Give a quiet hour to the records of how others came to Him. Begin with the eighth of St. Matthew, and trace out all through the Gospels how they came to Jesus with all sorts of different needs, and trace in these your own spiritual needs of cleansing, healing, salvation, guidance, sight, teaching. They knew what they wanted, and they knew Whom they wanted. And consequently they just *came*. Ask the Holy Spirit to show you what you want and Whom you want, and you will talk no more about

---

1 Isa. xxx. 30.  
4 John vi. 35.  
7 Hos. xiv. 2.  
2 Jer. iii. 22.  
5 Deut. xxx. 14.  
8 John vi. 37.  
3 Heb. xi. 6.  
6 Luke viii. 50.  

20

what it means, you will just *come* [1]  And then you will say, 'Now we believe, not because of thy saying; for we have heard Him ourselves, and know that this is indeed the Christ, the Saviour of the world;'[2] and you will say, '*My* Lord and *my* God.'[3]

———•———

## THIRD DAY.

———

## All Things are Ready.

'Come; for all things are now ready.'—LUKE xiv. 17.

*A*LL things!  God the Father is ready to save you.[4]  Jesus Christ is ready to receive you.[5] The Holy Spirit is ready to dwell in you.[6] Are you ready?

*All* things.  The 'great salvation' is ready for you.[7]  The full atonement is made for you.[8]  The eternal redemption is obtained for you.[9]  Are you ready?

*All* things.  The cleansing fountain is opened for you.[10]  The robe of righteousness is wrought for you.[11]  The way into the holiest is consecrated for you.[12]  Are you ready?

*All* things.  All things that pertain unto life and

---

1 John xii. 32.     2 John iv. 42.     3 John xx. 28.
4 Isa. xxxviii. 20.     5 John vi. 37.     6 Rom. viii. 9.
7 Heb. ii. 3.     8 Rom. v. 11.     9 Heb. ix. 12.
10 Zech. xiii. 1.     11 Rom. iii. 22.     12 Heb. x. 19, 20.

godliness are given you by His Divine power.[1]
Exceeding great and precious promises are given
you.[2] The supply of all your need is guaranteed
to you.[3] Strength and guidance, teaching and
keeping, are provided for you. Even the good
works in which you shall walk are prepared for
you.[4] A Father's love and care and a Saviour's
gift of peace are waiting for you. The feast is
spread for you.[5] All these things are ready for
you.[6] Are you ready for them?

Even if you did not heed nor believe any other
words of Jesus, could you—*can* you—doubt His
dying words? Surely they are worthy of all acceptation![7] What are they?

'IT IS FINISHED!'[8]

*What* is finished? 'I have finished the work
that Thou gavest Me to do.'[9] And what is that
work? Simply the work of our salvation. That is
the reason why all things are now ready, because
Jesus has finished that all-inclusive work. When
a thing is finished, how much is there left to do?
The question sounds too absurd with respect to ordinary things. We hardly take the trouble to answer, 'Why nothing, of course!' When Jesus has
finished the work, how much is there left for you to
do? Do you not see? *Nothing*, of course! You
have only to accept that work as really finished, and
accept His dying declaration that it is so.[10] What
further assurance would you have? Is not this
enough? Does your heart say Yes, or No?

---

1 1 Tim. iv. 8.  2 2 Pet. i. 3, 4.  3 Phil. iv. 19.
4 Eph. ii. 10.  5 Isa. xxv. 6.  6 Matt. xxii. 4.
7 1 Tim. i. 15.  8 John xix. 30.  9 John xvii. 4.
10 2 Tim. ii. 13.

'Do ye now believe?'[1] Settle that; and then what follows? Hear another word of the Faithful Witness.[2] Remember, it is no less true than the other. The Holy Lips that spoke that grand truth on the cross spoke nothing that could deceive or mislead. 'Verily, verily, I say unto you, He that believeth on Me hath everlasting life.'[3] What does this mean? Just what it says, and nothing less! It means that even if you never believed before—even if you never had a spark of faith or glimmer of hope before—yet if you have now given your heart-assent to Jesus and His finished work, you have now everlasting life![4] That heart-assent is believing;[5] and 'he that believeth on the Son hath everlasting life '[6] And this 'believing' is 'coming;'[7] and thus coming you shall find for yourself that all things are indeed ready.

What now? Shall praise be the only thing not ready? Will you not now prove your acceptance of the great gift of eternal life[8] by pouring out your thanks[9] at once for it, and prove your trust in the finished work[10] by praising the Saviour who died to finish it for you?[11]

> From the cross uplifted high,
> Where the Saviour deigns to die,
> What melodious sounds I hear,
> Bursting on my ravished ear!
> Love's redeeming work is done;
> Come, and welcome! sinner, come!

---

1 John xvi. 31; Mark ix. 24.   2 Rev. i. 5.   3 John vi. 47.
4 Acts viii. 32–39.   5 John iii. 16.   6 John iii. 36.
7 John vi. 35.   8 Rom. vi. 23; 2 Cor. ix. 15.   9 Cor. i. 12.
10 Isa. xii. 1, 2.   11 1 Pet. ii. 9.

Spread for thee the festal board,
See with richest dainties stored;
To thy Father's bosom pressed,
Yet again a child confessed,
Never from his house to roam;
Come, and welcome! sinner, come!

THOMAS HAWEIS.

---

# FOURTH DAY.

## Now.

'Come now.'—ISA. i. 18.

ALL things are *now* ready, therefore come *now!*

Experience does not run on rails laid regularly down, and readers do not always go hand in hand and heart to heart with the writer. I only wish they did. Then we might try to lead on more quickly, instead of reiterating the one call, in the hope that it may, first or last, be heard and obeyed.[1] Please do not imagine, because there are twenty-seven more chapters on the same subject, that there is any sort of slow necessary progress, any set of ideas and feelings to be gone or got through, gradually working up to the climax of 'coming.' This is all cut short by the simple word, 'Come *now!*' Nothing can be plainer. Therefore, if you postpone coming, you are calmly disobeying God. When we bid a child to 'come,' we do not

---

1 Isa. xxviii. 10.

count it obedience unless it comes at once, then
and there. It is not obedience if it stops to consider, and coolly tells you it is 'really thinking about
coming,' and waits to see how long you will choose
to go on calling it.[1]

What right have we to treat our holy Lord as we
would not think of letting a naughty child treat
us?[2] He says, 'Come now.' And 'now' does not
mean to-morrow.[3] 'To-day, if ye will hear His
voice, harden not your hearts.'[4]

Put it to yourself, what if *this night* God should
require your soul of you,[5] and you had not 'come?'
What if the summons finds you still far off, when
the Precious Blood was ready, by which you might
have been made nigh?[6] You do not know what a day
may bring forth.[7] There are plenty of things besides immediate death which may just as effectually
prevent your ever coming at all if you do not come
now. This might be your last free hour for coming. To-morrow the call may seem rather less
urgent, and the 'other things entering in'[8] may
deaden it, and the grieved Spirit may withdraw[9]
and cease to give you even your present inclination
to listen to it, and so you may drift on and on,
farther and farther from the haven of safety[10] (into
which you may enter *now* if you will), till it is out
of sight on the horizon. And then it may be too
late to turn the helm, and the current may be too
strong; and when the storm of mortal illness at

---

1 Rom. x. 21.  
2 Jer. vii. 13; Isa. lxv. 2.  
3 Jas. iv. 14.  
4 Heb. iv. 7.  
5 Luke xii. 20.  
6 Eph. ii. 13.  
7 Prov. xxvii. 1  
8 Mark iv. 19.  
9 Eph. iv. 30.  
10 Ps. li. 11.

last comes, you may find that you are too weak mentally or physically to rouse yourself even to hear, much less to come. What *can* one do when fever or exhaustion are triumphing over mind and body? Do not risk it. Come NOW! And 'though your sins be as scarlet, they shall be as white as snow; though they be red like crimson, they shall be as wool.'[1]

---

## FIFTH DAY.

## Coming into the Ark.

'Come thou, and all thy house, into the Ark.'—GEN. vii. 1.

NO need to repeat the story! We knew it all at six years old. To-day the words are sent to you, 'Come *thou!*'

We are either inside or outside the Ark. There is no half-way in this. Outside is death, inside is life.[2] Outside is certain, inevitable, utter destruction.[3] Inside is certain and complete safety.[4] Where are you at this moment? Perhaps you dare not say confidently and happily, 'I am inside;' and yet you do not like to look the alarming alternative in the face, and say, 'I am outside!' And you prefer trying to persuade yourself that you do not exactly know, and can't be expected to be able to

---

1 Isa. i. 18.      2 Deut. xxx. 15–19.
3 John iii. 36.      4 1 John v. 12.

answer such a question. And you say, perhaps with
a shade of annoyance, ' How *am* I to know ?'[1]
God's infallible Word tells you very plainly, 'If
any man be *in* Christ, he is a new creature : old
things are passed away ; behold, all things are
become new.'[2]   ' A very severe test !' you say.   I
cannot help that ; I can only tell you exactly what
God says.   ' I cannot reverse it,'[3] and you cannot
alter it.   So then, if old things have *not* passed
away in your life, and if you are *not* a new creature,[4]   ' born again,'[5] altogether different in heart
and life and love and aim,[6] you are not ' in Christ.'[7]
And if you are not ' *in* Christ,' you are *out* of
Christ,[8] outside the only place of safety.

  ' Come thou *into* the Ark !'   It is one of the
devices of the destroyer to delude you into fancy-
ing that no very decided step is necessary.   He is
very fond of the word ' gradually.'   You are to
become more earnest—gradually.   You are to find
salvation—gradually.   You are to turn your mind
to God—gradually.   Did you ever think that God
never once uses this word nor anything like it ?
Neither the word nor the sense of it occurs in any
way in the whole Bible with reference to salvation.[9]
You might have been ' gradually' approaching the
Ark, and ' gradually' making up your mind to
enter ; but unless you took the one step *into* the
Ark, the one step from outside to inside, what
would have been your fate when the door was shut ?[10]

---

1 1 John v. 13.          2 2 Cor. v. 17.          3 Num. xxiii. 20.
4 Gal. vi. 15.          5 John iii. 3..          6 1 John iii. 14.
7 Eph. ii. 12, 13.          8 Acts iv. 12.          9 Prov. xviii. 10.
10 Gen. vii. 21, 22.

' Come *thou* into the Ark ! ' I want the call to haunt you, to ring in your ears all day and all night, *till you come.*[1]

For at this moment, if you are not *in* the Ark, you are in more awful danger than you can conceive. Just because you know it is so awful, you shut your eyes and try *not* to think of it ! But there it is, all the same. Any moment the door may be shut for you.[2] Any hour may be the sunset of your day of grace, with no twilight of possibilities of salvation beyond.[3] And then, as the tree falleth, so it lieth.[4] As death finds you, so the judgment will find you.[5] Where it finds you, inside or outside the Ark, there the day of the Lord will find you, 'in the which the heavens shall pass away with a great noise, and the elements shall melt with fervent heat; the earth also, and the works that are therein, shall be burned up.'[6] What will you do then,[7] when neither heavens nor earth afford even a standing place for you ?[8]

But ' come thou *into the Ark !* ' Jesus is the Ark. He is the hiding-place[9] from that fiery tempest. 'I flee unto Thee to hide me '[10] ' from the wrath to come.'[11] ' Thou art my Hiding-place.'[12]

He who brings the flood[13] has provided the Ark. And the door is open. It *will* be shut some day —it may be shut to-morrow. What will you do if you find yourself not shut *in*,[14] but shut *out ?* Whose fault is it if you do not enter in and be saved?

---

1 Heb. xii. 25.
4 Eccl. xi. 3.
7 Jer. v. 31.
10 Ps. cxliii. 9.
13 Gen. vi. 17.

2 Matt. xxv. 10.
5 Rev. xx. 12.
8 Rev. vi. 17.
11 Matt. iii. 7.
14 Gen. vii. 16.

3 Luke xiii. 25–28.
6 2 Pet. iii. 10.
9 Isa. xxxii. 2.
12 Ps. xxxii. 7.

Noah did not put it off.  He and his family entered the self-same day into the Ark.[1]  I wonder if any of Noah's acquaintances were thinking about coming when the flood overtook them, and even coming 'gradually' nearer!  We are told that 'Noah *only*[2] remained alive, and they that were with him *in* the Ark.'  Then, once more, ' *Come* thou into the Ark,' that when the 'great and terrible day'[3] comes, you may be 'found of Him in peace,'[4] 'found *in* Him.'[5]

> The rising tempest sweeps the sky,
> The rain descends, the winds are high;
> The waters swell, and death and fear
> Beset thy path, no refuge near;
>      Haste, traveller, haste!
>
> Oh, haste! a shelter you may gain,
> A covert from the wind and rain,
> A hiding-place, a rest, a home,
> A refuge from the wrath to come:
>      Haste, traveller, haste!

W. B. COLLYER.

---

1 Gen. vii. 13.          2 Gen. vii. 23.          3 Joel ii. 31.
4 2 Pet. iii. 14.        5 Phil. iii. 9.

# SIXTH DAY.

---

## Drawn into the Ark.

'Thou shalt come into the Ark.'—GEN. vi. 18.

YOU would like to take this great step out of danger into safety; but you find it very hard, though it sounds very easy. You feel as if you had spiritual nightmare,—seeing the danger, and not able to stir hand or foot to escape it.[1]

Perhaps every one who comes to Christ has this sense of utter helplessness about it.[2] This is because the Holy Spirit must convince us that the whole thing is God's doing, and not ours, so that He may have *all* the glory of saving us from beginning to end.[3] It is not at all because He is not willing to save us, but just because He *is* willing, that He lets us find out for ourselves that our own will is so numb that it cannot rouse and move without the fire of His love and grace.[4]

Now just trust His promise, 'Thou shalt come into the Ark;' in other words, believe that His power and love are even now being exerted upon

---

[1] Rom. v. 6.
[3] Isa. xlii. 8; ib. lix. 16.
[2] Deut. xxxii. 36.
[4] Eph. ii. 1.

you, and that your sense of helplessness is only part of His wonderful way of drawing you to Jesus. God the Father is 'not willing that any should perish,[1] but that all should come to repentance.'[2]

Then why do any perish? Simply because they *won't* come; because they will not yield to the winning love and the 'drawing' power which is now being put forth to save you, if, as you read this, you *want* to be saved. There is no sadder word in the Bible than 'Ye *will* not come to Me, that ye might have life.'[3] But if you are saying, ever so feebly and faintly, 'I will,' God meets it with His strong and gracious 'Thou *shalt*.'[4]

Do not fear to take the '*Thou*' to yourself. Remember the great 'Whosoever will,'[5] and look up at this star of promise in the dark, 'Thou shalt come into the Ark.' Jesus said, 'All that the Father giveth Me *shall* come to Me.'[6] And the Father says, 'I will cause him to draw near, and he shall approach unto Me; for who is this that engaged his heart to approach unto Me?'[7] Whose heart? Is it not yours? You would hardly be reading these pages, if your heart were not at all engaged to approach unto Him. And if it is so engaged, who engaged it? Who but the God from whom alone *all* holy desires do proceed?

Then go on a few verses farther, and see the word of the Lord to you. 'Yea, I have loved thee with an everlasting love; *therefore* with loving-kindness

---

[1] 2 Pet. iii. 9.    [2] 1 Tim. ii. 4.    [3] John v. 40.
[4] Jer. iii. 19.    [5] Rev. xxii. 17.    [6] John vi. 37.
[7] Jer. xxx. 21.

have I drawn thee.'[1]  Now do not wrong, and wound, and insult that tremendous love by refusing to believe it.  He is at this moment giving you the personal proof of it, by 'drawing'[2] you even for these few minutes.  Do not resist the half-formed wish to come to Jesus.  It is very solemn to realize that this is no less than the Father's own drawing of you to His dear Son.[3]  Without it you could not come, because you know you would have refused to come;[4] but with it, if only you yield to it, 'thou *shalt* come into the Ark.'

When the dove found no rest for the sole of her foot, and returned to Noah because the waters were on the face of the whole earth, 'then he put forth his hand, and took her, and pulled her in'[5] (margin, 'caused her to come') 'unto him into the Ark.'  What a beautiful picture is this little helpless tired dove[6] of our helplessness and weariness, and the kind Hand, strong and tender, which does not leave us to flutter and beat against a closed window, but takes us, and *pulls* us '*unto* Him,'[7] *into* the Ark!'

So we have the willingness of the Father[8] in one part of the type,[9] and the willingness of the Son in another part,[10]—willingness to receive you into safety and rest.[11]  Then 'Come *thou* into the Ark!'[12]

---

1 Jer. xxxi. 3.  2 Hos. xi. 4.  3 John vi. 44.
4 Luke xiii. 34.  5 Gen. viii. 9.  6 Isa. lx. 8.
7 Luke xiv. 23.  8 Ezek. xviii. 23.  9 2 Cor. vi. 17.
10 Luke xv. 2.  11 John xii. 32.  12 Gen. vii. 1.

# SEVENTH DAY.

## Coming for Rest.

'Come unto Me, all ye that labour and are heavy laden, and
I will give you rest.'—MATT. xi. 28.

'THIS is *not* your rest.'[1] God says so, and
therefore it is no use seeking or hoping or
trying for it.[2] You may as well give up first as
last. The dove found no rest for the sole of her
foot till she came to the ark ;[3] and neither will you.
And the end of the dreary vista of unrest all
through the years of a life without Christ, is, ' They
have no rest day nor night.'[4]

'The people shall weary themselves for very
vanity.'[5] Do you know anything about that?
'They weary themselves to commit iniquity.'[6]
'Thou art wearied in the greatness of thy way.'[7]
Do these words come home to you? Or, ' But
now He hath made me weary ; Thou hast made
desolate all my company ? '[8] Whether it is the
weariness of sin or of sorrow, of vanity or of deso-
lation (and sooner or later the one must lead into

---

1 Mic. ii. 10.          2 Eccl. ii. 17-20.          3 Gen. viii. 9.
4 Rev. xiv. 11.        5 Hab. ii. 13.              6 Jer. ix. 5.
7 Isa. lvii. 10.        8 Job xvi. 7.

the other), the gentle call floats over the troubled waters, ' Come unto Me all ye that labor ' (or ' are weary ') ' and I will give you rest.'

But stay; you may, or rather you must, put in a double claim to the promise. You may not be consciously, particularly weary or labouring; but whether conscious of it or not, you *are* heavy laden, unless the one great burden of sin is taken away from you.[1] It is a fact, whether the Holy Spirit has convinced you of it or not as yet,[2] that unless your iniquity is taken away by personal washing in the only Fountain,[3] you are in the position described in the 38th Psalm, ' Mine iniquities are gone over my head: as an heavy burden, they are too heavy for me.'[4] So much too heavy for you, that if you do not accept Christ's offer of rest from that burden,[5] you will never be able to find or follow the path of life.[6] But why bear it one minute longer when Jesus says, ' Come unto Me, all ye that are heavy laden, and I will give you rest ' ?

' He hath given us rest by *His* sorrow, and life by His death ;' ' rest from *thy* sorrow and from thy fear, and from thy hard bondage wherein thou wast made to serve.'[7] Come and take the gift ! It is gloriously real. It is no mere slight and temporary sense of relief. ' We which have believed *do* enter into rest.'[8]

And He gives us ' rest on *every* side,'[9]—complete rest, guarded and sheltered all round.[10]

---

1 Isa. i. 4; ib. liii. 6.  2 John xvi. 8, 9.
3 Zech. xiii. 1 ; 1 John i. 7.  4 Ps. xxxviii. 4.
5 Ps. lv. 22 ; Ezek. xxxiii. 10.  6 Ps. xvi. 11 ; 1 Pet ii. 24.
7 Isa. xiv. 3.  8 Heb. iv. 3.
9 1 Chron. xxii. 18.  10 1 Kings v. 4.

It is not only rest *from* all the weariness and bur
dens, but rest *in* Himself.   Jesus is spoken of in
type as 'the Man of  Rest,'[1] 'and His rest shall be
glorious.'[2]   It is this, His own Divine rest, that He
will give.

'This is the rest wherewith ye may cause the
weary to rest.'[3]   Is it not worth having?   Will you
not come for it?   You *cannot* have it without coming to Jesus;[4] but only come, and it shall be yours
—for there stands His word—and ' in returning and
rest shall ye be saved.'[5]

*1/1/17*

I heard the voice of Jesus say,
  ' Come unto Me and rest ;
Lay down, thou weary one, lay down
  Thy head upon My breast.'
I came to Jesus as I was,
  Weary, and worn, and sad ;
I found in Him a resting-place,
  And He has made me glad.
                              DR. H. BONAR.

---

[1] 1 Chron. xxii. 9.      [2] Isa. xi. 10.         [3] Isa. xxviii. 12.
[4] Hos. xiii. 9.          [5] Isa. xxx. 15.

# EIGHTH DAY.

## Want of Will.

' Ye will not come to Me, that ye might have life.'—JOHN
V. 40.

IT is almost certain that some whose eyes glance
over these pages will be conscious that they do
not very much care to come to Christ, for this is at
once the commonest and the most fatal hindrance.
You cannot honestly say that you *want* to come.
You perhaps go as far as to say, with momentary
seriousness, ' I wish that I wished ! ' but no farther.
In your inmost heart you would rather be ' let
alone,'[1] not considering that *that* is the most terribly certain beginning of doom.  You are not per
fectly comfortable, but you are not so uncomfortable as to feel inclined to make any effort.  And
as long as you can keep from thinking about it, you
*say* you are ' very happy.'  Now believe me, yours
is a ten times worse and more dangerous state than
if you were a condemned murderer, knowing his
doom, realizing his sin and *therefore* seeking the

---

[1] Hos. iv. 17.

Saviour and coming to Him 'with all the desire of his mind.'[1]

For so long as you are not willing, *i.e.*, not actually and actively willing to come (for that is the meaning of the original), of course you cannot come. And without coming to Jesus you cannot have life.[2] And if you do not have life, there is nothing but death for you,—the second death with all its unknown terrors, into the realities of which any moment may plunge you.[3] Your not believing this makes no difference to the fact.[4] Your doubting it makes no difference to its certainty. I assert it on the authority of the Word of God. 'I call heaven and earth to record this day against you, that I have set before you life and death. Therefore choose life.'[5] For in not willing life, you are willing death, and 'why will ye die?'[6]

*Why?* Is it not utterly unreasonable? Would any but a lunatic walk with mirth and fun over the thin crust which hides unknown depths of boiling lava? Would you enjoy a picnic in the midst of it? Yet this is less mad than what you are doing.

Then you will say, 'I can't help it! I can't make myself care!' Exactly so ; and just in this fact lies, not your excuse, but your one hope and help. You cannot make yourself care to flee from the wrath to come.[7] You cannot rouse yourself to be willing to come to Christ for salvation. But One can.[8] And you may and can ask for the Holy

1 Deut. xviii. 6.　　　2 1 John v. 12.　　　3 Rev. xxi. 8.
4 Rom. iii. 3, 4.　　　5 Deut. xxx. 19; Jer. xxi. 8.
6 Ezek. xviii. 31.　　　7 Matt. iii. 7.　　　8 Hos. xiii. 9.

Spirit to make you willing. You can say, ' O God, give me Thy Holy Spirit to make me willing to come, for Jesus Christ's sake.' God makes no condition whatever as to giving this. The Blessed Spirit is promised most simply and unconditionally ' to them that ask Him.'[1] *This* promise says nothing even about desiring or thirsting; it premises absolutely nothing, but comes to the lowest depths of sin-paralyzed will—it is only and simply, ' *Ask.* '

Remember that one spirit or the other is now working in you. It is very awful to read of ' the spirit that now worketh in the children of disobedience; '[2] and what is more direct disobedience than not coming when Jesus calls? Therefore ' ask,' and ask at once, for the other spirit, the Holy Spirit, who can make you ' willing in the day of His power,'[3]—God the Holy Ghost, who ' worketh in us to will.'[4]

Think of Jesus saying, ' How often would I,' ' but ye would not '[5] *He* is willing.

May He give you ' one heart to do the commandment of the King ! '[6]

Come, Holy Spirit, heavenly Dove,
With all Thy quickening powers !
Come, shed abroad a Saviour's love,
And that shall kindle ours !
DR. WATTS.

---

1 Luke xi. 9-13.  2 Eph. ii. 2.  3 Ps. cx. 3.
4 Phil. ii. 13.  5 Luke xiii. 34.  6 2 Chron. xxx. 12.

# NINTH DAY.

---

# The Call of the Spirit.

'And the Spirit and the Bride say, Come.'—REV. xxii. 17.

HAVE you thought about 'the love of the Spirit'?[1]  Have you realized that God's 'loving Spirit'[2] says to you, 'Come'?  Are you conscious that if you refuse to listen to this gentlest call, you are 'grieving'[3] the Holy Spirit of God, —'vexing'[4] Him by the rebellion to which this refusal really amounts,—'resisting'[5] the Holy Ghost, whose power alone can work[6] in you the holiness without which you can never see the Lord?[7]

Every 'Come!' in the Bible is the call of the Spirit.  For 'all Scripture is given by inspiration of God,'[8] and the 'holy men of God spake as they were moved by the Holy Ghost.'[9]  And every time that a still small voice in your heart says 'Come,' it is the call of the Spirit.  Every time the remembrance of the Saviour's sweetest spoken word floats

---

1 Rom. xv. 30.          2 Ps. cxliii. 10, P. V. B.          3 Eph. iv. 30.
4 Isa. lxiii. 10.          5 Acts vii. 51.          6 2 Thess. ii. 13.
7 Heb. xii. 14.          8 2 Tim. iii. 16.          9 2 Pet. i. 21.

across your mind, it is the Holy Spirit's fulfilment of our Lord's promise that 'He shall bring all things to your remembrance, whatsoever I have said unto you.'[1] Last time those words, 'Come unto Me,' came into your mind, whether in some wakeful night hour, or suddenly and unaccountably amid the stir of the day, did you think that it was the very voice of the Holy Spirit speaking in your heart? Or did you let other voices drown it, not knowing that the goodness of God was leading you by it?[2]

Every time an ambassador of Christ[3] bids you come, and every time that any one who loves Him tries to speak a word for Jesus to you, it is the call of the Spirit and the Bride; for the Bride is the Church of Christ,[4] and she is the privileged instrument through which the clear music of the call is oftenest heard.

What makes you take the trouble to read this book? Why is there any attraction at all for you in the subject? Is it not that the Holy Spirit is causing your heart to vibrate, it may be but very feebly as yet, at the thrill of His secret call? Your awakening wish to come is the echo of that call. If you stop and listen, it will be heard more distinctly and winningly. The call will grow fuller and stronger as you turn and yield, and follow it. And the same blessed Spirit will give you power to do this.[5] He will show you your need of Jesus, and He will testify of Jesus to you, so that you shall be

---

1 John xiv. 26.    2 Rom. ii. 4.    3 2 Cor. v. 20.
4 Eph. v. 25-32 ; 2Chron. xxxvi. 15, 16.    5 1 Thess. v. 24.

willing to come.[1]   Do you feel very helpless about
it ?[2]   Do you wish you had the mighty aid of the
Almighty Spirit, so that you might rise and come
while Jesus of Nazareth passeth by ?[3]   Then why do
you not ask for it ?   Who is to blame if you do
not have what is to be had for the asking ?[4]   Christ
Himself has put the promise in the very plainest
words ·  'Ask, and it shall be given you,' and
'Every one that asketh receiveth.'[5]   What could
you wish Him to say more ?  What could He possibly say more ?   Clearly, if you have not, it is
because you ask not.[6]   But if you *are* asking for
the Holy Spirit in the name of Jesus, you have already the earnest of the Spirit,[7] and you shall have
more and more.[8]   So take courage !

But it is no light thing to put away a holy desire,
however feeble;   because it sprang not from your
own heart, but is the voice of the Spirit saying,
Come!   It will not always speak, if not obeyed.
Turn back from Revelation to Genesis, and you
find the shadow of the bright light of the winning
call in the unchanged warning note :  'My Spirit
shall not always strive with man.'[9]   Not *always*,
dear, unknown friend, whom I would fain win for
my Lord,—not *always !*   But He is striving now,
He is calling now, 'To-day, if ye will hear His
voice.'[10]   Listen, yield, come !

---

1 John xv. 26.        2 John v. 7.        3 Mark x  47-49.
4 Luke xi. 13.        5 Matt. vii. 7, 8.    6 Jas. iv. 2.
7 2 Cor. i. 22.       8 Matt. xiii. 12.     9 Gen. vi. 3 ; Prov. xxix. 1.
10 Heb. iv. 7.

# TENTH DAY.

---

# Come and See.

'He (Jesus) saith unto them, Come and see.'  'Philip saith unto him, Come and See.'—JOHN i. 39, 46.

WHEN Jesus had found Philip, Philip *knew* that he had found Him. And the next thing to knowing that 'we have found Him' is to find some one else, and say, 'Come and see!' I say it now to you, dear friend, known or unknown, '.We have found Him!'[1] 'We see Jesus!'[2] If you only knew the irresistible longing,[3] the very heart's desire[4] that you should find and see Him too, you would pardon all the pertinacity, all the insistence, with which again and again we say, 'Come and see!' The woman of Samaria left her water-pot, and went her way into the city with the same message: 'Come, see a man which told me all things that ever I did.'[5] And we to whom Jesus has said, 'I that speak unto thee am He,'[6] cannot do otherwise or less.

---

1 John i. 45.     2 Heb. ii. 9.     3 2 Cor. v. 14.
4 Rom. x. 1.      5 John iv. 28, 29.   6 John iv. 26 ; 1 Cor. ix. 16.

It is not always very easy to say it. You little know how much it sometimes costs us![1] You do not know that though the few words seem so easily spoken, and you take them as a matter of course from us, because you know we are of 'that way'[2] of thinking, they may have cost us not a little wrestling with God for faith and courage to utter them, and an effort which will leave us weary and exhausted. But 'we cannot but speak the things which we have seen and heard; '[3] 'we also believe, and *therefore* speak.'[4] We have seen Jesus,[5] and therefore we must tell you of the sight, and entreat you to ' come and see.' Understand or misunderstand us as you will, we must 'say, Come ! '[6]

But what is it that we are so burningly eager for you to see ? Very likely you suppose it is just that we have a certain set of views that we have taken up, and we want you to hold the same. You think it is merely that we want to bring you over to our opinions, and that we want to have the satisfaction of getting you to agree with us ! Oh, how wide of the mark ! It is no such thing. We are not speaking of what we think, but 'we speak that we do know, and testify that we have seen.'[7] We have seen by faith[8] the only sight that is worth gazing upon, the sight that satisfies the angels,[9] the sight that is enough for the joy and satisfaction of immortal vision throughout eternity. One thing we know, that, whereas we were blind, now we see.[10]

---

1 2 Sam. xxiv. 24.  2 Acts xix. 9; ib. ix. 2.  3 Acts iv. 20.
4 2 Cor. iv. 13.  5 1 John i. 3.  6 Rev. xxii. 17.
7 1 John iv. 14; John iii. 11.  8 Heb. xi. 27.  9 1 Tim. iii. 16.
10 John ix. 25.

We see Jesus, as our Lord and our God.[1]

We see Him as the very Saviour we need, and the very Friend we craved.

We see Him as ' the Son of God, who loved me and gave Himself for me '[2]

We see Him wounded for our transgressions, and bruised for our iniquities ;[3] our Substitute and our Sin-bearer.

We see Him, too, crowned with glory and honour,[4] and we rejoice in His glory and beauty ·[5] we make our boast of Him.[6]

If you say to us, ' What is thy Beloved more than another beloved?'[7] we reply, ' My beloved is the chiefest among ten thousand. Yea, He is altogether lovely.'

It is not at all only for your own sakes that we want you so very much to come and see. We do want you to look and be saved.[8] But our earnestness has a stronger spring than even that. We love our Lord, so that we cannot bear Him not to be esteemed aright. We cannot bear Him to be thought little of, and to be misunderstood ;[9] it is pain, real pain, to us when He is not appreciated and loved and adored,[10]—when all that He has done is treated as not worth whole-hearted gratitude and love,[11]—when His great and blood-bought salvation is neglected.[12] For His own beloved sake, for His own glory's sake, we want you to come and see, that you may love and bless and glorify Him !

---

1 John xx. 28.  2 Gal. ii. 20.  3 Isa. liii. 5.
4 Heb. ii. 9.  5 Zech. ix. 17.  6 Ps. xxxiv. 2.
7 Cant. v. 9, 10, 16.  8 Isa. xlv. 22.  9 1 Pet. ii. 4.
10 Isa. liii. 3.  11 Lam. i. 12.  12 Heb. ii. 3.

But, remember, this is not only our feeble human entreaty; it is Jesus Himself who first said, and still says, ' Come and see ! ' *He* says, ' Behold Me, behold Me ! '[1]

I know what you will say when you have come. You will say, ' Howbeit, I believed not their words *until* I came, and mine eyes had seen it: and, behold, the half was not told me.[2] Thou exceedest the fame that I heard ! '[3]

O Master, blessed Master, it is hard indeed to know
That thousands round our daily path misunderstand Thee so!
Despised and rejected yet, no beauty they can see,
O King of glory and of grace, beloved Lord, in Thee.

O Saviour, precious Saviour, come in all Thy power and
　　grace,
And take away the veil that hides the glory of Thy face!
Oh, manifest the marvels of Thy tenderness and love,
And let thy name be blessed and praised all other names
　　above.

---

[1] Isa. lxv. 1.　　　[2] 1 Kings x. 7.　　　[3] 2 Chron. ix. 6.

## ELEVENTH DAY.

## 𝕿𝖍𝖊 𝕾𝖆𝖋𝖊 𝖁𝖊𝖓𝖙𝖚𝖗𝖊.

'Bid me come unto Thee.　.　.　.　And He said,
Come.'—MATT. xiv. 28, 29.

IF Jesus says, 'Come!' don't you think you
may venture?

Perhaps it is night in your soul,[1]—as dark as
ever it can be. It would not be so bad if you
could even distinctly see the waves of the troubled
sea[2] on which you are tossing. You do not know
where you are. All seems vague and uncertain and
wretched and confused.[3] And though the Lord
Jesus is very near you, though He has come to you
walking on the water, and has said, 'It is I, be not
afraid,'[4] you cannot see Him, and you are not at
all sure it is His voice;[5] or if it is, that He is
speaking to you. So of course you are 'troubled '[6]

And if, in this trouble, you go on trying to steer
and row for yourself, these same waves will prove

1 Ps. cvii. 14.　　　2 Job. xvi. 16.　　　3 Jer. xvii. 9.
4 Matt. xiv. 25.　　　5 Matt. xiv. 27.　　　6 Matt. xiv. 26.

themselves to be awful realities, and you will be lost in the storm. Do not venture that; but venture out through the darkness and upon the waves at the bare word of Jesus.

You do not need even to say, 'Lord, bid me come to Thee!' for He has done that already. Jesus *has* bid you 'Come!'[1] and the bidding would be no more real if He opened the heavens, and said it again to you from the right hand of the throne of God. So the only question is, Will you venture?

True, it is but a word, but think Whose word![2] Could the word that Jesus Christ Himself uttered be a vain deceit?[3] Is not the Person the guarantee of the word?[4] 'The word only,'[5] of the Son of God has proved enough for every one of the great multitude that no man could number,[6] and it will be enough for you.

It does not matter in the least that you cannot see, and that you cannot feel, and that you cannot hear or distinguish anything else at all.[7] It does not matter in the least that you feel miserable and confused, and that you don't know what will come next.[8] It does not matter in the least that you cannot exactly understand how this simple coming can result in calm, and peace, and safety, and finding yourself at the land.[9] It does not matter in the least that the waters are casting up all the mire and dirt[10] of all the sinfulness of heart and life, the 'old

---

1 Matt. xi. 28.     2 Matt. xxiv. 35.     3 John xii. 48.
4 Num. xxiii. 19.     5 Matt. viii. 8.     6 Rev. vii. 9.
7 Isa. l. 10.     8 Isa. ix. 5; 2 Chron. xx. 12.
9 John vi. 21.     10 Isa. lvii. 20.

sins,"[1] and the besetting sins.[2] It does not matter in the least that all the winds of doubt seem let loose upon you, boisterous and blowing from every point to which you turn.[3] All this, and everything else that is 'contrary,'[4] is only so much the more reason for the simple venture. Just only you 'come!' And even if in the very act of coming you are afraid,[5] and think you are beginning to sink, come on with the cry, 'Lord, save me!'[6] and immediately Jesus will save you, and with the strong grasp of His hand the unanswerable question will come, 'Wherefore didst thou doubt?'[7] You need not say, 'If I perish, I perish,'[8] for you will not perish, and cannot perish, in this blessed venture of your soul upon His word.[9] He 'will cause you to know His hand and His might;'[10] 'He will save, He will rejoice over thee with joy; *He* will rest in His love,'[11] and *you* shall rest in His love, now and for ever.

'They shall know in that day that I am He that doth speak; behold, it is I.'[12]

> Come, ye weary, heavy laden,
> Lost and ruined by the fall;
> If you tarry till you're better,
> You will never come at all.
> Not the righteous,
> Sinners Jesus came to call.
>
> Lo! the incarnate God, ascended,
> Pleads the merit of His blood;

---

1 2 Pet. i. 9.      2 Heb. xii. 1.      3 2 Tim. ii. 13.
4 Matt. xiv. 24.    5 Mark v. 33.      6 Matt. xiv. 30.
7 Matt. xiv. 31.    8 Esth. iv. 16.    9 John x. 27, 28.
10 Jer. xvi. 21.    11 Zeph. iii. 17.  12 Isa. lii. 6.

Venture on Him, venture wholly,
Let no other trust intrude.
None but Jesus
Can do helpless sinners good.

JOSEPH HART.

---

# TWELFTH DAY.

---

## Coming Boldly.

'Let us therefore come boldly unto the throne of grace, that
we may obtain mercy, and find grace to help in time of need.'
—HEB. iv. 16.

'THEREFORE!' because we have 'such an
High Priest,'[1] touched with the feeling of
our infirmities, and in all points tempted like as we
are;[2] because He is 'a Priest upon His throne,'[3] ever
living, with His royal power to save to the utter
most,[4] and His priestly power to make intercession;
'let us *therefore* come boldly unto the throne of
grace.'[5]

Boldness and faith go together; fear and unbe
lief go together.[6] 'If ye will not believe, surely
ye shall not be established.'[7] It is always want of
faith that is at the bottom of all fear. 'Why are
ye fearful?' is the question for those 'of little

---

1 Heb. vii. 26.      2 Heb. iv. 14, 15.      3 Zech. vi. 13.
4 Heb. vii. 25.      5 Heb. iv. 16.      6 Rev. xxi. 8.
7 Isa. vii. 9.

faith.'[1] So, in order to come boldly, and therefore joyfully, all we need is more faith in the Great
High Priest who sits upon the throne of grace.

Now, do not sigh, 'Ah, I wish I had more faith!'
It will not come to you by languid lamentations
about your want of faith. 'It is the gift of God.'[2]
And if thou knewest this gift of God,[3] and who it
is that only waits to be inquired of,[4] that He may
give it thee, surely thou wouldst ask of Him! For
He giveth to all men liberally, and upbraideth not,[5]
—not even with all your neglect of Him and His
gifts. Just *ask!* and he says, 'It shall be given
you.'[6] 'Ye have not, because ye ask not.'[7] And
let the least glimmer of dawning faith in your heart
lead you to go on asking, and to pray continually,
'Lord, increase our faith.'[8] Then you will be able
to come boldly; for 'in Christ Jesus our Lord
we have boldness and access with confidence by the
faith of Him.'[9]

People do not come for what they do not want.
Until the Holy Spirit shows us our need of mercy,
and puts reality into the Litany prayer, 'Have
mercy upon us miserable sinners,'[10] we shall never
come to the throne of grace to obtain mercy.

> 'He that into God's kingdom comes,
> Must enter by this door.'

So, if you have never yet felt that you could sincerely say, 'God be merciful to *me* a sinner'[11] (or,

---

| | | |
|---|---|---|
| 1 Matt. viii. 26. | 2 Eph. ii. 8. | 3 John iv. 10. |
| 4 Ezek. xxxvi. 37. | 5 Jas. i. 5. | 6 Matt. vii. 7. |
| 7 Jas. iv. 2. | 8 Luke xvii. 5. | 9 Eph. iii. 11, 12. |
| 10 Ps. li. 1. | 11 Luke xviii. 13. | |

as the Greek has it more emphatically, ' to me, *the*
sinner '), and therefore have never yet felt particularly anxious to come to the throne of grace to obtain it, I would urgently entreat you to pray,
' Lord, show me myself!' When the Holy Spirit
answers that prayer, you will be eager enough to
come and obtain mercy! It will be the one thing[1]
then that you will be particularly anxious about.

Obtaining mercy comes first; *then* finding grace
to help in time of need. You cannot reverse
God's order. You will not find grace to help in
time of need till you have sought and found mercy
to save. You have no right to reckon on God's
help and protection and guidance, and all the other
splendid privileges which He promises to 'the children of God by faith in Jesus Christ,'[2] until you
have this first blessing, the mercy of God in Christ
Jesus; for it is ' *in* ' Jesus Christ that all the promises of God are yea, and Amen.[3] But He is ' rich
in mercy,'[4] and ' delighteth in mercy.'[5] All who
have come to the throne of grace for it ' are now
the people of God, which had not obtained mercy,
but now have obtained mercy.'[6] And then no less
surely will they, and do they, ' find grace to help
in every time of need.'[7]

' Let *us* therefore come boldly ! '

> Behold the throne of grace !
> The promise calls me near;
> There Jesus shows a smiling face,
> And waits to answer prayer.

---

1 Luke x. 42.     2 Gal. iii. 26.     3 2 Cor. i. 19, 20,
4 Eph. ii. 4.     5 Mic. vii. 18.     6 1 Pet. ii. 10.
7 Heb. iv. 16.

My soul, ask what thou wilt,
  Thou canst not be too bold;
Since His own blood for thee He spilt,
  What else can He withhold?

JOHN NEWTON.

---

## THIRTEENTH DAY.

---

## A Hindrance.

' First be reconciled to thy brother, and then come and offer thy gift.'—MATT. v. 24.

IT is a strange gift that we have to bring,—so strange, that it is in one sense ' nothing,' and yet in another sense everything. He asks us for it, saying, ' Give Me thine heart;'[1] and this heart of ours, this gift that we are to bring, worthless and yet priceless,[2] is one mass of sins and burdens.[3] Jesus asks for it just as it is, with all the sins and all the burdens; and the moment it is given over to Him, the sins are cleansed and the burdens are borne for us.

Do you wish to come to Him with it, and yet find that there seems something preventing you from really doing so? If so, the verse at the head of this chapter may throw God's light upon the secret obstacle. ' Is there any secret thing with *thee ?* '[4]

---

[1] Prov. xxiii. 26.
[2] Jer. xvii. 9.
[3] Matt. xv. 19.
[4] Job xv. 11.

22

Christ will either accept the gift altogether, or not at all.[1] If there is something which you do not really mean to do right about,—some sin which you have no real intention of giving up,—it will be a fatal barrier. He forgives all or none. If you are but willing, His precious blood shall cleanse you from *all* sin.[2] But He does not save by halves; and if there is a sin knowingly kept back, then 'ye are yet in your sins,'[3] and 'thou hast neither part nor lot in this matter; *for* thy heart is not right in the sight of God.'[4]

This may seem a very stern way of putting it; but when such tremendous issues hang upon it, is it not folly to shrink from looking the matter straight in the face? The Lord says, 'First be reconciled to thy brother, and *then* come and offer thy gift.'

This may be literally your case. Some one may have somewhat against you,—an old quarrel, or a fresh misunderstanding,—and you are too proud to acknowledge your fault, or your share of it;[5] or you are too timid, or even too idle to do so. When there are faults on both sides, it is pretty often the one most in fault who is the least ready to forgive. Now do look into the matter, and see if you are truly[6] 'in love and charity with all men.'[7] It is no use trying to explain away your daily words, 'Forgive us our trespasses, as we forgive them that trespass against us,'[8] for Christ Himself has explained and emphasized them. He said, 'But if ye forgive not men their trespasses, neither will your

---

1 Hos. x. 2.       2 1 John i. 7.       3 1 Cor. xv. 17; ib. iii. 3.
4 Acts viii. 21.       5 Jas. v. 16.       6 Heb. xii. 14, 15.
7 1 John iii. 10, 15.       8 Matt. vi. 15.

Father forgive your trespasses.' There is no evading this. There is absolutely *no* forgiveness for you, if you do not forgive; for 'who can forgive sins but God only?'[1]

And it is no use saying, 'Well, I will forgive, but I can't forget!' You know quite well in your heart that the very tone in which you say that, shows that you are not really forgiving, and God knows what is at the bottom of your 'can't *forget!*'

Don't turn round fiercely, and say, 'But if I can't, I can't!' For 'the things which are impossible with men, are possible with God.'[2]

Read the 45th of Genesis, and see how Joseph forgave;[3] and remember that the same Spirit of God which was in him is freely promised to you for the asking.

And then look at the still greater example of perfect forgiveness,—hear the smitten King in His lonely death-agony saying, 'Father, forgive them!'[4] 'For He knew that forgiveness would raise them to the very level of His throne; so He must have literally loved His murderers with the love wherewith His Father loved Him.'[5] Oh, it is hard to forgive anything, when one looks away to the forgiveness of Jesus.[6]

*Then* come and offer thy gift.

---

[1] Mark ii. 7.   [2] Luke xviii. 27.   [3] Gen. xlv. 1-15.
[4] Luke xxiii. 34.   [5] John xvii. 26.   [6] Eph. iv. 32.

# FOURTEENTH DAY.

---

## The Entreaty to Come.

'Come near to me, I *pray* you.'—GEN. xlv. 4.

'THERE stood no man with him, while Joseph made himself known to his brethren. And he wept aloud.'[1] They had hated him, conspired against him to slay him, very nearly killed him, sold him into exile and slavery, and here was the brother's recompense for all this—love ! No such exquisite story of love and forgiveness was ever imagined by any writer ; no such climax of tenderness as Joseph's words through his tears, ' Come near to me, I pray you.' Only one thing surpasses the type, and that is the antitype.

Our Elder Brother was more than ' very nearly killed.' He poured out His soul unto death.[2] We are not innocent of His blood ;[3] for ' He was wounded for *our* transgressions, He was bruised for *our* iniquities.'[4] ' Christ died *for our sins*.'[5] Mark that,—not merely ' for us,' but '*for our sins*,'

---

1 Gen. xlv. 1.　　　　2 Isa. liii. 12.　　　　3 Zech. xiii. 6.
4 Isa. liii. 5.　　　　5 1 Cor. xv. 3.

for *yours.* And where has been the love and
gratitude that you have owed Him all this time?[1]
Where has been the mere acknowledgment of what
He has suffered for your sins?[2] He did this for
you, and because of you. And what have you done
for Him, and because of Him?[3]

And what could you now expect from Him?
What did Joseph's brothers expect after their be-
havior to him? Well may the Lord say, 'I know
the thoughts that I think towards you—thoughts of
peace, and not of evil.'[4] For just as Joseph's words
to his brethren were not, 'Go away, I will have no
more to do with you,' so the Lord Jesus 'upbraideth
not,' but says, 'Come near to Me, I *pray* you.'

His whole life says it. It is the epitome of all
He said and did,—winning, beseeching, entreating
the far-off to come nigh, giving His own blood that
they might be made nigh.[5]

What is the eloquence of 'those wounds in
Thine hands?'[6] Are they not always saying, 'I
*pray* you'? For 'all day long I have stretched forth
My hands unto a disobedient and gainsaying
people.'[7]

'All day long,' while you are dressing, and eat-
ing, and talking, and laughing, and working or
amusing yourself, Jesus is stretching forth His
hands to you, calling you, waiting for you, looking
for the first little thrill of recognition from you,
saying, 'I am Jesus whom thou persecutest,[8] whom
thou neglectest, whom thou grievest.'

---

1 Ps. cxvi. 12 ; 2 Cor v. 15.        2 1 Pet. iii. 18.
3 Phil. iii. 8.     4 Jer. xxix. 11.     5 Eph. ii. 13.
6 Zech. xiii. 6.     7 Rom. x. 21.     8 Acts ix. 5.

Joseph's brethren were troubled at his presence.[1]
Do *you* reply, ' Therefore I am troubled at His
presence ; when I consider, I am afraid of Him '?[2]
Would you, honestly, rather flee from His presence ?[3]
Stay and listen.

' Come near to Me, I pray you.'

There is forgiveness with Him ;[4] will **you** not
come and receive it ?—Forgiveness for you, though
every sin of yours that is forgiven had to be borne
in His dying agony.[5]  His love has not changed
from the moment when He said, ' Father, forgive
them '[6]  What must that love have been !  And
what must it be for you and me, for whom He cannot make the gracious excuse, ' They know not
what they do ! '

Come *alone* to Him, and Jesus will make **known**
Himself[7] and His forgiving love to you.

> One there is above all others,
>     Well deserves the name of Friend;
> His is love beyond a brother's,
>     Costly, free, and knows no end :
> They who once His kindness prove
> Find it everlasting love.
>
> JOHN NEWTON.

---

1 Gen. xlv. 3.     2 Job xxiii. 15.     8 Ps. cxxxix. 7.
4 Ps. cxxx. 4.     5 1 Pet. ii. 24.     6 Luke xxiii. 34.
7 Gen. xlv. 1.

## FIFTEENTH DAY.

## The Command to Come

'Come unto me. . . . Now thou art commanded, this do ye, . . . and come.'—GEN. xlv. 18, 19.

WE are too much inclined to forget that 'Come' is not merely an invitation, but a command. An ordinary invitation can be accepted or refused; but a Royal Invitation[1] is always a Royal Command, giving no option, but requiring obedience. Therefore, just so long as we are hanging back, just so long as we have not come to Jesus, we are living in a state of actual disobedience to Him.

Joseph, whose dealings with his brethren are among the most beautiful types, was to say to them not only, 'Come unto me,' but 'Now thou art *commanded*, this do ye,—and come!'

The Lord Jesus, the King of Glory, has said the very same words, 'Come unto Me!'[2] to you and me. And so we *are* commanded. There is no excusing ourselves by any uncertainty about it.

1 Matt. xxii. 2, 3.      2 Matt. xi. 28.

The very moment that 'Come'[1] first fell on our heart, the command was upon us, and we were responsible for obeying it. And every moment since, we have been disobeying the plainest and sweetest word of command that ever fell on mortal ear, unless we have really and truly 'come to Jesus.'

So it is not at all a light thing, but a heavy and tremendous sin in which we are living,—the sin of direct and continued disobedience to Christ.

If one *single* and *sudden* act of disobedience was enough to lose Paradise[2] and lead to incalculable consequences of misery,[3] what about this persistence in refusal[4] to obey this strong and gentle command, clearly understood, continually reiterated, and unmistakably personal, Christ's personal command to you personally? 'Death without mercy' is as terrible a punishment as can well be imagined; but what must be the 'much sorer punishment' than *that*, which is denounced by the Word of our God on those who, instead of merely 'despising Moses' law,' have 'trodden under foot the Son of God?'[5]

We must not and dare not leave out of sight, the awful revelation that it is the Lord Jesus Himself,[6] the very same tender Saviour who now bids you 'Come,' who will take vengeance in flaming fire on them 'that obey not the gospel of our Lord Jesus Christ,'[7] who shall be punished with everlasting destruction from the presence of the Lord.'[8]

---

1 Deut. xxx. 11, 14.    2 Gen. iii. 24.    3 Rom. v. 19.
4 Prov. i. 24-26.    5 Heb. x. 28, 29.    6 Acts i. 11.
7 2 Thess. i. 7-9.    8 Matt. xxv. 41, 46.

When I began to write this little book, I never meant to say all this. I only wanted to win you by the sweet, sweet music of my Master's call. I only meant to tell you of His patient, forbearing love,[1] waiting so long for you, wanting you to come to Him.[2] But what can I do? Half a truth is not 'the truth.' You may not like it; but I dare not speak to you only smooth things,[3] I dare not shun to declare unto you the whole counsel of God[4] in this matter. 'I cannot go beyond the word of the Lord my God to do *less.*'[5] I should come under the awful condemnation of those who ' take away from the words of the book,'[6] if I did not tell the whole message. The Lord has said, ' Diminish not a word,'[7] and so I entreat you to look for yourselves at the passages I have quoted, and ' *hear* the word of the Lord' in them.

Oh, ' see that ye refuse not Him that speaketh !'[8] If you do not obey the ' Come unto Me,' there remaineth nothing for you but the ' Depart from Me.'[9]

Life alone is found in Jesus,
Only there 'tis offered thee,
Offered without price or money,
'Tis the gift of God sent free:
Take salvation,
Take it now, and happy be.
ALBERT MIDLANE.

---

1 Rom. x. 21.  2 Rom. ii. 4.  3 Isa. xxx. 10.
4 Acts xx. 27.  5 Num. xxii. 18.  6 Rev. xxii. 19.
7 Jer. xxvi. 2.  8 Heb. xii. 25.  9 Matt. xxv. 41.

# SIXTEENTH DAY.

## Royal Largesse.

'Come unto Me : and I will give you the good of the land of
Egypt, and ye shall eat the fat of the land. . . . Also
regard not your stuff; for the good of all the land of Egypt is
yours.'—GEN. xlv. 18, 20.

'IF I become a Christian, I shall have to give up
so many things!'[1]   Spoken or unspoken, this
is the invariable thought of every one who has not
found Christ.  The presence of this thought is an
actual test as to whether you have come to Him or
not; for the moment you have really come, you
will know better!

'Giving up'[2] this, that, and the other, is a down-
right *unfair* way of putting it; unless, indeed, the
magnificent gain is distinctly set against the paltry
loss.  As well talk of an oak tree 'giving up' the
withered leaves which have clung to the dry twigs
all the winter, when the sap begins to rise fresh and
strong, and the promise of all the splendour of
summer foliage is near !

---

1 Matt. xix. 22.              2 Phil. iii. 7.

The sons of Jacob were called away from their famine-stricken fields by their brother, that they might be 'nourished '[1] by him, and share his prosperity, and dwell 'in the best of the land;'[2] receiving from his hand a place and possessions far beyond what they had 'given up.' Of course they could not have all this till they had actually come to him! Before they came, they had only his bare word for it.[3] But they considered his word enough, and they came; and he kept his word to the full.[4]

Not less, but infinitely more, does the Lord Jesus, our Lord and Brother, hold forth to you. Is His word worthy of less belief? Over and above the unspeakable gift of eternal life,[5] He promises to those who leave anything for His sake that they 'shall receive an hundred-fold *now, in this time !*'[6] Do you suppose He did not mean what He said?

Listen again to the twin promises, negative and positive, in their all-inclusive simplicity: 'No good thing will He withhold from them that walk uprightly;'[7] and 'The Lord will give that which is good.'[8] And yet your secret feeling is, that if you come and give yourself up to Him, you will have to go without all sorts of things that you fancy are good and nice and pleasant, and that you will find yourself let in for all sorts of things which do not seem to you 'good' at all![9] Is this fair, when he has said positively just the opposite?

---

1 Gen. xlv. 11.  2 Gen. xlvii. 11, 27.  3 Gen. xlvi. 31.
4 Gen. xlvii. 11, 12.  5 2 Cor. ix. 15.  6 Mark x. 30.
7 Ps. lxxxiv. 11.  8 Ps. lxxxv. 12; Matt. vii. 11.
9 Ps. xxxiv. 10.

Listen again to what He says to those who *have* come, and who are His own · 'Whether . . . the world, or life, or death, or things present, or things to come; *all are yours!*'[1]   What do you make of that?   It is not figurative, but perfectly true and literal.   Only you will never be able to understand it, until the next verse is true of you: 'Ye are Christ's.'[2]   *Then* another verse will be true of you: 'Now we have received, not the spirit of the world, but the spirit which is of God; that we might *know* the things which are freely given to us of God.'[3]   Ask for that blessed Spirit of God, and you will receive it,[4] and *then* you will understand.[5]

Knowing what he was purposing to do for them as soon as they came, Joseph naturally said to his brethren, 'Also regard not your stuff; for the good of all the land of Egypt is yours.'[6]   Take this advice, 'regard not your stuff!'   However much you have or may have to give up for Christ, oh, *do* believe the words of His prophet: 'The Lord is able to give thee *much more* than this!'[7]

Can you not instinctively feel what a thrill of deep triumphant joy there is in St. Paul's words. 'Yea, doubtless, and I count all things but loss for the excellency of the knowledge of Christ Jesus my Lord!'[8]   Did you ever feel anything like as glad as that?   Christ Jesus my Lord is willing and waiting to give that same fulness of gladness and blessing to every one who will take Him at His word and come to Him.

---

1 1 Cor. iii. 22.          2 1 Cor. iii. 23.          3 1 Cor. ii. 12..
4 Luke xi. 13.          5 Prov. xxviii. 5.          6 Gen. xlv. 20.
7 2 Chron. xxv. 9.     8 Phil. iii. 8.

Yes, to *you !*

> Oh, the happiness arising
>   From the life of grace within,
> When the soul is realizing
>   Conquests over hell and sin !
>     Happy moments !
>     Heavenly joys on earth begin.
>
> On the Saviour's fulness living,
>   All His saints obtain delight ;
> With the strength which He is giving,
>   They can wrestle, they can fight.
>     Happy moments,
>     When King Jesus is in sight !
>
> JOSEPH IRONS.

---

# SEVENTEENTH DAY.

---

# Tarry Not.

'Come down unto me, tarry not.'—GEN. xlv. 9.

IT is just this 'tarrying' that is hindering so many from coming to the Saviour. What reason could there be for Joseph's brethren to 'tarry,'[1] and go on starving a little longer in their own land, when Joseph was waiting to settle them and their father and their whole families in the land of Goshen 'in the best of the land ?'[2] And what reason can

---

1 Gen. xliii. 1, 2.　　　　2 Gen. xlvii. 11.

there be for you to tarry, and go on starved and
unsatisfied a little longer, when the Lord Jesus is
waiting to receive you into the 'pleasant land'[1] of
His all-satisfying love? Why tarry in the ' far
country'[2] with the husks and the heart-loneliness?
'Ye shall haste!' said Joseph, for his heart was
eager to do great things for them

If you grant the reality of Christ's love at all, do
you not see that delay in coming down to Him, and
hesitation in letting Him save you in His own way
(and there is no other), and putting Him off from
day to day, must be wounding His love?[3]

Why *do* you tarry? Have you any reason whatever to give Him? 'What wilt thou say?'[4] Do not
flatter yourself that all this delay and putting off is
any preparation for coming, much less any part of
coming to Him. There are no steps in coming to
Jesus. Either you come, or you do not come.
There is only the 'one step, out of self, into Christ.'
There are no gradations of approach marked out in
His Word. If you think there are, search and see;
do not take my word for it; look for yourself, and
see what is the Lord's word about it.[5]

You have nothing to gain, but very much, perhaps everything, to lose by 'tarrying.' You are
accumulating the guilt of disobedience. You are,
it may be very unconsciously, hardening your
heart,[6] and making the great step more and more
difficult. Instead of being in a better position for
coming to-morrow, you will be in a worse one.[7]

---

1 Ps. cvi. 24.      2 Luke xv. 13, 16.      3 Cant. v. 2, 6.
4 Jer. xiii. 21.      5 Acts xvii. 11, 12.      6 Acts xxiv. 25.
7 Heb. iii. 7, 8.

While you are doing nothing, the enemy is very busy strengthening his toils around you, and they will be stronger to-morrow than to-day.

While you are, as you fancy, only lying still, you are drifting fast down the stream into the stronger current, nearing the rapids, nearing the fatal fall.

It is a question of life and death. ' Escape for thy life; look not behind thee, neither stay thou in all the plain.'[1] It is the old story of

> ' If you tarry till you're better,
> You will never come at all.'

I do not know any one promise in all the Bible for the lingerers. And if you put yourself out of the sphere of God's promises, what have you to found any hope at all upon ?

' Tarry not ! '[2] Oh, if I could but reach you and rouse you !

> 'And if I care
> For one unknown, oh how much more doth He !'[3]

For one who perishes through straightforward refusal, there are probably thousands who perish through *putting off*.[4] 'How shall we escape if we' *refuse*—no, if we merely '*neglect*—so great salvation ?'[5]

> Yet there is room ! The Lamb's bright hall of song,
> With its fair glory, beckons thee along.

> Yet there is room ! Still open stands the gate,
> The gate of love ; it is not yet too late.

---

1 Gen. xix. 17.    2 Heb. iv. 7.    3 2 Pet. iii. 9.
4 Matt. xxii. 3, 5.    5 Heb. xii. 25 ; Heb. ii. 3.

Pass in, pass in !　That banquet is for thee;
That cup of everlasting love is free.

Ere night that gate may close, and seal thy doom;
Then the last, low, long cry,—' No room, no room !'
Dr. H. Bonar.

---

# EIGHTEENTH DAY.

---

# Without Christ.

'At that time ye were without Christ.'—Eph. ii. 12.

I COULD not do without Thee,
　O Saviour of the lost !
Whose precious blood redeemed me
　At such tremendous cost.
Thy righteousness, Thy pardon,
　Thy precious blood—must be
My only hope and comfort,
　My glory and my plea.

I could not do without Him !
　Jesus is more to me
Than all the richest, fairest gifts
　Of earth could ever be.
But the more I find Him precious,
　And the more I find Him true,

The more I long for you to find
  What He can be to you.

You need not do without Him,
  For He is passing by ,
He is waiting to be gracious,
  Only waiting for your cry.
He is waiting to receive you,—
  To make you all His own !
Why will you do without Him,
  And wander on alone ?

Why will you do without Him !
  Is He not kind indeed ?
Did He not die to save you?
  Is He not all you need ?
Do you not want a Saviour ?
  Do you not want a Friend ?
One who will love you faithfully,
  And love you to the end ?

Why will you do without Him ?
  The word of God is true :
The world is passing to its doom,
  And you are passing too
It may be, no to-morrow
  Shall dawn for you or me,
Why will you run the awful risk
  Of all eternity ?

What will you do without Him
  In the long and dreary day
23

Of trouble and perplexity,
   When you do not know the way;
And no one else can help you,
   And no one guides you right,
And hope comes not with morning,
   And rest comes not with night?

You could not do without Him,
   If once He made you see
The fetters that enchain you
   Till He hath set you free;
If once you saw the fearful load
   Of sin upon your soul,—
The hidden plague that ends in death
   Unless He makes you whole!

What will you do without Him
   When death is drawing near,
Without His love—the only love
   That casts out every fear;
When the shadow-valley opens,
   Unlighted and unknown,
And the terrors of its darkness
   Must all be passed alone?

What will you do without Him
   When the great White Throne is set,
And the Judge who never can mistake,
   And never can forget,—
The Judge whom you have never here
   As Friend and Saviour sought,
Shall summon you to give account
   Of deed, and word and thought?

What will you do without Him
 When He hath shut the door,
And you are left outside, because
 You would not come before;
When it is no use knocking,
 No use to stand and wait,
For the word of doom tolls through **your**
  heart,
 That terrible ' Too late ' ?


You cannot do without Him!
 There is no other name
By which you ever *can* be saved,—
 No way, no hope, no claim!
Without Him—everlasting loss
 Of love, and life, and light!
Without Him—everlasting woe,
 And everlasting night.


But with Him—oh! *with Jesus !*—
 Are any words so blest?
With Jesus—everlasting joy
 And everlasting rest!
With Jesus—all the empty heart
 Filled with His perfect love!
With Jesus—perfect peace below,
 And perfect bliss above!


Why should you do without Him?—
 It is not yet too late;
He has not closed the day of grace,
 He has not shut the gate.

He calls you!—hush! He calls **you**!—
　　He would not have you go
Another step without Him,
　　Because He loves you so.

Why will you do without Him?
　　He calls and calls again—
'Come unto Me! Come unto Me!'
　　Oh, shall He call in vain?
He wants to have you with Him;
　　Do you not want Him too?
You cannot do without Him,
　　And He wants—even you!

---

## NINETEENTH DAY.

## Come Away.

'My beloved spake, and said unto me, Rise up, my love, my
fair one, and come away.'—CANT. ii. 10.

WHAT a loving call! What astonishing condescension, that the Heavenly Bridegroom
should use such words to—whom? Would you not
like to be able to fill up that blank, and say, 'My
Beloved spake, and said unto *me!*'
　Perhaps you think this is too much for *you.* You
feel too sinful and unworthy to be so loved,—too
defiled to be called 'my fair one.' If so, will you

turn to a wonderful picture of those upon whom He
sets His love,[1] and of what His love does for them,
asking the Holy Spirit to open your eyes while you
read it, that you may behold wondrous things out
of it.[2]

I will not quote it here, because I want you to go
to His own Book for it. See in it how the Lord
Jesus goes down to the very depths, and begins at
the very beginning.[3] Your case is not deeper than
those depths; for it is even when we are *dead*[4] in
sins that the great love wherewith God loved us
reaches and raises us.[5] He says, 'Awake, thou that
sleepest, and rise *from the dead*, and Christ shall
give thee light.'[6] You cannot be worse than 'dead;'
and the very sense of sin and death working in
you[7] 'is a proof' that He has said unto you,
'Live!'[8]

The call to arise and come away is a proof that
He is passing by.[9] And when Jesus passes by, He
looks upon you, though you are not yet able to see
Him. And He says that when He does this, it is
'the time of love.'[10] And oh, what *that* implies!
What will He not do, when the bright, warm, powerful rays of the love which passeth knowledge[11] are
focussed upon you, and He says even to you, 'My
love!' giving you the glorious right to respond, 'My
beloved!'[12]

Read on, and see what He will do 'then!' '*Then*'
the 'thoroughly' washing[13] and the anointing which

---

1 Ezek. xvi. 5, 14.    2 Ps. cxix. 18.    3 Ps. xl. 2.
4 Eph. ii. 1.    5 Eph. ii. 4, 5.    6 Eph. v. 14.
7 Rom. vii. 13.    8 Ezek. xvi. 6.    9 Luke xviii. 37.
10 Ezek. xvi. 8.    11 Eph. iii. 19.    12 Cant. ii. 16.
13 Ps. li. 2.

prepares you for the delight of the King.[1] 'Then'
the clothing, the girding, and the covering, each
with their treasures of significance.[2]   Then 'also'
the decking and the crowning, and the being made
'exceeding beautiful' and 'perfect through My
comeliness which I had put upon thee, saith the
Lord God!'[3]   When He puts the beauty of the Lord
our God upon us,[4] then He can indeed say, 'My
fair one!'[5] 'Fair' *only* with His comeliness;[6] otherwise the fairest natural character that was ever seen
is 'black as the tents of Kedar,'[7]—those miserable
goats'-hair tents, which are to this day the very type
of the filthiest blackness.   Yet with it, whatever
your natural character, and whatever your added
deformity through having been 'accustomed to do
evil,'[8] you will be 'comely as the curtains of Solomon,'—the type of all that is costly and beautiful
in colours and workmanship.

*Let* Him do all this for you![9]   Rise up and come
away from all that pollutes and separates you from
Him.   'Shake thyself from the dust, and arise!'[10]
'Arise, shine, for thy Light is come!'[11]   'Though
ye have lien among the pots, yet' (when you come
to the Light that is come so close to you), 'yet
shall ye be as the wings of a dove covered with
silver, and her feathers with yellow gold,'[12] shining
and gleaming as you rise and come away, resplendent in the beams of the Sun of righteousness.[13]
'Rise, He calleth thee!'[14] 'Come away!'

---

1 Esth. ii. 12–14.        2 Isa. lxi. 10; Ps. xlv. 13.        3 Ezek. xvi. 14.
4 Ps. xc. 17.        5 Cant. iv. 7.        6 Rom. viii. 7.
7 Cant. i. 5.        8 Jer. xiii. 23.        9 Phil. ii. 13.
10 Isa. lii. 2.        11 Isa. lx. 1.        12 Ps. lxviii. 13.
13 Mal. iv. 2.        14 Mark x. 49.

## TWENTIETH DAY.

---

## Coming after Jesus.

'Come and follow Me.'—MATT. xix. 21.

FOLLOWING is the only proof of coming. There is hardly a commoner lamentation than this : ' I do not know whether I have come or not ! '[2] And nobody ever says that with a happy smile. It is always with a dismal look ; and no wonder ! When so much hinges upon it,—poverty or riches, safety or danger, life or death,—uncertainty must and will be miserable. Now, do you really want to know whether you have come or not ? Our Lord gives you the test, ' Come *and follow* Me ! '[3]

If you are willing for that, willing with the will that issues in act and deed, then the coming is real.[4]

If you are not willing to follow, then you may dismiss at once any idea that perhaps you have come or are coming : there is no reality in it, and there is nothing for you but to go away sorrowful,

---

1 Ezek. xxxiii. 31.  2 1 Kings xviii. 21.
3 John x. 27.  4 Matt. xx. 34.

as the rich young man did, who ' came,' but would not ' follow.'[1]

The following will be just as real and definite as the coming, if there is any reality in you at all; and if you are not deluding yourself with a deceitful cloudland of sentimental religion, without foundation and without substance, which is but a refuge of lies which the hail shall sweep away.[2] Do not sit down in this most serious state of uncertainty, but ' give diligence to make your calling and election sure.'[3]

But you say, ' How am I to know whether I am following?' Well, following is not standing still. Clearly it is not staying just where you always were. You cannot follow one thing without coming away from something else.[4] Apply this test. What have you *left* for Jesus?[5] What have you left off doing for His sake?[6] If you are moving onward, some things must be left behind. What are ' the things which are behind '[7] in *your* life? If the supposed coming has made no difference in your practical daily life,[8] do not flatter yourself that you have ever yet really come at all.[9] Jesus says, ' If any man will come after Me, let him deny himself, and take up his cross and follow Me.'[10] What light does that saying throw upon your case? Be honest about it; all true coming *to* Jesus must issue in thus coming *after* Him.[11]

---

1 Matt. xix. 22.    2 Isa. xxviii. 17.    3 2 Pet. i. 10.
4 Rom. vi. 2, 4, 13, 22.    5 Matt. iv. 18-20.    6 Matt. ix. 9.
7 Phil. iii. 13.    8 Matt. vii. 21.    9 2 Cor. v. 17.
10 Matt. xvi. 24.    11 Luke xiv. 27.

Then look at it from the positive side. He has left us ' an example that ye should follow His steps.'[1] As the beautiful collect puts it, ' Give us grace that we may daily endeavour ourselves to follow the blessed steps of His most holy life.'[2] Now, what are those steps? Perhaps you are not even looking to see what they are, let alone following them! Following the *steps* is quite a different thing from thinking to follow one's own idea of the general direction of a course. If you would only take one Gospel, and read it through with the earnest purpose of noting, by the Holy Spirit's guidance, what the steps of Jesus are, you would soon see clearly whether you are following or not,[3] far more clearly than by reading any amount of books about it, or consulting any number of human counsellors. Take for to-day only one indication of what those steps were ' Who went about doing good.'[4] Do your steps correspond with that?[5] It is not, ' went about doing no harm,' but actively and positively ' doing good.'

Oh, dear friends, they are ' blessed ' steps in all senses of the word! For His ways are ways of pleasantness, and all His paths are peace.[6] Once fairly and fully entered, the paradox is always solved, the self-denial is lost in the greater joy of pleasing Him,[7] the cross becomes a sceptre in the hand of His ' kings and priests.'[8] Then you

---

1 1 Pet. ii. 21.    2 John xiii. 15.    3 Matt. xi. 29.
4 Acts x. 38.    5 1 John ii. 6.    6 Prov. iii. 17.
7 Phil. iii. 7.    8 Rev. i. 6.

shall 'continue following the Lord your God.'[1] And the end of the following is, 'that where I am, there shall also My servant be.'[2]

---·---

## TWENTY-FIRST DAY.

---

## Coming with Jesus.

'Come with Me.'—CANT. iv. 8.

'COME away'[3] is not all that the Lord Jesus has to say to us. 'Come unto Me'[4] and 'Come after Me,'[5] only lead up to the even more gracious invitation, 'Come *with* Me.'[6]

'Ye see your calling;'[7] it is nothing less than to come *with* Jesus. The enviable privilege of the twelve whom Jesus ordained 'that they should be with Him,'[8] is freely offered to you. Will you avail yourself of it? Will you come with Jesus, walking with Him[9] from this day every step of the way? Will you accept Him as the Guide with whom you will go, the Friend with whom you will commune by the way?[10] It will be no dreamy or nominal coming with Him, if only you are willing to come. You will find it very real in all respects.'

You can never be so *really always* with any earthly friend as you can be with Jesus, and as you

---

1 1 Sam. xii. 14.　2 John xii. 26; Rev. xiv. 4.　3 Cant. ii. 10.
4 Matt. xi. 28.　5 Matt. xvi. 24.　6 2 Sam. xix. 33.
7 1 Cor. i. 26.　8 Mark iii. 14.　9 Rev. iii. 4, 21.
10 John vi. 68; Ex. xxxiii. 14.

*will* be, if you accept the invitation.[1] For there are two sides to that 'with.' If you will but *come with* Him, He will come unto you and *abide with* you.[2] Your natural fear lest, even when you consent to come to be with Him, you might not remain with Him, is met and completely settled by His promise, 'I will never leave thee.'[3] And of course if He *never* leaves you, you will always be with Him. And if He has *said* that, of course He will do it.[4] So do not let *that* objection come up again!

It is a very common experience in great things and small, that the person or thing we most want is not there just when we most want him or it. Never shall we have to complain of this as to the promised perpetual presence of our Lord;[5] for He says, 'I will be with him in trouble.'[6] 'When thou passest through the waters, I will be with thee.'[7] And in the deepest need of all, in the valley of the shadow of death, the soul that has yielded to the present call will be able to say, 'Thou art with me.'[8]

I do not think we consider enough how we disappoint the love of Jesus when we refuse to come with Him.[9] For He does truly and literally desire us to be with Him.[10] Would He have made it the very climax of His great Prayer, representing it as the very culmination of His own rest and glory that His people should be *with Him*,[11] if He did

---

1 Prov. xviii. 24.    2 John xiv. 23.    3 Heb. xiii. 5.
4 Num. xxiii. 19.    5 Matt. xxviii. 20.    6 Ps. xci. 15.
7 Isa. xliii. 2.    8 Ps. xxiii. 4.    9 Luke xiii. 34.
10 Cant. v. 2.    11 John xvii. 24.

not so very much care about it, and was only seeking and saving us out of bare pity? No, it was in
His *love* as well as in His pity that He redeemed
us![1] And love craves nearness. This is the very
thing that differences love from the lesser glow of
mere pity, or kindness, whatever their degrees or
combinations. The Lord Jesus would not say,
'Come *with* Me,' if He did not feel towards us
something far beyond any degree of pity and kindness. It is the Royal Invitation of His kingly
love.

But now, what are you going to do about it?
Hearing it, and thinking it very gracious, and all
that, is not enough. You must come to a point
about it.[2] You must give as definite an answer to
this as mere common courtesy demands to any
earthly invitation. Giving *no* answer is an acknowledged insult. Will you treat the King thus? And
if not what shall your answer be? You must give
it yourself. Christ Himself is waiting for it.[3]

There is a beautiful type[4] which tells us how a
maiden was chosen to be the bride of the son of a
'mighty prince'[5] in a far-off land. She was to
answer for herself about it, and so 'they said, We
will call the damsel and enquire at her mouth. And
they called Rebekah, and said, Wilt thou go with
this man? And she said, *I will go.*'[6]

Shall this be *your* answer to-day?

---

1 Isa. lxiii. 9.        2 1 Kings xviii. 21.        3 John vi. 67.
4 Gen. xxiv.        5 Gen. xxiii. 6.        6 Gen. xxiv. 57, 58.

## TWENTY-SECOND DAY.

---

## The Living Water.

'If any man thirst, let him come unto Me, and drink.'
—JOHN vii. 37.

THE Invitation could not have been given in any wider form. Neither could it have been given in any form which so certainly concentrates all its light and warmth on one point, that point yourself!

First, there is the grand sweep of the '*any*' man. Instead of amplifying this into a list of all possible varieties of 'rich or poor, old or young,' and so on, just never mind about these usual human paraphrases, which may or may not seem to include you, and come face to face with the magnificently simple word of our Lord, 'Any!' and know that it means '*you!*' for you cannot possibly get outside of this great circle, described by the hand of Infinite Love. You cannot possibly say it does not include you. Words mean nothing, if this word does not mean that you, whose eyes now rest upon it, are included and intended. To you the Lord Jesus says, 'Let him come unto Me.'

But another word is appended which seems at first sight to be a limitation. 'If any man *thirst,*

let him come.'[1]  *Is* it a limitation? Ask your own
heart! Is there *any* one who does not thirst?[2] In
other words, is there any one who can say before
God who searches the heart,[3] 'I am satisfied. I
have no sense of thirst, no nameless craving'? Are
*you* satisfied? I do not mean, are you tolerably
contented and comfortable on the whole and in a
general way when things are at their best? But,
*satisfied!*—the deep under-the-surface rest and complete satisfaction of the very heart, the filling of its
emptiness, the stilling of all its cravings; and this
not during the false frothing of excitement or business, but when you are alone, when you lie awake
in the night, when you are shut away from any
fictitious filling of your cup, and when the broken
cisterns have leaked out,[4] as they will, and do, and
must,—are you satisfied then? Verily, He who
knew what was in man[5] knew that He was not nar-
rowing the invitation when He said, 'Let him that
is athirst, come!'[6]

Did you ever think *why* it is so utterly hopeless
and useless to try to quench that inner thirst with
anything but the living water, 'the supply of the
Spirit of Jesus Christ'?[7] He has said plainly and
positively that you shall not succeed![8] He hath
said, 'Whosoever drinketh of this water *shall* thirst
again.'[9] You see there is no chance for you, for
His word cannot be broken, and He says you '*shall*
thirst again.'[10] There are only two issues of that

---

1 Rev. xxi. 6.  2 Ps. cvii. 5.  3 Ezek. xi. 5.
4 Jer. ii. 13.  5 John ii. 25.  6 Rev. xxii. 17.
7 Phil. i. 19.  8 John vii. 39.  9 John iv. 13.
10 John x. 35.

perpetual thirst. One is the unanswered entreaty for a drop of water, only so much as the tip of a finger may bear, not to .quench the unquenchable thirst, but only to *cool* a flame-tormented tongue[1] The other, the *only* other, is, ' Whosoever drinketh of the water that I shall give him shall never thirst.'[2] And lest our slow perceptions should fail to grasp the fact in the figure, the Lord Jesus repeats the promise, and says, 'He that believeth on Me shall never thirst.'[3] Never! for ' He satisfieth the longing soul.'[4]

'Let him come *unto Me*, and drink.'[5] You see there is only this one way of drinking of the living water : you must come to Jesus Himself, personally and really. Knowing all about it is not enough. Consulting Christian friends, and reading good books, and doing any amount of religious duties and exercising any amount of self-denial, will not stay the more or less conscious heart-thirst. The Lord says not a word about any channels ; He only says, 'If any man thirst, let him come unto Me, and drink.' And ' Whosoever will, let him take of the water of life freely.'[6] Will not *you* come ?

---

1 Luke xvi. 24.    2 John iv. 14.    3 John vi. 35.
4 Ps. cvii. 9.    5 John vii. 37.    6 Rev. xxii. 17.

## TWENTY-THIRD DAY.

---

## The Bread and Wine.

' Come, eat of my bread, and drink of the wine which I have
mingled.'—Prov. ix. 5.

IN several chapters of Proverbs the Lord Jesus
Christ is beautifully described under the figure of
Wisdom. For He is ' the Wisdom of God,' and He
is ' made unto us Wisdom '[1]

In this verse He gives a double Invitation,—to
eat of His bread, and drink of His wine. These
are the symbols of life and joy—His life and His
joy.

' Come, eat of My bread.' ' Feed on Him in thy
heart by faith, with thanksgiving.' For Jesus Himself is the true Bread from heaven.[2] And he that
eateth of this Bread shall live for ever. For He
is the Bread of Life, life-giving and life-sustaining.[3]

How shall we eat? It is the old story,—only
coming, only believing ! For ' he that cometh to
Me shall never hunger,'[4] and ' we are made partakers of Christ, if we hold the beginning of our
confidence steadfast unto the end.'[5]

---

1 1 Cor i. 24, 30.        2 John vi. 51.        3 John vi. 48 ; Gal. ii. 20.
4 John vi. 35.        5 Heb. iii. 14.

It is not a mere tasting or a bare subsisting to which Christ invites us. He says, ' Eat, O friends ; drink, yea, drink abundantly, O beloved.'[1] For 'I am come that they might have life, and that they might have it more abundantly ;'[2] fulness and vigour of life, abounding pulses of vitality, fresh and strong; life that shall not and cannot fail, for 'He ever liveth ;'[3] and 'because I live, ye shall live also.'[4]

How often we have sung, ' He hath filled the hungry with good things! '[5] Are you hungry ?[6] Come, eat of His bread, leaving the husks and ashes, and you shall know what it is to be filled with good things.[7] For ' He filleth the hungry soul with goodness.'[8]

It is not only the solid life-need of bread that is provided at the feast which the Lord has made for us, but Wine, the symbol of joy, ' that maketh glad the heart of man.'[9] ' Come, buy wine and milk without money and without price,'[10] because the price is already paid for it. His sorrow was the price of the joy offered to us. He poured out His soul unto death,[11] that He might pour out His joy into our lives.[12] He emptied the cup which His Father gave Him,[13] that He might fill ours till it runs over.[14] Without price to us,—but oh, the price to Him !

The Lord Jesus says it is wine which He has *mingled*. Not all one kind, but mingled by Divine care and skill into a perfect draught of manifold

---

1 Cant. v. 1.          2 John x. 10.          3 Heb. vii. 25
4 John xiv. 19.        5 Luke i. 53.          6 Luke xv. 16; Isa. xliv. 20.
7 Jer. xxxi. 14, 25.   8 Ps. cvii. 9.         9 Ps. civ. 15.
10 Isa. lv. 1.          11 Isa. liii. 12.      12 John xv. 11.
13 John xviii. 11.      14 Ps. xxiii. 5.

24

gladness: 'If they obey and serve Him, they shall spend their days in prosperity, and their years in pleasures.'[1]    *That* is the heritage of the servants of the Lord !'[2]    Did you think it was so pleasant ?    Did you know that He meant you to spend your years in pleasures *here,*[3] as well as to give you the pleasures for evermore hereafter?[4]    'Come, drink of the wine that He has mingled,' and you will find out what these pleasures are, and how exceedingly real they are !    No wonder you are a little skeptical about it! for 'eye hath not seen, nor ear heard, neither have entered into the heart of man, the things which God hath prepared for them that love Him; *but,*' notice now exactly what is said, ' *God* HATH *revealed them unto us by His Spirit.*'[5]    So, unless or until God reveals them to you by His Spirit, you cannot see or conceive what these pleasures are which He has prepared for those who love Him,—what this wine is which He has mingled for those who come to Him.    Oh taste and see ![6] Come and put your trust under the shadow of His wings ;[7] and *then* you shall be abundantly satisfied with the fatness of His house,[8] and he shall **make** you drink of the *river* of His pleasures.

---

1 Job xxxvi. 11 ; Ps. xc. 14.
3 Ps. iv. 7 ; Prov. iii. 17.
5 1 Cor. ii. 9, 10.
7 Ps. xxxvi. 7, 8.

2 Isa. lxv. 13, 14.
4 Ps. xvi. 11.
6 Ps. xxxiv. 8.
8 Ps. lxiii. 5.

## TWENTY FOURTH DAY.

---

## 𝔚𝔦𝔩𝔩 𝔜𝔬𝔲 𝔑𝔬𝔱 𝔠𝔬𝔪𝔢?

'Thou hast received gifts for men; yea, for the rebellious also.'—Ps. lxviii. 18.

WILL you not come to Him for life?
　　Why will ye die, oh why?
He gave His life for you, for you!
The gift is free, the word is true!
　　Will you not come? oh, why will you die?

Will you not come to Him for peace—
　　Peace through His cross alone?
He shed His precious blood for you;
The gift is free, the word is true !
　　He is our Peace! oh, is He your own?

Will you not come to Him for rest?
　　All that are weary, come !
The rest He gives is deep and true;
'Tis offered now, 'tis offered you!
　　Rest in His love, and rest in His home.

Will you not come to Him for joy,—
　　Will you not come for this?
He laid His joys aside for you,

To give you joy, so sweet, so true!
  Sorrowing heart, oh drink of the bliss!

Will you not come to Him for love—
  Love that can fill the heart,
Exceeding great, exceeding free?
He loveth you, He loveth me!
  Will you not come? Why stand you apart?

Will you not come to Him for *all?*
  Will you not 'taste and see'?
He waits to give it all to you;
The gifts are free, the words are true!
  Jesus is calling, 'Come unto Me!'

---

## TWENTY-FIFTH DAY.

## Come Near.

'Come ye near unto Me.'—ISA. xlviii. 16.

'SHE obeyed not the voice; . . . she trusted not in the Lord, she drew not near to her God.'[1] What was her portion? 'Woe to her!'[2]
'But, beloved, we are persuaded better things of you, though we thus speak.'[3] For Jesus says that if He is lifted up, He will draw all men unto Him.[4]

---

1 Zeph. iii. 2.    2 Zeph. iii. 1.    8 Heb. vi. 9.    4 John xii. 32.

And it is the Lord Jesus Himself (see context) who says, 'Come ye near unto Me, hear ye this!'[1] No matter how far off you may be, this call of peace is to you who are far off.[2] And if you hearken, then shall your peace be as a river. [3] And if you have already come to Jesus, still He says to them that are nigh, 'Now ye have consecrated yourselves to the Lord, come near,'[4]—nearer still, closer and closer to the Lord who loves you.

There is only one way of coming near or being made near, but that way is open for you. Not into the outer court of religious profession, but 'into the Holiest,' into the reality of most sacred nearness to your Lord, you may enter 'by the blood of Jesus.'[5] The moment you claim by faith the power of that precious blood,[6]—the moment you let your Great High Priest put it upon you,[7] that moment 'ye who sometimes were far off are made nigh by the blood of Christ.'[8] Then, having this High Priest,[9] and having this one blessed and unfailing means of access, 'let us draw near with a true heart, in full assurance of faith.'[10]

Do not be discouraged from coming near because you feel far off. Take that rather as your very claim to be included in the call, for He says, 'Hear ye that are far off, what I have done!'[11] and take it as your very reason for coming; come just because you *are* 'a great way off,' for He says, 'They that are far off shall come.'[12]

---

[1] Isa. xlviii. 16.  [2] Isa. lvii. 19.  [3] Isa. xlviii. 18.
[4] 2 Chron. xxix. 31.  [5] Heb. x. 19.  [6] Heb. xiii. 12.
[7] Lev. xiv. 14; Heb. ix. 13, 14.  [8] Eph. ii. 13.
[9] Heb. iv. 14.  [10] Rom. v. 9; Eph. iii. 12; Heb. x. 21, 22.
[11] Isa. xxxiii. 13.  [12] Zech. vi. 15.

If you feel very powerless about it, plead and claim the promise of His enabling grace, ' I will cause him to draw near.'[1] And then you will find that ' blessed' is the man whom Thou choosest, and causest to approach unto Thee ; "[2] and your experience will be, ' It is good for me to draw near unto God. '[3]

He who causes you to come near will keep you near. Joseph did not only say to his brethren, ' Come near to me,'[4] in that moment of tenderest love when he made himself known to them, but his promise was, 'And thou shalt be near unto me.'[5] This is your calling. Never to be far off any more ! Never any more distance and separation ![6] Never any more wandering in the far country[7] without God,[8] but henceforth to be 'a people near unto Him !'[9] ' No more strangers and foreigners, but fellow citizens with the saints, and of the household of God,'[10] having found the very home of the weary heart, from which you shall no more go out.[11]

---

1 Jer. xxx. 21.  2 Ps. lxv. 4.  3 Ps. lxxiii. 28.
4 Gen. xlv. 4.  5 Gen. xlv. 10.  6 Rom. viii. 35-39.
7 Luke xv. 13.  8 Eph. ii. 12.  9 Ps. cxlviii. 14.
10 Eph. ii. 19.  11 Rev. iii. 12.

## TWENTY-SIXTH DAY.

---

## To the Uttermost.

'But this man, because He continueth ever, hath an unchangeable priesthood. Wherefore He is able also to save
them to the uttermost that come unto God by Him.'—HEB. vii.
24, 25.

'AND suppose I do come, what then? Suppose I
do receive all this blessedness to-day, what
about to-morrow?' Something like this thought is
very often in the minds of those who see the lions
not only outside but inside the doors of the House
Beautiful. But it is all met by that wonderful word,
'to the uttermost.'

This does not only mean that the Lord Jesus is
able to save out of the uttermost depth of need and
misery and sin, and that He is able to save from the
uttermost regions of distance and despair. It means
all that, but more besides. It is not only bringing
you up out of the horrible pit and miry clay, but
setting your feet upon a rock, and establishing your
goings.[1]

The word is one of those remarkable compound
ones for which we have no equivalent. It means
that He is able to save unto all completeness, unto
the total perfection of saving.[2]

---

1 Ps. xl. 2.  2 Eccl. iii. 14; Isa. xlv. 17; Jer. xvii. 14.

Suppose I were drowning, and you drew me out of the deepest water, just in time to save my life, but then left me wet and shivering and exhausted on-the bank, to run the more than risk of wretched after-effects of cold and rheumatism, from which I might never entirely recover! That would not be saving 'to the uttermost' in this sense of the word. But if you did the thing completely,—carrying me home, and doing everything necessary to restore me, and avert ill effects, and that effectually; never relaxing in care and effort, nor letting me go, till you had me safe and well, however long and difficult it might be, then you would have saved me 'to the uttermost,' in the true meaning of it.

This is what Jesus is able to do for you. Your first coming to Him is only like letting Him grasp you in your terrible danger, and draw you out of the fatal depths. But 'because He continueth ever,'[1] always the same loving and faithful Saviour, He will complete what He begins.[2] For we are 'confident of this very thing, that He which hath begun a good work in you will perform it until the day of Jesus Christ.'[3] Having saved you from destruction, His very name[4] is the guarantee that He will not leave you to struggle helplessly with your sins, much less to 'continue '[5] in them, but that He shall save you from them.[6] You will find it a daily continual salvation, by which He will keep you by the power of God through faith,[7] unto the consummated salvation of body and soul, 'ready to be revealed in the last time.'[8]

---

1 Heb. vii. 24.　　2 1 Thess. v. 24.　　3 Phil. i. 6.
4 Matt. i. 21.　　5 Rom. vi. 1.　　6 Ps. ciii. 3-5.
7 2 Pet. i. 4.　　8 1 Pet. i. 5.

# TWENTY-SEVENTH DAY.

## Ⓣbe Ⓟroof of Ⓒbrist's Ⓐbility to Ⓢave.

'Wherefore He is able also to save them to the uttermost that come unto God by Him, seeing He ever liveth to make intercession for them.'—HEB. vii. 25.

SEE what is the proof that the Lord Jesus Christ is able to save you thus, 'to the uttermost.' It is that He ever liveth to make intercession. For whom? For them 'that come unto God by Him.' Or, as He Himself said, in that wonderful prayer when He lifted the veil from His own Divine communing with the Father, and let us hear His mighty intercession: 'Neither pray I for these alone, but for them also which shall believe on Me through their word,'[1]—thus again identifying 'coming' with believing. Then, if you come, the perpetual intercession of our ascended High Priest will be for you, always for you.[2] Only think that this is what Jesus is now living for,—'liveth to make intercession'[3] for you! Should we ever have dared to imagine such grace and love? Should we ever have conceived that such a privilege could be ours?

---

[1] John xvii. 20.    [2] Heb. iv. 14.    [3] Rom. viii. 34; Heb. ix. 24.

Only think what security there must be in it!
If the Lord Jesus is praying for you, can you perish?[1] If He is praying for you, will not the
Father's answer of blessing be beyond anything
you would ask for yourself? Is not this enough to
answer all your misgivings as to what you will find
and how you will get on when you have come?

There is a solemn side to it. He not only says
nothing about making intercession for those who do
*not* come, but He plainly and positively says, 'I
pray *not* for the world, but for them which Thou
hast given Me;'[2] the proof of having been *given*
to Christ being the *coming* to Him, for 'all that the
Father giveth Me shall come to Me.'[3] Then face
the terrible position which is yours, if you will not
come! Christ will *not* pray for you! you shut
yourself out from the prayer of Him whom the
Father heareth *always*.[4] He prays *not* for all alike,
but only for those who receive His words. He says
'I pray for them; I pray *not* for the world.' You
dare not and cannot explain this away. It is no
mere inference, no question of differing 'views,'
but spoken by Him whose words can never pass
away.[5] Will you not 'come,' and share in this unspeakable privilege of Christ's intercession?

We must not overlook the fact that it is for those
who 'come unto God by Him.' Your coming to
Jesus is also coming to your Father. In our right
earnestness to have clear views of the Trinity, we
are liable to forget the *Unity* of the Godhead. 'I
and My Father are one,'[6] saith the Lord Jesus; and

---

1 John x. 28.          2 John xvii. 9.          3 John vi. 37.
4 John xi. 42.          5 Luke xxi. 33.          6 John x. 30.

this blessed and glorious unity is our key to many
an apparent difficulty. Yet there is a Divine order
in the approach which we invert at our eternal
peril. It must be ' by Him,' or it is no coming at
all. For He hath said, ' No man cometh unto the
Father but by Me.'¹ The redemption of Christ is
for them ' who *by Him* do believe in God.'² You
*cannot* be made nigh to God except by the blood
of Christ ³ You *cannot* reach the Father except
through the Son, for it is through Him and in Him
that we alone have access.⁴ You *cannot* offer
thanks, any more than prayer, to God, except in
the same way, for it is ' by Him ' that we are to
offer it.⁵ In one word, you cannot be saved any
other way at all, except by Jesus,⁶ and it is no use
talking about being simply saved by God's mercy,
for God's own Word says, ' There is none other
name under heaven given among men whereby we
must be saved,'⁷ so that fallacy is disposed of forever. So 'diminish not a word ;'⁸ do not venture
to leave out the words ' by Him,' but come in
God's own appointed way, and you shall be saved
in His own grand and perfect way, ' to the uttermost ! '

---

1 John xiv. 6.  2 1 Pet. i. 21.  3 Eph. ii. 13.
4 Eph. ii. 18.  5 Heb. xiii. 15.  6 Rom. v. 9, 10.
7 Acts iv. 12.  8 Deut. xii. 32.

## TWENTY-EIGHTH DAY.

—

## Continual Coming.

'To whom coming, as unto a living stone, disallowed indeed of men, but chosen of God, and precious, ye also, as lively stones, are built up, a spiritual house, an holy priesthood, to offer up spiritual sacrifices, acceptable to God by Jesus Christ.' —I PET. ii. 4.

'To whom *coming*.' Here is the secret of advance in the narrow way, after we have entered by the Strait Gate.[1] It is not the having come once and to begin with, but the coming continually to Jesus. When we have once really come to Him, it is not only our privilege, but our constant joy, to come to Him about everything—to go on drinking at the fountain. It is a beautiful paradox which is realized and reconciled in the experience of those who come, that we may be continually coming afresh without ever going away, —always *at* the fountain-head, and yet always *coming* to it.

As the first coming to Jesus gives us the true and only foundation,[2] so by the very same coming, continued with ever fresh peace and joy, we shall be built up in Him.[3] It is *as* we have received Christ Jesus the Lord that we are to walk in Him, and

---

1 Matt. vii. 14.　　2 1 Cor. iii. 11.　　3 Col. ii. 6, 7.

then we shall be rooted and built up in Him.[1] Think what this building up implies ! Coming to Him, you individually, as well as all who come collectively, shall be builded together for an habitation of God through the Spirit,[2] that Christ may dwell in your hearts by faith,[3] that your bodies may be the temple of the Holy Ghost.[4] Coming to Him, you shall no longer be a loose stone, lying about and getting weatherworn, but you 'shall be built in the midst of My people,' saith the Lord.[5]

Coming to Him, you shall also be built up as a holy and royal priesthood.[6] For He that loved us and washed us from our sins in His own blood, hath made us kings and priests unto God.[7] What does this priesthood involve, which the Lord has 'given unto you as a service of gift' ?[8] Does it not involve the very point on which you had a misgiving, namely, 'if I do come to-day, what about to-morrow?' for the priests had everything provided for them.[9] When they were set apart to the priest's office, they did not need to have a thought or a care about their maintenance in it all the rest of their lives.[10] When once this 'service of gift' was theirs, they were joined unto the high priest himself, and shared his privileges and his provision; they were given to him, and he was given to them.[11] This provision for them was 'all the *best* of the oil, and all the *best* of the wine, and of the wheat, and the first-fruits,' besides 'all the *best* thereof' of other

---

1 1 Pet. ii. 5.    2 Eph. ii. 22.    3 Eph. iii. 17.
4 1 Cor. vi. 19    5 Jer. xii. 16.    6 1 Pet. ii. 5, 9.
7 Rev. i. 5, 6; ib. v. 10.      8 Num. xviii. 7.
9 Num. xviii. 9, 14.    10 Ezek. xliv. 28–30; 2 Cor. vi. 10.
11 Num. xviii. 2, 4.

things ;[1] 'for it is your reward for your service.'[2] And the Lord says, 'I will satiate the soul of my priests with fatness '[3] They shall be abundantly 'satisfied with the plenteousness of Thy house.'[4] For 'His divine power hath given unto us *all* things that pertain unto life and godliness.'[5]

Coming to Him, you shall 'offer up spiritual sacrifices, acceptable to God by Jesus Christ.'[6] You will offer by Him the sacrifice of praise continually ;[7] and what can the angels do more? Continual praise *must* be continual gladness.[8] And when you are able to say, 'O Lord, I will praise Thee ; though Thou wast angry with me, Thine anger is turned away, and Thou comfortedst me ; behold, God is my salvation ;' then, and '*therefore*, with joy shall ye draw water out of the wells of salvation.'[9]

This is what is before you, as soon as you come to Jesus. Thenceforth it shall be continual coming, and that will be continual rest, continual peace, continual joy.[10]

---

1 Num. xviii. 12.   2 Num. xviii. 29, 31.   3 Jer. xxxi. 14.
4 Ps. xxxvi. 8, P.B.V.   5 2 Pet. i. 3.
6 1 Pet. ii. 5 ; Rom. xii. 1.   7 Heb. xiii. 15.
8 Ps. lxxi. 6, 14 ; ib. xxxiv. 1.   9 Isa. xii. 1–3.
10 Phil. iv. 4, 6, 7.

# TWENTY-NINTH DAY.

## fellowship and Cleansing.

'Come ye, and let us walk in the light of the Lord.'—
Isa. ii. 5.

IT is not only the Spirit but the Bride who says,
'Come.'[1] And it is remarkable that the Bride
is never found saying 'Come' without including
herself. 'Come with *us;* '[2] 'Come, and let *us* join
ourselves unto the Lord; '[3] 'Come, and let *us* return unto the Lord ·'[4] 'Let *us* come boldly.'[5] It
is always 'us,' expressed or implied, though the
speaker be patriarch, prophet, or apostle. And
you may be very sure that those who venture to
'say, Come' to you, are truly and deeply feeling
the need of continual coming for themselves. If
the Master's call were not sounding very fresh
and sweet in their own hearts, they would not be
constrained to sound it out to you.[6]

'Come ye,' then, 'and let us walk in the light of
the Lord.'[7] This is one of the blessed results and
tests of true following, as following is of coming.
For the Lord says, 'He that followeth Me shall not

---

1 Rev. xxii. 17.  2 Num. x. 29.  3 Jer. l. 5.
4 Hos. vi. 1.  5 Heb. iv. 16.  6 2 Cor. v. 14.
7 Isa. ii. 5.

walk in darkness, but shall have the light of life."[1]
And the results of this walking in the light are
fellowship and cleansing; and these, when fully
accepted, are all that we can need for the brightest,
happiest pilgrim course. 'If we walk in the light,
as He is in the light, we have fellowship one with
another; and the blood of Jesus Christ His Son
cleanseth us from all sin.'[2] This is not merely
fellowship with other Christians, though that, with
all its warmth and pleasantness, is no doubt included.[3] But scholars tell us that the true meaning is
that we and the Lord have fellowship *with each
other*—a marvellous mutual interchange of sympathy,
interest, and love. 'Truly our fellowship is with
the Father, and with His Son Jesus Christ.'[4] Fellowship implies a good deal more than even friendship; the word is really 'communion,' in its
widest and yet closest sense. It is literally having
all things in common. It is the Lord saying,
'Thou art ever with Me, and all that I have is
thine.'[5] It is our responding, 'My Beloved is
mine, and I am His.'[6] It is, 'All are yours, and ye
are Christ's, and Christ is God's.'[7] It is the present
fact, which yet we cannot fully apprehend,[8] till 'at
that day ye shall know that I am in My Father,
and ye in Me, and I in you.'[9] 'Come ye, and let
us walk in the light of the Lord,' that this glorious
fellowship may be ours.[10]

But there can be no fellowship without the cleansing. For how 'can two walk together, except they

---

1 John viii. 12.     2 1 John i. 7.     3 1 John iii. 14.
4 1 John i. 3.     5 Luke xv. 31.     6 Cant. ii. 16.
7 1 Cor. iii. 22, 23.     8 Phil. iii. 12.     9 John xiv. 20.
10 Isa. ii. 5; Gen. v. 22; Rev. iii. 4.

be agreed?'[1]  And sin is the one great obstacle to this agreement.  God never makes peace with sin.[2] No armistice, no truce, no compromise is possible! If you would read through Jeremiah or Ezekiel with your eyes open to observe what God thinks of sin, you would be perfectly startled.  It leaves the impression that no language can convey His indignant loathing of ' this abominable thing  which I hate.'[3] But this one precious promise shows  it all  in a moment.  'The blood of Jesus Christ His Son cleanseth us from all sin!'[4]  If anything less than the blood of His own Son *could* have cleansed us, would He not have spared Him?[5]  Nothing shows us the exceeding sinfulness of  sin like this one word.

But oh, thank God for the ' all '!  As nothing less than  the blood  of Christ is needed for one single sin, so  nothing more is needed  for *all* sin.[6] Ask the Holy Spirit to open out this one word to you.[7]  'All' the sin  cleansed by it,[8]—'all' that separated between you and God put away by it,[9]— you yourself made nigh by it, and sanctified by it,[10]— the fellowship will be unbroken,  the light  will be unclouded, the following will be faithful,[11] and the coming will be sealed.[12]

---

1 Amos iii. 3.  2 Ps. lxvi. 18.  3 Jer. xliv. 4.
4 1 John i. 7.  5 Rom. viii. 32.  6 Heb. ix. 22.
7 Ps. cxix. 19.  8 Isa. lix. 2.  9 Eph. ii. 13.
10 Heb. xiii. 12.  11 Eph. v. 8.  12 Zech. x. 12.

25

## THIRTIETH DAY

---

## The Perpetual Covenant

'Come, and let us join ourselves to the Lord in a perpetual covenant that shall not be forgotten.'—JER. l. 5.

THIS is no external joining of church or congregation. 'He that is joined unto the Lord is one spirit.'[1]   To this we are invited,[2]—to be so joined that nothing shall separate;[3] to be made one with Christ in blessed and eternal union.[4]   The instrument, so to speak, of the joining, is our consent, in faith and obedience, to the perpetual covenant that shall not be forgotten.[5]

Herein lies the answer to all the distressing doubts about persevering in which we 'err, not knowing the scriptures, nor the power of God.'[6] For see what the terms of the new covenant are l 'I will put My laws into their mind, and write them in their hearts: and I will be to them a God, and they shall be to Me a people.'[7]   This seems all one-sided.   It is all what God undertakes to do.   Not a word about what we undertake to do.   How different from any human covenant !

---

1 1 Cor. vi. 17.          2 Num. xviii. 2.          3 Rom. viii. 39.
4 Eph. v. 30; John xvii. 23.                        5 Jer. l. 5.
6 Matt. xxii. 29.         7 Heb. viii. 10.

Ah, the Lord tried us with the other way, and we failed; and so the old covenant of works came to naught.[1] It was not only the children of Israel who ' continued not '[2] in God's covenant; we have done just the same. We have proved in our own experience that we cannot keep any one condition of it, let alone the whole l[3] And so the Lord makes a new covenant, in which the marvellous terms are that He undertakes our part as well as His own, by promising to put His laws into our minds and write them upon our hearts, so that we may keep them and really obey them.[4]

And when He says He will be to us a God,[5] He has promised in that one word more than mortal thought or mortal desire can reach. And when He says we *shall* be to Him a people,[6] He guarantees us all the safety and happiness, and all the privileges and blessings, in all certainty and perpetuity, which He promises to His people.[7] He knows our total weakness,[8] and our utter inability to persevere,[9] and so He stoops to undertake the whole thing for us, if we will only ' come, and join ourselves to the Lord,' consenting to His perpetual covenant, and accepting these wonderful provisions in simple faith.

But remember, there is no such thing as drifting into this covenant. We shall never ' happen ' to find ourselves included in it by waiting to see what turns up, or by dint of admiringly contemplating it. We must ' *come ;* ' and we must join ourselves to

1 Jer. xxxi. 32.   2 Heb. viii. 9.   3 Rom. iii. 19, 23.
4 Isa. xxxviii. 14.   5 2 Cor. vi. 16; Rev. xxi. 3.
6 Deut. xxxiii. 29.   7 2 Cor. i. 20.   8 Ps. ciii. 14.
9 Jude 24.

the Lord in it by our own voluntary act and deed.[1]
Each must 'subscribe with his hand unto the
Lord.'[2] This covenant requires the free individual
signature of each participator, so that each shall be
able to say, 'Yet hath He made with *me* an everlasting covenant, ordered in all things and sure.'[3]
Do you ask for some proof that you *may* thus come
and share its blessedness?—some distinct evidence
that the covenant is meant for you? The Lord,
who has given all the rest, has given this too. You
know the freeness of the call, 'Ho, *every one* that
thirsteth, come ye to the waters.'[4] That is only
the beginning of the Invitation. It goes on, without a break, still to *every* one,—'Incline your ear,
and come unto Me; hear, and your soul shall live;
and I will make an everlasting covenant with *you*.'[5]

> Oh, happy day that fixed my choice
>    On Thee, my Saviour and my God!
> Well may this glowing heart rejoice,
>    And tell its raptures all abroad.
>
> 'Tis done! the great transaction's done.
>    I am my Lord's, and He is mine;
> He drew me, and I followed on,
>    Charmed to obey the Voice Divine.
>
>                 DODDRIDGE.

---

[1] 2 Cor. viii. 5.      [2] Isa. xliv. 5.      [3] 2 Sam. xxiii. 5.
[4] Isa. lv. 1.      [5] Isa. lv. 3.

# THIRTY-FIRST DAY.

## Tbe Consummation of tbe Invitation.

'Then shall the King say unto them on His right hand, Come, ye blessed of My Father, inherit the kingdom prepared for you from the foundation of the world.'—MATT. xxv. 34.

'THEN!' when the sure but as yet unseen hope of the Church is fulfilled, and Jesus comes in His glory:[1] 'then!' when all are gathered before Him, and 'He shall separate them one from another:' '*then* shall the King say unto them on His right hand, Come!'[2]

The King—'this same Jesus,'[3] who now says, 'Come unto Me,' 'whom I shall see for myself, and mine eyes shall behold, and not another'[4] (margin, *not a stranger*)—He shall utter with His own gracious lips[5] the same sweet call; and we shall hear it, no longer by faith, but literally.

The call will be no longer, 'Come unto Me, all ye that are weary and heavy laden;'[6] for the weariness and the burdens that have been cast upon Jesus will be at an end for ever.[7]   It will be, 'Come, ye

---

1 Tit. ii. 13.   
3 Acts i. 11.   4 Job xix. 27.   5 Luke iv. 22.   2 Matt. xxiv. 30, 31 ; ib. xxv. 32.   
6 Matt. xi. 28.   7 Ps. lv. 22 ; ib. xxxviii. 4.

blessed!' Not 'blessed' then for the first time, but
'ye' whose position already is that of 'the blessed
of the Lord.'[1]    Every one who comes to Jesus takes
that glorious position, and possesses all its manifold
privileges.[2]    If you are only come to-day for the
first time, 'thou art *now* the blessed of the Lord,'[3]
and you shall be among the blessed ones who stand
in their lot at the end of the days.[4]    You are *now*
made kings and priests unto God by Him who loved
you and washed you from your sins in His own
blood;[5] and *then* the King will call you to 'inherit
the kingdom.'    For 'by faith in Christ Jesus'
(which is the same thing, in other words, as coming
to Christ), you are 'the children of God.'[6]    'And
if children, then heirs; heirs of God, and joint-
heirs with Christ.'[7]    He will make you inherit the
throne of His glory, and grant you to sit with Him
in His throne,[8] for it is your Father's good pleasure
to give you the kingdom.[9]    Confess now, that this
is doing for you exceeding abundantly above all you
asked or thought![10]    To be permitted just to escape
the terrible doom of 'everlasting punishment,'[11]—
just to get inside the door of the palace,[12]—a sort of
standing afar off, even in heaven,—is about as much
as you really thought of!    But look at the grandeur
of *His* thought, and the riches of His love for you!
He has prepared not only 'a place,'[13] and 'a city,'[14]
but a kingdom for you, and that not since you began to pray for salvation, but from the foundation

---

1 Ps. cxv. 15.      2 Eph. i. 3.      3 Gen. xxvi. 29.
4 Dan. xii. 12, 13.      5 Rev. i. 5, 6.      6 Gal. iii. 26.
7 Rom. viii. 17.      8 Rev. iii. 21.      9 Luke xii. 32.
10 Eph. iii. 20.      11 Matt. xxv. 46.      12 Ps. xlv. 15.
13 John xiv. 2.      14 Heb. xi. 16.

of the world.[1]   And all this time this splendid and
amaranthine inheritance has been reserved in heaven
for you,[2] and you are being kept by the power of
God for it![3]  Have you thanked Him for this?  It is
not too soon to do so.

This is indeed the consummation of the Royal
Invitation,—the King on the throne of His glory
inviting you to come and reign with Him![4]

And 'this same Jesus' says to you to-day, 'Him
that cometh to Me, I will in no wise cast out.'[5]

Still shall the keyword ringing, echo the same sweet ' Come !'
' Come ' with the blessed myriads, safe in the Father's home ;
'Come !' for the toil is over ; ' come !' for the feast is spread ;
' Come !' for the crown of glory waits for the weary head.

---

1 Matt. xxv. 34 ; Eph. i. 4.　　　　　　2 1 Pet. i. 4, Gr.
3 1 Pet. i. 5.　　　　4 Rev. v. 10.　　　5 John vi. 37

# LOYAL RESPONSES

OR

## DAILY MELODIES

FOR

### The King's Minstrels

# FIRST DAY.

---

## Consecration Ibymn.

' Here we offer and present unto Thee, O Lord, ourselves,
our souls and bodies, to be a reasonable, holy, and lively sacrifice unto Thee.'

TAKE my life, and let it be
    Consecrated, Lord, to Thee.

Take my moments and my days;
Let them flow in ceaseless praise.

Take my hands, and let them move
At the impulse of Thy love.

Take my feet, and let them be
Swift and ' beautiful ' for Thee.

Take my voice, and let me sing
Always, only, for my King.

Take my lips, and let them be
Filled with messages from Thee.

Take my silver and my gold;
Not a mite would I withhold.

(391)

Take my intellect, and use
Every power as Thou shalt choose.

Take my will, and make it Thine;
It shall be no longer mine.

Take my heart, it *is* Thine **own**;
It shall be Thy royal throne.

Take my love; my Lord, I pour
At Thy feet its treasure-store.

Take myself, and I will be
Ever, *only*, ALL for Thee.

———•———

## SECOND DAY.

———

## Set Apart.

'Know that the Lord hath set apart him that is godly for
Himself.'—Ps. iv. 3.

### I.

SET apart for Jesus!
　　Is not this enough,
Though the desert prospect
　　Open wild and rough?
Set apart for His delight,
　　Chosen for His holy pleasure,
　　Sealed to be His special treasure!
Could we choose a nobler joy?—and would **we if**
　　**we** might?

## II.

Set apart to serve Him !
Ministers of light,
Standing in His presence,
Ready day or night !
Chosen for the service blest,
He would have us always willing,
Like the angel host fulfilling
Swiftly and rejoicingly each recognized behest.

## III.

Set apart to praise Him,
Set apart for this !
Have the blessed angels
Any truer bliss ?
Soft the prelude, though so clear :
Isolated tones are trembling ;
But the chosen choir, assembling,
Soon shall sing together, while the universe shall
hear.

## IV.

Set apart to love Him,
And His love to know !
Not to waste affection
On a passing show.
Called to give Him life and heart,
Called to pour the hidden treasure,
That none other claims to measure,
Into His belovèd hand ! thrice blessèd 'set apart !'

## V.

Set apart for ever
  For Himself alone !
Now we see our calling,
  Gloriously shown.
Owning, with no secret dread,
  This our holy separation,
  Now the crown of consecration
Of the Lord our God shall rest upon our willing
    head !¹

————•————

# THIRD DAY.

————

# The Secret of a Happy Day.

'The secret of the Lord is with them that fear Him.'
Ps. xxv. 14.

## I.

JUST to let thy Father do
    What He will;
  Just to know that He is true,
    And be still.
  Just to follow hour by hour
    As He leadeth;
  Just to draw the moment's power
    As it needeth.

———————————————————
        •       1 Num. vi. 7.

Just to trust Him, this is all !
Then the day will surely be
Peaceful, whatsoe'er befall,
Bright and blessèd, calm and free.

## II.

Just to let Him speak to thee
Through His Word,
Watching, that His voice may be
Clearly heard.
Just to tell Him everything
As it rises,
And at once to Him to bring
All surprises.
Just to listen, and to stay
Where you cannot miss His voice.
This is all ! and thus to-day,
Communing, you shall rejoice.

## III.

Just to ask Him what to do
All the day,
And to make you quick and true
To obey.
Just to know the needed grace
He bestoweth,
Every bar of time and place
Overfloweth.
Just to take thy orders straight
From the Master's own command.
Blessèd day ! when thus we wait
Always at our Sovereign's hand.

## IV.

Just to recollect His love,
　　Always true;
Always shining from above,
　　Always new.
Just to recognize its light,
　　All-enfolding;
Just to claim its present might,
　　All-upholding.
Just to know it as thine own,
　　That no power can take away.
Is not this enough alone
　　For the gladness of the day?

## V.

Just to trust, and yet to ask
　　Guidance still;
Take the training or the task,
　　As He will.
Just to take the loss or gain,
　　As He sends it;
Just to take the joy or pain,
　　As He lends it.
He who formed thee for His praise
　　Will not miss the gracious aim;
So to-day and all thy days
　　Shall be moulded for the same.

## VI.

Just to leave in His dear hand
　　*Little* things,
All we cannot understand,
　　All that stings.

Just to let Him take the care
　Sorely pressing,
Finding all we let Him bear
　Changed to blessing.
This is all! and yet the way
　Marked by Him who loves thee best;
Secret of a happy day,
　Secret of His promised rest.

———•———

## FOURTH DAY.

———

# Tbe Unfailing One.

'He faileth not.'—ZEPH. iii. 5.

### I.

HE who hath led, will lead
　　All through the wilderness;
He who hath fed, will feed;
　He who hath blessed, will bless·
He who hath heard thy cry,
　Will never close His ear;
He who hath marked thy faintest sigh,
　Will not forget thy tear.
He loveth always, faileth never;
So rest on Him, to-day, for ever !

### II.

He who hath made thee whole
　Will heal thee day by day;
He who hath spoken to thy soul
　Hath many things to say.

He who hath gently taught
   Yet more will make thee know ;
He who so wondrously hath wrought
   Yet greater things will show.
He loveth always, faileth never ;
So rest on Him, to-day, for ever !

### III.

He who hath made thee nigh
   Will draw thee nearer still ;
He who hath given the first supply
   Will satisfy and fill.
He who hath given thee grace
   Yet more and more will send ;
He who hath set thee in the race
   Will speed thee to the end.
He loveth always, faileth never ;
So rest on Him, to-day, for ever !

### IV

He who hath won thy heart
   Will keep it true and free ;
He who hath shown thee what thou **art**
   Will show Himself to thee.
He who hath bid thee live,
   And made thy life His own,
Life more abundantly will give,
   And keep it His alone ,
He loveth always, faileth never ;
So rest on Him, to-day, for ever !

## V.

Then trust Him for to-day
 As thine unfailing Friend,
And let Him lead thee all the way,
 Who loveth to the end.
And let the morrow rest
 In His belovèd hand ;
His good is better than our best,
 As we shall understand,—
If, trusting Him who faileth never,
We rest on Him, to-day, for ever !

---

# FIFTH DAY.

---

# On the Lord's Side.

‘ Thine are we, David, and on thy side, thou son of Jesse.’—
I CHRON. xii. 18.

## I.

WHO is on the Lord's side ?
 Who will serve the King ?
Who will be His helpers,
 Other lives to bring ?
Who will leave the world's side ?
 Who will face the foe ?
Who is on the Lord's side ?
 Who for Him will go ?

*Response.*    By Thy call of mercy,
         By Thy grace divine,
      We are on the Lord's side;
         Saviour, we are Thine.

## II.

Not for weight of glory,
   Not for crown and palm,
Enter we the army,
   Raise the warrior-psalm;
But for Love that claimeth
   Lives for whom He died:
He whom Jesus nameth
   *Must* be on His side.
*Response.*    By Thy love constraining,
         By Thy grace divine,
      We are on the Lord's side;
         Saviour, we are Thine.

## III.

Jesus, Thou hast bought us,
   Not with gold or gem,
But with Thine own life-blood,
   For Thy diadem.
With Thy blessing filling
   Each who comes to Thee,
Thou hast made us willing,
   Thou hast made us free.
*Response.*    By Thy grand redemption,
         By Thy grace divine,
      We are on the Lord's side;
         Saviour, we are Thine.

### IV.

Fierce may be the conflict,
  Strong may be the foe,
But the King's own army
  None can overthrow.
Round His standard ranging,
  Victory is secure,
For His truth unchanging
  Makes the triumph sure.
*Response.* Joyfully enlisting
      By thy grace divine,
      We are on the Lord's side ;
      Saviour, we are Thine.

### V.

Chosen to be soldiers
  In an alien land ;
' Chosen, called, and faithful,'
  For our Captain's band ;
In the service royal
  Let us not grow cold ;
Let us be right loyal,
  Noble, true, and bold.
*Response.* Master, Thou wilt keep us,
      By Thy grace divine,
      Always on the Lord's side,
      Saviour, always Thine.

## SIXTH DAY.

---

# True-hearted, Whole-hearted.

### I.

TRUE-HEARTED, whole-hearted, faithful and
    loyal,
  King of our lives, by Thy grace we will be !
Under Thy standard, exalted and royal,
  Strong in Thy strength, we will battle for Thee !

### II.

True-hearted, whole-hearted ! Fullest allegiance
  Yielding henceforth to our glorious King ;
Valiant endeavour and loving obedience
  Freely and joyously now would we bring.

### III.

True-hearted ! Saviour, Thou knowest our story ;
  Weak are the hearts that we lay at Thy feet,
Sinful and treacherous ! yet, for Thy glory,
  Heal them, and cleanse them from sin and deceit.

### IV.

Whole-hearted ! Saviour, belovèd and glorious,
  Take Thy great power, and reign Thou alone,
Over our wills and affections victorious,
  Freely surrendered, and wholly Thine own.

## V.

*Half*-hearted, *false*-hearted ! Heed we the warning !
  Only the whole can be perfectly true ;
Bring the whole offering, all timid thought scorning,
  True-hearted only if whole-hearted too.

## VI.

Half-hearted ! Saviour, shall aught be withholden,
  Giving Thee part who hast given us all ?
Blessings outpouring, and promises golden
  Pledging, with never reserve or recall.

## VII.

Half-hearted ! Master, shall any who know Thee
    Grudge Thee their lives, who hast laid down
      Thine own ?
Nay ; we would offer the hearts that we owe
    Thee,—
  Live for Thy love and Thy glory alone.

## VIII.

Sisters, dear sisters, the call is resounding,
  Will ye not echo the silver refrain,
Mighty and sweet, and in gladness abounding,—
  ' True-hearted, whole-hearted ! ' ringing again ?

## IX.

Jesus is with us, His rest is before us,
  Brightly His standard is waving above.
Brothers, dear brothers, in gathering chorus,
  Peal out the watchword of courage and love !

### X.

Peal out the watchword, and silence it never,
  Song of our spirits, rejoicing and free!
'True-hearted, whole-hearted, now and for ever,
  King of our lives, by Thy grace we will be!'

———•———

## SEVENTH DAY

———

## '**By Thy Cross and Passion.**'

' He hath given us rest by His sorrow, and life by His death.'
—JOHN BUNYAN.

### I.

WHAT hast Thou done for me, O mighty Friend,
      Who lovest to the end!
Reveal Thyself, that I may now behold!
      Thy love unknown, untold,
Bearing the curse, and made a curse for me,
That blessed and made a blessing I might be.

### II.

Oh, Thou wast crowned with thorns, that I might
      wear
      A crown of glory fair;
'Exceeding sorrowful,' that I might be
      Exceeding glad in Thee;
'Rejected and despised,' that I might stand
Accepted and complete on Thy right hand.

## III.

Wounded for my transgression, stricken sore,
    That I might 'sin no more;'
Weak, that I might be always strong in Thee;
    Bound, that I might be free;
Acquaint with grief, that I might only know
Fulness of joy in everlasting flow.

## IV.

Thine was the chastisement, with no release,
    That mine might be the peace;
The bruising and the cruel stripes were Thine,
    That healing might be mine;
Thine was the sentence and the condemnation,
Mine the acquittal and the full salvation.

## V

For Thee revilings, and a mocking throng,
    For me the angel-song;
For Thee the frown, the hiding of God's face,
    For me His smile of grace;
Sorrows of hell and bitterest death for Thee,
And heaven and everlasting life for me.

## VI.

Thy cross and passion, and Thy precious death,
    While I have mortal breath,
Shall be my spring of love and work and praise,
    The life of all my days;
Till all this mystery of love supreme
Be solved in glory—glory's endless theme!

# EIGHTH DAY.

---

## The Opened Fountain.

' A fountain opened for sin and for uncleanness. . . .
Wounded in the house of My friends.'—ZECH. xiii. 1, 6.

### I.

AND I have wounded Thee—oh, wounded
Thee !—
Wounded the dear, dear Hand that holds me
fast !
Oh, to recall the word ! That cannot be !
Oh, to unthink the thought that out of reach
hath passed !

### II.

Sorrow and bitter grief replace my bliss ;
I could not wish that any joy should be ;
There is no room for any thought but this,
That I have sinned—have sinned—have wounded
Thee !

### III.

How *could* I grieve Thee so ! Thou couldst have
kept ;
My fall was not the failure of Thy word.
Thy promise hath no flaw, no dire 'except,'
To neutralize the grace so royally conferred.

### IV.

Oh, the exceeding sinfulness of sin!
Tenfold exceeding in the love-lit light
Of Thy sufficient grace, without, within,
Enough for every need, in never-conquered
might!

### V.

With all the shame, with all the keen distress,
Quick, 'waiting not,' I flee to Thee again;
Close to the wound, belovèd Lord, I press,
That Thine own precious blood may overflow the
stain.

### VI.

O *precious* blood! Lord, let it rest on me!
I ask not only pardon from my King,
But cleansing from my Priest. I come to Thee
Just as I came at first,—a sinful, helpless thing.

### VII.

Oh, cleanse me now! My Lord, I cannot stay
For evening shadows and a silent hour:
*Now* I have sinned, and *now*, with no delay,
I claim Thy promise and its total power.

### VIII.

O Saviour, bid me ' go and sin no more,'
And keep me always 'neath the mighty flow
Of Thy perpetual fountain; I implore
That Thy perpetual cleansing I may fully know.

## NINTH DAY.

———

# The Precious Blood of Jesus.

### I.

PRECIOUS, precious blood of Jesus,
Shed on Calvary ;
Shed for rebels, shed for sinners,
Shed for me.

### II.

Precious blood, that hath redeemed us !
All the price is paid ;
Perfect pardon now is offered,
Peace is made.

### III.

Precious, precious blood of Jesus,
Let it make thee whole ;
Let it flow in mighty cleansing
O'er thy soul.

### IV.

Though thy sins are red like crimson,
Deep in scarlet glow,
Jesus' precious blood can make them
White as snow.

## V.

Now the holiest with boldness
    We may enter in,
For the open fountain cleanseth
    From all sin.

## VI.

Precious blood ! by this we conquer
    In the fiercest fight,
Sin and Satan overcoming
    By its might.

## VII.

Precious, precious blood of Jesus,
    Ever flowing free !
O believe it, O receive it,
    'Tis for thee !

## VIII.

Precious blood, whose full atonement
    Makes us nigh to God !
Precious blood, our song of glory,
    Praise and laud !

# TENTH DAY.

---

# ¶ Remember Thee.

'Thus saith the LORD, I remember thee, the kindness of thy youth, the love of thine espousals.'—JER. ii. 2.

## I.

MY Lord, dost Thou indeed remember me,
  Just *me*, the least and last?
With all the names of Thy redeemed,
And all Thy angels, has it seemed
As though my name might perhaps be overpassed;
Yet here I find Thy word of tenderest grace,
True for this moment, perfect for my case,—
'Thus saith Jehovah, I remember thee!'

## II.

My Lord, dost Thou remember *this* of me,
  The kindness of *my* youth?—
• The tremulous gleams of early days,
 The first faint thrills of love and praise,
Vibrating fitfully?  Not much, in truth,
Can I bring back at memory's wondering call;
Yet Thou, my faithful Lord, rememberest all,—
'Thus saith Jehovah, I remember thee!'

## III.

My Lord, dost Thou remember this of me,
  My love, so poor, so cold?
Oh, if I had but loved Thee more!
Yet Thou hast pardoned.  Let me pour

My life's best wine for Thee, my heart's best gold
(Worthless, yet all I have), for very shame
That Thou should'st tell me, calling me by
    name,—
'Thus saith Jehovah, I remember thee!'

### IV.

My Lord, dost Thou remember this of me,
    The day of Thine own power?
  The love of *mine* espousals sweet,
  The laying wholly at thy feet
Of heart and life, in that glad, willing hour?
That love was Thine—I gave Thee but Thine own,
And yet the Voice falls from the emerald throne,—
'Thus saith Jehovah, I remember thee!'

### V.

My Lord, dost Thou remember *this* of me?
    Forgetting every fall,
  Forgetting all the treacherous days,
  Forgetting all the wandering ways,
With fulness of forgiveness covering all;
Casting these memories, a hideous store,
Into the crimson sea, for evermore,
And only saying, 'I remember thee!'

### VI.

My Lord, art Thou indeed remembering me?
    Then let me not forget!
  Oh, be Thy kindness all the way,
  Thy everlasting love to-day,

In sweet perpetual remembrance set
Before my view, to fill my marvelling **gaze,**
And stir my love, and lift my life to praise,
Because Thou sayest, ' I remember thee ! '

---

## ELEVENTH DAY.

## Knowing.

### I.

I KNOW the crimson stain of sin,
   Defiling all without, within;
But now rejoicingly I know
That He has washed me white as snow.
I praise Him for the cleansing tide,
Because I know that Jesus died.

### II.

I know the helpless, hopeless plaint,
' The whole head sick, the whole heart faint;'
But now I trust His touch of grace,
That meets so perfectly my case,
So tenderly, so truly deals;
Because I know that Jesus heals.

### III.

I know the pang of forfeit breath,
When life in sin was life in death;

But now I know His life is mine,
And nothing shall that cord untwine,
Rejoicing in the life He gives,
Because I know that Jesus lives.

## IV.

I know how anxious thought can press,
I know the weight of carefulness;
But now I know the sweet reward
Of casting all upon my Lord,
No longer bearing what He bears,
Because I know that Jesus cares.

## V.

I know the sorrow that is known
To the tear-burdened heart alone;
But now I know its full relief
Through Him who was acquaint with grief,
And peace through every trial flows,
Because I know that Jesus knows.

## VI.

I know the gloom amid the mirth,
The longing for the love of earth;
But now I know the Love that fills,
That gladdens, blesses, crowns and stills,
That nothing mars and nothing moves,—
I know, I know that Jesus loves!

## VII.

I know the shrinking and the fear,
When all seems wrong, and nothing clear;

But now I gaze upon His throne,
And faith sees all His foes o'erthrown,
And I can wait till He explains,
Because I know that Jesus reigns.

---

## TWELFTH DAY.

---

## Trusting Jesus.

### I.

I AM trusting Thee, Lord Jesus,
    Trusting only Thee ;
Trusting Thee for full salvation,
    Great and free.

### II.

I am trusting Thee for pardon ;
    At Thy feet I bow,
For Thy grace and tender mercy,
    Trusting now.

### III.

I am trusting Thee for cleansing
    In the crimson flood ;
Trusting Thee to make me holy
    By Thy blood.

### IV.

I am trusting Thee to guide me;
   Thou alone shalt lead !
Every day and hour supplying
   All my need.

### V.

I am trusting Thee for power;
   Thine can never fail !
Words which Thou Thyself shalt give me,
   Must prevail.

### VI.

I am trusting Thee, Lord Jesus;
   Never let me fall !
I am trusting Thee for ever,
   And for all.

---

## THIRTEENTH DAY.

---

## 𝕷ooking unto 𝕵esus.

### I.

LOOKING unto Jesus !
   Battle-shout of faith,
Shield o'er all the armour,
   Free from scar or scathe.

Standard of salvation,
  In our hearts unfurled,
Let its elevation
  Overcome the world !

### II.

Look away to Jesus !
  Look away from all ;
Then we need not stumble,
  Then we shall not fall.
From each snare that lureth
  Foe or phantom grim,
Safety this ensureth
  Look away to Him.

### III.

Looking into Jesus !
  Wonderingly we trace
Heights of power and glory,
  Depths of love and grace.
Vistas far unfolding,
  Ever stretch before,
As we gaze, beholding
  Ever more and more.

### IV.

Looking up to Jesus
  On the emerald throne !
Faith shall pierce the heavens
  Where our King is gone.
Lord, on Thee depending,
  Now, continually,
Heart and mind ascending,
  Let us dwell with Thee.

# FOURTEENTH DAY.

---

## Shining.

### I.

ARE you *shining* for Jesus, dear one?
    You have given your heart to Him;
But is the light strong within it,
    Or is it but pale and dim?
Can *everybody* see it,—
    That Jesus is all to you?
That your love to Him is burning
    With radiance warm and true?
Is the seal upon your forehead,
    So that it *must* be known
That you are 'all for Jesus,'—
    That your heart is all His own?

### II.

Are you shining for Jesus, dear one?
    You remember the first sweet ray,
When the sun arose upon you
    And brought the gladsome day;
When you heard the gospel message,
    And Jesus Himself drew near,
And helped you to trust Him simply,
    And took away your fear.

When the darkness and the shadows
　　Fled like a weary night,
And you felt that you could praise Him,
　　And everything seemed bright.

### III.

Are you shining for Jesus, dear one,
　　So that the holy light
May enter the hearts of others,
　　And make them glad and bright?
Have you spoken a word for Jesus,
　　And told to some around,
Who do not care about Him,
　　What a Saviour *you* have found?
Have you lifted the lamp for others,
　　That has guided your own glad feet?
Have you echoed the loving message,
　　That seemed to you so sweet?

### IV.

Are you shining for Jesus, dear one,—
　　Shining for Him all day,
Letting the light burn always
　　Along the varied way?
Always,—when those beside you
　　Are walking in the dark?
Always,—when no one is helping,
　　Or heeding your tiny spark?
Not idly letting it flicker
　　In every passing breeze
Of pleasure or temptation,
　　Of trouble or of ease?

## V.

Are you shining for Jesus, dear one,—
　Shining just everywhere,
Not only in easy places,
　Not only just here or there?
Shining in happy gatherings,
　Where all are loved and known?
Shining where all are strangers?
　Shining when quite alone?
Shining at home, and making
　True sunshine all around?
Shining abroad, and faithful—
　Perhaps among faithless—found?

## VI.

Are you shining for *Jesus*, dear one,
　Not for yourself at all?
Not because dear ones, watching,
　Would grieve if your lamp should fall?
Shining because you are walking
　In the Sun's unclouded rays,
And you cannot help reflecting
　The light on which you gaze?
Shining because it shineth
　So warm and bright above,
That you *must* let out the gladness,
　And you *must* show forth the love?

## VII.

*Are* you shining for Jesus, dear one?
　Or is there a little sigh

That the lamp His love had lighted
   Does not burn clear and high?
Is the heavenly crown that waits you,
   Still, still without a star,
Because your light was hidden,
   And sent no rays afar?
Do you feel you have not loved Him
   With a love right brave and loyal,
But have faintly fought and followed
   His banner bright and royal?

VIII.

Oh, come again to Jesus!
   Come as you came at first,
And tell Him all that hinders,
   And tell Him all the worst;
And take His sweet forgiveness
   As you took it once before,
And hear His kind voice saying,
   'Peace! go, and sin no more!'
Then ask for grace and courage
   His name to glorify,
That never more His precious light
   Your dimness may deny.

IX.

Then rise, and, 'watching daily,'
   Ask Him your lamp to trim
With the fresh oil He giveth,
   That it may not burn dim.
Yes, rise and shine for Jesus!
   Be brave, and bright, and true

To the true and loving Saviour,
  Who gave Himself for you.
Oh, shine for Jesus, dear one,
  And henceforth be your way
Bright with the light that shineth
  Unto the perfect day !

———•———

# FIFTEENTH DAY.

———

# 𝔊rowing.

### I.

UNTO him that hath, Thou give**st**
  Ever 'more abundantly,'
Lord, I live because Thou livest,
  Therefore give more life to me ;
Therefore speed me in the race ;
Therefore let me grow in grace.

### II.

Deepen all Thy work, O Master,
  Strengthen every downward root,
Only do Thou ripen faster,
  More and more, Thy pleasant fruit.
Purge me, prune me, self abase,
Only let me grow in grace.

### III

Jesus, grace for grace outpouring,
  **Show me** ever greater things ;

Raise me higher, sunward soaring,
    Mounting as on eagle-wings.
By the brightness of Thy face,
Jesus, let me grow in grace.

### IV.

Let me grow by sun and shower,
    Every moment water me;
Make me really hour by hour
    More and more conformed to Thee.
That Thy loving eye may trace,
Day by day. my growth in grace.

### V.

Let me then be always growing,
    Never, never standing still;
Listening, learning, better knowing
    Thee and Thy most blessèd will.
Till I reach Thy holy place,
Daily let me grow in grace.

# SIXTEENTH DAY.

---

# Resting.

'This is the rest wherewith ye may cause the weary to rest; and this is the refreshing.'—Isa. xxviii. 12.

### I.

RESTING on the faithfulness of Christ our
    Lord;
Resting on the fulness of His own sure word;
Resting on His power, on His love untold;
Resting on His covenant secured of old.

### II.

Resting 'neath His guiding hand for untracked
    days;
Resting 'neath His shadow from the noontide rays;
Resting at the eventide beneath His wing;
In the fair pavilion of our Saviour King.

### III.

Resting in the fortress while the foe is nigh;
Resting in the lifeboat while the waves roll high;
Resting in His chariot for the swift, glad race;
Resting, always resting in His boundless grace.

### IV.

Resting in the pastures, and beneath the Rock;
Resting by the waters where He leads His flock;
Resting, while we listen, at His glorious feet;
Resting in His very arms!—O rest complete !

### V.

Resting and believing, let us onward press;
Resting in Himself, the Lord our Righteousness;
Resting and rejoicing, let His saved ones sing,
Glory, glory, glory be to Christ our King !

———————•———————

## SEVENTEENTH DAY.

———

## Filling.

'Filled with all the fulness of God.'—Eph. iii. 19.

### I.

HOLY Father, Thou hast spoken
　　Words beyond our grasp of thought,—
Words of grace and power unbroken,
　　With mysterious glory fraught.

## II.

Promise and command combining,
  Doubt to chase and faith to lift;
Self renouncing, all resigning,
  We would claim this mighty gift.

## III.

Take us, Lord, oh, take us truly,
  Mind and soul and heart and will;
Empty us and cleanse us throughly,
  Then with all thy fulness fill.

## IV.

Lord, we ask it, hardly knowing
  What this wondrous gift may be,
But fulfil to overflowing,—
  *Thy* great meaning let us see.

## V.

Make us in Thy royal palace
  Vessels worthy for the King;
From Thy fulness fill our chalice,
  From Thy never-failing spring.

## VI.

Father, by this blessèd filling,
  Dwell Thyself in us, we pray;
We are waiting, Thou art willing,
  Fill us with Thyself to-day!

# EIGHTEENTH DAY.

---

## Increase our Faith.

'Lord, increase our faith.'—LUKE xvii. 5.

### I.

INCREASE our faith, belovèd Lord!
    For Thou alone canst give
The faith that takes Thee at Thy word,
    The faith by which we live.

### II.

Increase our faith!  So weak are we,
    That we both may and must
Commit our very faith to Thee,
    Entrust to Thee our trust.

### III.

Increase our faith! for there is yet
    Much land to be possessed;
And by no other strength we get
    Our heritage of rest.

### IV.

Increase our faith!  On this broad shield
    '*All*' fiery darts be caught;

We must be victors in the field
  Where Thou for us hast fought.

### V.

Increase our faith, that we may claim
  *Each* starry promise sure,
And *always* triumph in Thy name,
  And to the end endure.

### VI.

Increase our faith, O Lord, we pray,
  That we may not depart
From Thy commands, but *all* obey
  With free and loyal heart.

### VII.

Increase our faith—increase it still—
  From heavenward hour to hour
And in us gloriously ' fulfil
  The work of faith with power.'

### VIII.

Increase our faith, that never dim
  Or trembling it may be,
Crowned with the ' perfect peace' of him
  ' Whose mind is stayed on Thee.'

### IX.

Increase our faith, for Thou hast prayed
  That it should never fail ;
Our steadfast anchorage is made
  With Thee, within the veil.

## X.

Increase our faith, that unto Thee
 More fruit may still abound ;
That it may grow ' exceedingly,'
 And to Thy praise be found.

## XI.

Increase our faith, O Saviour dear,
 By Thy sweet sovereign grace,
Till, changing faith for vision clear,
 We see Thee face to face !

---

# NINETEENTH DAY.

## ' Nobody Knows but Jesus.'

### I.

' NOBODY knows but Jesus !'
 'Tis only the old refrain
Of a quaint, pathetic slave-song,
 But it comes again and again.

### II.

I only heard it quoted,
 And I do not know the rest ;
But the music of the message
 Was wonderfully blessed.

### III.

For it fell upon my spirit
  Like sweetest twilight psalm,
When the breezy sunset waters
  Die into starry calm.

### IV.

' Nobody knows but Jesus !'
  Is it not better so,
That no one else but Jesus,
  My own dear Lord, should know?

### V.

When the sorrow is a secret
  Between my Lord and me,
I learn the fuller measure
  Of His quick sympathy.

### VI.

Whether it be so heavy,
  That dear ones could not bear
To know the bitter burden
  They could not come and share ;

### VII.

Whether it be so tiny,
  That others could not see
Why it should be a trouble,
  And seem so real to me;

28

## VIII.

Either, and both, I lay them
  Down at my Master's feet,
And find them, alone with Jesus,
  Mysteriously sweet.

## IX.

Sweet, for they bring me closer
  To the dearest, truest Friend;
Sweet, for He comes the nearer,
  As 'neath the cross I bend;

## X.

Sweet, for they are the channels
  Through which His teachings flow;
Sweet, for by these dark secrets
  His heart of love I know.

## XI.

'Nobody knows but Jesus!'
  It is music for to-day,
And through the darkest hours
  It will chime along the way.

## XII.

'Nobody knows but Jesus!'
  My Lord, I bless Thee now
For the sacred gift of sorrow
  That no one knows but Thou.

## TWENTIETH DAY.

---

## He is Thy Life.

### I.

JESUS, Thy life is mine !
　　Dwell evermore in me ;
　　And let me see
That nothing can untwine
　　My life from Thine.

### II.

Thy life in me be shown !
Lord, I would henceforth seek
　　To think and speak
Thy thoughts, Thy words alone,
　　No more my own.

### III.

Thy love, Thy joy, Thy peace,
Continuously impart
　　Unto my heart
Fresh springs, that never cease
　　But still increase.

### IV.

The blest reality
Of resurrection power,
    Thy Church's dower,
Life more abundantly,
    Lord, give to me!

### V.

Thy fullest gift, O Lord,
Now at Thy feet I claim,
    Through Thy dear name!
And touch the rapturous chord
    Of praise forth poured.

### VI.

Jesus, my life is Thine,
And evermore shall be
    Hidden in Thee!
For nothing can untwine
    Thy life from mine.

----•----

## TWENTY-FIRST DAY.

## Enough.

### I.

I AM so weak, dear Lord, I cannot stand
    One moment without Thee!
But oh! the tenderness of Thine enfolding.

And oh! the faithfulness of Thine upholding,
And oh! the strength of Thy right hand!
   That strength is enough for me!

## II.

I am so needy, Lord, and yet I know
   All fulness dwells in Thee;
And hour by hour that never-failing treasure
Supplies and fills, in overflowing measure,
My least, my greatest need; and so
   Thy grace is enough for me!

## III.

It is so sweet to trust Thy word alone:
   I do not ask to see
The unveiling of Thy purpose, or the shining
Of future light on mysteries untwining:
Thy promise-roll is all my own,—
   Thy word is enough for me!

## IV.

The human heart asks love; but now I know
   That my heart hath from Thee
All real, and full, and marvellous affection,
So near, so human; yet divine perfection
Thrills gloriously the mighty glow!
   Thy love is enough for me!

## V.

There were strange soul-depths, restless, vast, and
    broad,
   Unfathomed as the sea;

An infinite craving for some infinite stilling;
But now Thy perfect love is perfect filling!
Lord Jesus Christ, my Lord, my God,
    Thou, Thou art enough for me!

---

## TWENTY-SECOND DAY.

---

### All.

#### I.

GOD'S reiterated 'ALL!'
    O wondrous word of peace and power!
Touching with its tuneful fall
    The rising of each hidden hour,
             **All the day.**

#### II.

Only *all* His word believe,
    *All* peace and joy your heart shall fill,
*All* things asked ye shall receive:
    This is thy Father's word and will,
             **For to-day.**

#### III.

' *All* I have is thine,' saith He.
    ' *All* things are yours,' He saith again;

*All* the promises for thee
  Are sealed with Jesus Christ's Amen,
             For to-day.

## IV.

He shall *all* your need supply,
  And He will make *all* grace abound ;
*Al*ways *all* sufficiency
  In Him for *all* things shall be found,
             For to-day.

## V.

*All* His work He shall fulfil,
  *All* the good pleasure of His will,
Keeping thee in *all* thy ways,
  And with thee always, ' *all* the days,'
             And to-day !

---

# TWENTY-THIRD DAY.

---

# 𝕺𝔫𝔩𝔶.

## I.

ONLY a mortal's powers,
  Weak at their fullest strength ;
Only a few swift-flashing hours,
  Short at their fullest length.

## II.

Only a page for the eye,
　Only a word for the ear,
Only a smile, and by and by
　Only a quiet tear.

## III.

Only one heart to give,
　Only one voice to use;
Only one little life to live,
　And only one to lose.

## IV.

Poor is my best and small:
　How could I dare divide?
Surely my Lord shall have it all,
　He shall not be denied!

## V.

All! for far more I owe
　Than all I have to bring;
All! for my Saviour loves me so!
　All! for I love my King!

## VI.

All! for it is His own,
　He gave the tiny store;
All! for it must be His alone;
　All! for I have no more.

## VII.

All ! for the last and least
  He stoopeth to uplift :
The altar of my great High Priest
  Shall sanctify my gift.

———•———

# TWENTY-FOURTH DAY.

———

# 𝔐𝔶 𝔐𝔞𝔰𝔱𝔢𝔯.

'I love my master ; . . . I will not go out free.
And he shall serve him for ever.'—Ex. xxi. 5, 6.

## I.

I LOVE, I love my Master,
  I will not go out free,
For He is my Redeemer,
  He paid the price for me.

## II.

I would not leave His service,
  It is so sweet and blest ;
And in the weariest moments
  He gives the truest rest.

## III.

I would not halve my service,
  His only it must be,—
His *only*, who so loved me
  And gave Himself for me.

### IV.

My Master shed His life-blood
  My vassal life to win,
And save me from the bondage
  Of tyrant self and sin.

### V.

He chose me for His service,
  And gave me power to choose
That blessed, 'perfect freedom'
  Which I shall never lose:

### VI.

For He hath met my longing
  With word of golden tone,
That I shall serve for ever
  Himself, Himself alone.

### VII.

'Shall serve Him' hour by hour,
  For He will show me how;
My Master is fulfilling
  His promise even now!

### VIII.

'Shall serve Him,' and 'for ever;'
  O hope most sure, most fair!
The perfect love outpouring
  In perfect service there!

## IX.

Rejoicing and adoring,
  Henceforth my song shall be ·
I love, I love my Master,
  I will not go out free !

———•———

# TWENTY-FIFTH DAY.

———

# 𝔓erfect 𝔓eace.

## I.

L IKE a river glorious
    Is. God's perfect peace,
Over all victorious
  In its bright increase.
Perfect—yet it floweth
  Fuller every day ;
Perfect—yet it groweth
  Deeper all the way.
*Chorus.* Stayed upon Jehovah,
      Hearts are fully blest,
    Finding, as He promised,
      Perfect peace and rest.

## II.

Hidden in the hollow
  Of His blessèd hand,

Never foe can follow,
  Never traitor stand.
Not a surge of worry,
  Not a shade of care,
Not a blast of hurry
  Touch the spirit there.
*Chorus.* Stayed upon Jehovah,
    Hearts are fully blest,
    Finding, as He promised,
    Perfect peace and rest.

## III.

Every joy or trial
  Falleth from above,
Traced upon our dial
  By the Sun of Love.
We may trust Him solely
  All for us to do ;
They who trust Him wholly,
  Find Him wholly true.
*Chorus.* Stayed upon Jehovah,
    Hearts are fully blest,
    Finding, as He promised,
    Perfect peace and rest.

## TWENTY-SIXTH DAY.

---

## I am with Thee.

### I.

' I AM with thee ! '   He hath said it
    In His truth and tender grace ;
Sealed the promise, grandly spoken,
With how many a mighty token
    Of his love and faithfulness.

### II.

He is with thee !—In thy dwelling,
    Shielding thee from fear of ill ;
All thy burdens kindly bearing,
For thy dear ones gently caring,
    Guarding, keeping, blessing still.

### III.

He is with thee !—In thy service
    He is with thee ' certainly,'
Filling with the Spirit's power,
Giving in the needing hour
    His own messages by thee.

### IV.

He is with thee!—With thy spirit,
　　With thy lips, or with thy pen;
In the quiet preparation,
In the heart-bowed congregation,
　　Nevermore alone again!

### V.

He is with thee!—With thee always,
　　All the nights and all the days;
Never failing, never frowning,
With His loving-kindness crowning,
　　Tuning all thy life to praise.

### VI.

He is with thee!—Thine own Master,
　　Leading, loving to the end;
Brightening joy and lightening sorrow,
*All* to-day, yet *more* to-morrow,
　　King and Saviour, Lord and Friend.

### VII.

He is with thee!—Yes, for ever,
　　Now, and through eternity;
Then with Him for ever dwelling,
Thou shalt share His joy excelling,
　　Thou with Christ and Christ with thee!

## TWENTY SEVENTH DAY.

## Trust and Distrust.

### I.

DISTRUST thyself, but trust His grace;
　　It is enough for thee !
In every trial thou shalt trace
　　Its all-sufficiency.

### II.

Distrust thyself, but trust His strength;
　　In Him thou shalt be strong:
His weakest ones may learn at length
　　A daily triumph-song.

### III.

Distrust thyself, but trust His love;
　　Rest in its changeless glow:
And life or death shall only prove
　　Its everlasting flow.

### IV.

Distrust thyself, but trust alone
　　In Him, for all—for ever !
And joyously thy heart shall own
　　That Jesus faileth never.

## TWENTY EIGHTH DAY.

——

## Without Carefulness.

'I would have you without carefulness.'—1 Cor. vii. 32.

### I.

MASTER! how shall I bless Thy name
    For Thy tender love to me,
For the sweet enablings of Thy grace,
    So sovereign, yet so free,
That have taught me to obey Thy word
    And cast my care on Thee!

### II.

They tell of weary burdens borne
    For discipline of life,
Of long anxieties and doubts,
    Of struggle and of strife,
Of a path of dim perplexities
    With fears and shadows rife.

### III.

Oh, I have trod that weary path,
    With burdens not a few,
With shadowy faith that Thou wouldst lead
    And help me safely through,
Trying to follow and obey,
    And bear my burdens too.

### IV.

Master! dear Master, Thou didst speak,
  And yet I did not hear,
Or long ago I might have ceased
  From every care and fear,
And gone rejoicing on my way
  From brightening year to year.

### V.

Just now and then some steeper slope
  Would seem so hard to climb,
That I *must* cast my load on Thee;
  And I left it for a time,
And wondered at the joy at heart,
  Like sweetest Christmas chime.

### VI.

A step or two on wingèd feet,
  And then I turned to share
The burden Thou hadst taken up
  Of ever-pressing care;
So that I would not leave with Thee
  Of course I had to bear.

### VII.

At last Thy precious precepts fell
  On opened heart and ear,
A varied and repeated strain
  I could not choose but hear,
Enlinking promise and command,
  Like harp and clarion clear

29

## VIII.

' No anxious thought upon thy brow
　　The watching world should see ;
No carefulness !　O child of God,
　　For *nothing* careful be !
But cast thou *all* thy care on Him
　　Who always cares for thee.'

## IX.

Did not Thy loving Spirit come
　　In gentle, gracious shower,
To work Thy pleasure in my soul
　　In that bright, blessèd hour,
And to the word of strong command
　　Add faith and will and power?

## X.

It was Thy word, it was Thy will—
　　That was enough for me !
Henceforth no care shall dim my trust,
　　For all is cast on Thee;
Henceforth my inmost heart shall praise
　　The grace that set me free.

## XI.

And now I find Thy promise true,
　　Of perfect peace and rest ;
I cannot sigh—I can but sing
　　While leaning on Thy breast,
And leaving everything to Thee,
　　Whose ways are always best.

## XII.

I never thought it could be thus,—
　Month after month to know
The river of Thy peace without
　One ripple in its flow;
Without one quiver in the trust,
　One flicker in its glow.

## XIII.

Oh, Thou hast done far more for me
　Than I had asked or thought!
I stand and marvel to behold
　What Thou, my Lord, hast wrought,
And wonder what glad lessons yet
　I shall be daily taught.

## XIV.

How shall I praise Thee, Saviour dear,
　For this new life so sweet,
For taking all the care I laid
　At Thy belovèd feet.
Keeping Thy hand upon my heart
　To still each anxious beat!

## XV.

I want to praise, with life renewed,
　As I never praised before;
With voice and pen, with song and speech,
　To praise thee more and more,

And the gladness and the gratitude
  Rejoicingly outpour.

### XVI.

I long to praise Thee more, and yet
  This is no care to me ·
If Thou shalt fill my mouth with songs,
  Then I will sing to Thee;
And if my silence praise Thee best,
  Then silent I will be.

### XVII.

Yet if it be Thy will, dear Lord,
  Oh, send me forth, to be
Thy messenger to careful hearts,
  To bid them taste and see
How good Thou art to those who cast
  All, all their care on Thee!

# TWENTY NINTH DAY.

## 𝕿𝖍𝖞 𝕽𝖊𝖎𝖌𝖓

'Righteousness, and peace, and joy in the Holy Ghost.'—
ROM. xiv. 17.

### I.

THY reign is righteousness,
   Not mine, but Thine !—
A covering no less
Than the broad, bright waves of Thy great sea,
   That roll triumphantly
From line to pole, and pole to line;
A reign where every rebel thought
   In sweet captivity
To Thine obedience is brought.

### II

Thy reign is perfect peace;
   Not mine, but Thine !—
A stream that cannot cease,
For its fountain is Thy heart.  O depth unknown!
   Thou givest of Thine own,
Pouring from Thine and filling mine.
The 'noise of war' hath passed away;
   God's peace is on the throne,
Ruling with undisputed sway.

### III.

Thy reign is joy divine;
    Not mine, but Thine;
  Or else not any joy to me!
For a joy that flowed not from Thine own,
    Since Thou hast reigned alone,
  Were vacancy or misery.
O sunshine of Thy realm, how bright
    This radiance from Thy throne,
Unspeakable in calmest light!

### IV.

Thy reign shall still increase!
    I claim Thy word,—
  Let righteousness and peace
And joy in the Holy Ghost be found,
    And more and more abound
  In me, through Thee, O Christ my Lord;
  Take unto Thee Thy power, who art
    My Sovereign, many-crowned!
Stablish Thy kingdom in my heart.

# THIRTIETH DAY.

## Tried, Precious, Sure.

JESUS
CHRIST

'The Same yesterday, and to-day, and for ever.'—
HEB. xiii. 8.
'A stone, a tried stone, a precious corner stone, a
sure foundation.'—ISA. xxviii. 16.

### I.

THROUGH the yesterday of ages,
Jesus, Thou hast been The Same;
Through our own life's chequered pages,
Still the one dear changeless Name.
Well may we in Thee confide,
Faithful Saviour, proved and ' TRIED ! '

### II.

Joyfully we stand and witness
Thou art still to-day The Same;
In Thy perfect, glorious fitness,
Meeting every need and claim.
Chiefest of ten thousand Thou !
Saviour, O most ' PRECIOUS,' now!

### III.

Gazing down the far for ever,
Brighter glows the one sweet Name,

Steadfast radiance, paling never,
  Jesus, Jesus! still The Same.
Evermore 'Thou shalt endure,'
Our own Saviour, strong and 'SURE!'

----------•----------

# THIRTY-FIRST DAY.

## Just when Thou Wilt.

### I.

JUST when Thou wilt, O Master, call,
    Or at the noon, or evening fall,
Or in the dark, or in the light,—
Just when Thou wilt, it must be right.

### II.

Just when Thou wilt, O Saviour, come,
Take me to dwell in Thy bright home!
Or when the snows have crowned my head,
Or ere it hath one silver thread.

### III.

Just when Thou wilt, O Bridegroom, say,
'Rise up, my love, and come away!'

Open to me Thy golden gate,
Just when Thou wilt, or soon, or late.

### IV.

Just when Thou wilt—Thy time is best—
Thou shalt appoint my hour of rest,
Marked by the Sun of perfect love,
Shining unchangeably above.

### V

Just when Thou wilt !—no choice for me !
Life is a gift to use for Thee ;
Death is a hushed and glorious tryst,
With Thee, my King, my Saviour, Christ !

# Index.

## MY KING.

## ROYAL COMMANDMENTS.

## THE ROYAL BOUNTY.

## ROYAL INVITATION.

---

## LOYAL RESPONSES.

CPSIA information can be obtained
at www.ICGtesting.com
Printed in the USA
FSOW03n0948041216
28150FS